W9-AGN-603

teach yourself...

UNIX

3rd Edition

Kevin Reichard and **Eric F. Johnson**

MIS: *PRESS*

A Subsidiary of
Henry Holt and Co., Inc.

Copyright © 1995 by Kevin Reichard and Eric Johnson

MIS:Press
a subsidiary of Henry Holt and Company, Inc.
115 West 18th Street
New York, NY 10011

All rights reserved. Reproduction or use of editorial or pictorial content in any manner is prohibited without express permission. No patent liability is assumed with respect to the use of the information contained herein. While every precaution has been taken in the preparation of this book, the publisher assumes no responsibility for errors or omissions. Neither is any liability assumed for damages resulting from the use of the information contained herein.

Throughout this book, trademarked names are used. Rather than put a trademark symbol after every occurrence of a trademarked name, we used the names in an editorial fashion only, and to the benefit of the trademark owner, with no intention of infringement of the trademark. Where such designations appear in this book, they have been printed with initial caps.

Third Edition—1995

Printed in the United States of America.

Reichard, Kevin.
    Teach yourself — UNIX / Kevin Reichard, Eric F. Johnson, — 3rd ed.
        p.   cm.
    Includes index.
    ISBN 1-55828-418-4
    1. Operating systems (Computers)   2. UNIX (Computer file)
I. Johnson, Eric F.   II. Title.
QA76.76.063R443   1995
005.4'3—dc20   95-1180
                                                                       CIP

10 9 8 7 6 5 4 3 2

MIS:Press books are available at special discounts for bulk purchases for sales promotions, premiums, fund-raising, or educational use. Special editions or book excerpts can also be created to specification.

For details contact: Special Sales Director
                        MIS:Press
                        a subsidiary of Henry Holt and Company, Inc.
                        115 West 18th Street
                        New York, New York 10011

Editor-in-Chief: Paul Farrell
Managing Editor: Cary Sullivan
Development Editor: Laura Lewin
Production Editor: Eileen Mullin
Technical Editor: Mike Wexler
Copy Editor: Suzanne Ingrao

Dedication

From Kevin:

For Penny, Sean, and Geisha.

From Eric:

To, well, you know who you are.

Table of Contents

Section II: Hello, Neighbor! 165

Chapter 8: Electronic Mail 167

Chapter 9: Extending Your Reach with Networking 181

Chapter 10: The Usenet, the Internet, and the World Wide Web 197

Introduction: What is UNIX?

Welcome to *Teach Yourself UNIX* and the UNIX operating system! If there's any operating system that has been consistently attacked for being obscure and hard to use, it's UNIX—and hence the need for a book that lays out the basics in a clear easy-to-read format. Truth be told, UNIX isn't that complicated once you take the time to learn its underlying concepts. In other words, if you take the time to learn why things are the way they are, UNIX becomes much more logical.

We hope this book teaches you the basics of UNIX, while at the same time providing a logical explanation of how and why things work. You'll find *Teach Yourself UNIX* useful if:

▼ You're a beginning computer user and need to learn UNIX.

▼ You've used computers before but not necessarily UNIX. Since many computer users have already used DOS on some level, we'll make parallels to DOS when applicable.

▼ You've used UNIX in the past and need a refresher course.

▼ You're a programmer and want to learn more about programming UNIX applications.

▼ You're a student who needs to know more about the university UNIX system.

▼ You're in charge of your corporate computing system and want to know the ins and outs of UNIX usage and setups before making a purchasing decision.

In this introduction we'll run through the basic structure of UNIX and introduce you to some basic UNIX concepts. Don't worry if you fail to immediately grasp the intricacies of UNIX after reading this introduction; we'll put these concepts into practical use throughout the remainder of the book.

What's New in the Third Edition

This is the third edition of *Teach Yourself UNIX*. You might be wondering exactly how this book differs from the second edition, which came out three years ago. After all, UNIX really hasn't changed—System V Release 4.2 is still the most modern version of UNIX available.

What's changed, however, is how people are using UNIX—and specifically, how companies and universities are using UNIX. Connectivity has been built into UNIX from the beginning; it has always been comparatively easy to connect UNIX computers in different locations.

This easy connectivity, by and large, led to one of the most important computing phenomena of the 1990s: the rise of the Internet, a global network of interconnected computers. The Internet and its components (the World Wide Web, the Usenet) suddenly became the darlings of the media, as newspapers rushed to assign reporters covering "cyberspace" and companies installed support mechanisms via web pages.

That's why the most important changes in this book concern electronic mail and the Internet. Electronic mail, which has always been part of UNIX and is suddenly ubiquitous in the corporate and personal-computing worlds, has been given its own chapter. Virtually everyone connected to the Internet has electronic mail (indeed, for most Internet users, electronic mail is their *only* connection to the Internet). Electronic mail is the real killer app that UNIX backers have been searching for, while other Internet tools certainly have that capability. Chapter 9 covers older UNIX tools like **ftp**, **telnet**, and **uucp**, while Chapter 10 covers the hot and trendy in the Internet world, including the Usenet, web browsers, the World Wide Web, and various searching tools.

This is not to say that we spent all of our time cruising the 'Net in a tax-deductible fashion. When we wrote the second edition, the X Window System was just reaching maturity in terms of being a viable development environment; today, you'll find X on more and more UNIX systems as it continues to gain popularity. As a result, we beefed up our coverage of X and moved it nearer the beginning of the book. We have divided other UNIX connectivity into two chapters.

In addition, we've made a host of changes to other chapters. We've devoted much more space to topics like permissions, which is difficult for almost every UNIX beginner. We have extended our discussion of advanced tools with a primer of **awk** and a short discussion of **perl**. Intermediate users will get more out of beefed-up chapters on shell programming and C programming.

What Exactly is UNIX?

UNIX is an *operating system* in the same way MS-DOS and OS/2 are operating systems: software that controls the physical computer and interprets your commands.

An operating system performs many functions:

▼ **It actually runs a program**. When you enter a program's filename at the command line, the operating system takes over by loading the program into your computer's memory and runs it. Adjustments in the operating system can affect the actual performance of the programs.

▼ **It controls all input and output on the computer**. When you delete a file, the operating system goes ahead and eliminates a record of that file. When you save a file, the operating system makes sure your file isn't written on top of an existing file. The operating system also controls what's displayed on your monitor (or monitors) and allows you to input commands with a keyboard and mouse.

UNIX carries out these functions through three separate, but closely integrated, parts: the file system, the shell, and the kernel.

The *kernel* is responsible for all basic operating-system functions. At its most basic level, the kernel manages the computer's memory and how software instructions are allocated to that memory, executes all commands, oversees the file systems of files and directories, handles errors, and more. The kernel is launched when the computer is turned on and remains running no matter what software or shells you run. In many ways you as a user won't have to think about the kernel; you just need to know that it works.

The file system tracks files and where they are located. Everything in UNIX, whether it's a file created in a text processor or a driver used to send instructions to a printer, is contained in a file. If you're moving from a DOS or Macintosh background, you'll notice some striking similarities between DOS subdirectories and UNIX directories. We'll cover files and directories in depth in Chapter 2.

The shell, or command-line interpreter, is the part of UNIX you'll actually be using most of the time. Essentially, the shells takes your instructions and translates them into instructions the kernel understands. When you run a program, you're telling the shell to execute a program from the kernel.

Why UNIX?

UNIX has developed into a very popular operating system for a variety of reasons:

▼ ***UNIX is portable***. Because UNIX is written in the C programming language and not tied to any specific computer hardware, it has been ported to virtually every type of computer. PCs, Amigas, Macintoshes, workstations, minicomputers, mainframes, and supercomputers of all kinds run the UNIX operating system.

This means that software written on one computer can be transferred to another computer. Companies are not tied to single computer vendors any longer. Ever hear the buzzphrase "open systems"? In many ways this is a synonym for UNIX. You are free to buy computer hardware and software that should be able to be integrated into your grand computing scheme. Yes, there will always be problems when mixing different hardware types and architectures, but at least you're not tied to buying all your computer equipment from a single vendor who has you over a barrel with proprietary hardware and software.

▼ ***UNIX features powerful applications***. No one buys an operating system because it's such a wonderful operating system. Instead, you commit to an operating system because it runs the applications you want. UNIX features very powerful applications in virtually every software type, ranging from electronic publishing to industrial control to basic office automation.

▼ ***UNIX is a multiuser operating system***. More than one user can be using the UNIX system at one time. Precious hardware resources, like printers and large file servers, can be used by many.

▼ ***UNIX is a multitasking operating system***. You can be performing two tasks simultaneously: For instance, you can be formatting a text file in the background while reading through your electronic mail. While multitasking is probably not as important to most users as it is to computer theorists, it is a handy function to have at times.

▼ ***UNIX has networking built in***. Today one of computing's biggest challenges is to link different types of computers across small and large areas. With UNIX, the networking is built in with various programs and utilities. As long as we're discussing buzzphrases, we'll bring up another one: distributed processing, where (in theory) the computer power is matched to the location where it's needed. To distribute this processing power, networking is needed.

A History of UNIX Development

UNIX's long and checkered history is a study in perseverance, the quirky twists of software developments, and the triumph of good technology over the sometimes anarchical way the computer industry treats good products.

Flash back to the 1960s, when computer development was the domain of a few industrial leaders and leading universities. In this era much leading-edge research was being done at Bell Labs, MIT, and General Electric (at the time a leading computer manufacturer). The three had collaborated on an operating system called MULTICS (Multiplexed Information and Computing Systems) for the GE 645 mainframe computer. MULTICS was not exactly a triumph, and so it met with a deserved death (as did GE's computer efforts).

In 1969 Ken Thompson, a Bell Labs researcher and one of the MULTICS developers, had written a MULTICS game called Space Travel. In those days of timesharing, users had to pay for their time spent on the mainframe. Space Travel may have been a neat game, but it didn't run too well on a GE mainframe and cost $75 to play. Even for a research lab this was a tremendous waste of money, so Thompson and his colleague Dennis Ritchie rewrote the game to run on a DEC PDP-7 computer sitting unused at Bell Labs. But in order to port Space Travel to the DEC, Thompson had to write a new operating system for it—the roots of today's UNIX.

This operating system was dubbed UNICS (for Uniplexed Information and Computer Systems) by fellow Bell researcher Brian Kernighan. Along the way it became known as UNIX and was ported to more powerful computers. By 1972 there were exactly 10 computers running UNIX, and in the following year Thompson and Ritchie rewrote UNIX in the C programming language, a more portable language that helped establish UNIX as an operating system that could be run on many different types of computers.

As a product, UNIX was hampered by its corporate parent, AT&T, being barred by the government from introducing computer products commercially; this was before AT&T was broken up into regional Bell operating companies, and the fear was that AT&T's deep pockets would allow it to drive other players from the computer market. Because of demand, AT&T essentially gave UNIX away (charging a nominal cost to defray the cost of materials) to universities, the government, and some companies.

During the period of 1974 and 1979, UNIX was really a research product, becoming popular in universities for teaching purposes. The UNIX of 1974 was not very similar to the UNIX of 1979; during that period many utilities and tools were added to UNIX, while the computer industry expanded rapidly, increasing the potential market for UNIX.

At this time UNIX development was not limited to Bell Labs and AT&T. The University of California-Berkeley began work on UNIX in 1974 and came up with Berkeley Software Distribution. BSD included many common utilities we find in today's UNIX, such as the text editor **vi** and the C shell. Research on BSD continues to this day.

However, one of BSD's architects, Bill Joy, cofounded Sun Microsystems and developed his own UNIX research and development there. Today Sun is one of the leaders in the UNIX workstation market (its SPARCstation series is synonymous with UNIX workstation for many people), and SunOS is merely an extended version of BSD.

Many other companies took Sun's lead and developed their own versions of UNIX. IBM's AIX, DEC's Ultrix, and Hewlett-Packard's HP-UX are all examples of semiproprietary UNIX. Some versions, like Coherent from The Mark Williams Company, aren't really UNIX at all—just software that responds to UNIX commands the same way a real UNIX would.

UNIX also became available for microcomputer users in 1980, when Microsoft released a scaled-down version of UNIX called XENIX. Microsoft is perhaps more famous for creating an alliance with IBM that made its DOS (Disk Operating System) the most popular microcomputer operating system. XENIX development was taken over by the Santa Cruz Operation (a company partially owned by Microsoft), and SCO UNIX is now an important product in the UNIX world.

But we're jumping ahead of ourselves. Before 1983, UNIX suffered because it was not an officially supported product; AT&T made no guarantees about its future availability. That changed in 1983, when AT&T released UNIX System V Release 1 and promised that software created for it would be compatible with all future versions of UNIX from AT&T.

But what about all the other versions of UNIX? In the course of UNIX development, a number of incompatibilities had crept into the various versions, making uniform software development somewhat difficult—and no matter how good the operating system is, if there are no useful applications, no one will buy and use the operating system.

That's why AT&T embarked on what it calls The Grand Unification: UNIX System V Release 4. This newest version of UNIX combines the most popular and most used commands from UNIX System V Release 3.2, BSD, SunOS, and Xenix.

UNIX is now owned by Novell, which acquired UNIX as part of its purchase of UNIX System Labs. However, UNIX transcends the control of one corporation, as the UNIX industry works together to determine standards. Novell has even ceded the UNIX brand to X/Open, an industry group.

Still, there are different versions of UNIX floating around the marketplace. We have Solaris from Sun available for Sun workstations and Intel-based personal computers. We have Unixware available from Novell. And many users are discovering the power of UNIX with Linux, a freely available UNIX workalike written for personal computers.

As a user, system administrator or software developer, you don't really need to worry overwhelmingly about these various products and if they will cause you many problems. These disparate releases have one thing common: adherence to standards. Indeed, you can't find a more popular operating system today whose future is in the hands of so many.

Why are standards important to you? Because they ensure that an application developed for one type of computer and adhering to standards will run on your other type of computer. Various groups contribute to UNIX standards: UNIX System Labs, American National Standards Institute (ANSI, which oversees POSIX standards with the Institute for Electrical and Electronic Engineers, or IEEE), and X/Open.

In this book we are not going to dwell too much on the different versions of UNIX. The commands and procedures we document here should be applicable to most old and new versions of UNIX. Most of the discrepancies we detail will be due to various versions of the UNIX shell—Korn, Bourne, and C. As a user, it's much more important for you to know what shell you're using than to delve into the differences between operating-systems versions.

This Book

We've organized this book to reflect how you'll actually use UNIX. Each chapter builds on the concepts and procedures introduced in the previous chapter.

Section I of *Teach Yourself UNIX* covers the basics of UNIX usage. Chapter 1 covers a standard UNIX session, logging you onto a UNIX-based computer and performing many standard tasks. Chapter 2 introduces you to UNIX's method of organizing files and directories on a hard disk, and runs down the many tools providing shortcuts to efficient file management. Chapter 3 describes several handy UNIX utilities, such as **grep, sort, uniq,** and **cal.** Chapter 4 explains the shell and how you interact with it, while Chapter 5 covers the popular C and Korn shells in some detail. Chapter 6 explains how UNIX deals with more than one job at a time, and how you can harness this power to your benefit. Finally, Chapter 7 introduces The X Window System, a graphical windowing environment currently used in many UNIX installations.

Section II covers UNIX tools for connectivity. Chapter 8 covers UNIX's outstanding support of electronic mail. Chapter 9 covers established UNIX communications and networking tools like **uucp, telnet,** and **ftp.** Chapter 10 covers the hottest area of the computer world at the moment—the Internet, the Usenet, and the World Wide Web.

Section III focuses on how UNIX's tools solve many problems. Chapters 11 and 12 describe text editing and processing tools, including **vi, ed, emacs, troff,** and other text-processing packages. In Chapter 13 we cover shell programming basics, including changing shells, executing scripts, and creating a daemon. Chapter 14 introduces basic C programming tools. Chapter 15 covers assorted administrative topics, including system backup, setup procedures, and dealing with emergencies. Chapter 16 covers advanced and additional UNIX tools like **awk** and **perl**.

Typographical Conventions

We'll use the monospaced font to denote commands you enter directly into the computer at a command prompt:

```
$ cd /bin
```

When the name of a program or command appears in the text, it will be marked with **bold** type.

The name of a new concept is *italicized*.

Keyboard Conventions

UNIX relies heavily on key combinations for entering commands. For example, when we specify **Ctrl-L**, it means you should hold down the **Ctrl** key and press the **L** key. (Why not **Ctrl-l** instead of **Ctrl-L**? We have no idea.) This is true of all **Ctrl**-key combinations.

UNIX sometimes denotes these **Ctrl**-key combinations with a carat: **^L**, for example, means the same as **Ctrl-L**.

When we specify a command or filename, be sure to type the command or filename *exactly as printed*. UNIX is very fussy about the case of such commands (which are lowercase most of the time) and filenames (which usually mix upper- and lowercase letters).

Drop Us a Line

We'd love to hear your comments about *Teach Yourself UNIX*. You can drop us a note via electronic mail (*reichard@mr.net*).

UNIX from the Ground Up

UNIX has a reputation for being difficult to use and even more difficult to master. Forget that you have ever heard about this bad reputation, as you're about to discover that UNIX is only as tough as you make it.

We'll begin your UNIX education in this section with a series of tutorials covering the basics of UNIX usage. Chapter 1 begins with a standard UNIX session, logging you onto a UNIX-based computer and performing many standard tasks. Next, Chapter 2 introduces you to UNIX's method of organizing files and directories, while explaining shortcuts to efficient file management; virtually everything UNIX does can be related to file management of some sort, and the more you know about the subject the better.

UNIX can also be seen as a collection of tools, and in Chapter 3 you'll learn about several handy UNIX utilities, such as **grep**, **sort**, **uniq**, and **cal**. Chapter 4 explains the shell and how you interact with it, while Chapter 5 covers the popular C and Korn shells in some detail.

In Chapters 6 and 7 we start to get into some areas where you'll want to pay close attention, as you'll be dealing with their underlying concepts more than you may anticipate. Chapter 6 explains how UNIX deals with more than one job at a time, and how you can harness this power to your benefit. Chapter 7 introduces the X Window System, a graphical windowing environment currently used in many UNIX installations. Neither are easy to master, but some well-chosen tip should get you up and running in no time.

Getting Started with UNIX

This chapter covers:

- ▼ The basics of a typical UNIX session
- ▼ Logging in a UNIX system
- ▼ Choosing a login name and password
- ▼ Dealing with system prompts
- ▼ An explanation of UNIX commands
- ▼ Changing your password on the fly
- ▼ Logging off a UNIX system

3

Let's Start at the Very Beginning

This chapter covers the basics of a typical UNIX session. We'll begin with you logging onto your UNIX system, and then we'll guide you through some of the basic functions you'll use often in UNIX.

Because we believe that the best way to learn something is to actually use it, we'd recommend that you go through this chapter while actually in front of a computer running UNIX. To get to this beginning point is not as simple as it sounds, though. First of all, you'll need to learn about your system's configuration—and more specifically, if it's a multiuser or single-user system.

If you're using a multiuser system, you'll use a *terminal* to login a UNIX system. As we covered in the introduction, UNIX can be running on virtually any kind of computer—anything from a microcomputer to a supercomputer. You'll have to approach the idea of a multiuser system somewhat abstractly—the actual computer may be located in your office, in another room, or (if you've connected via modem or local-area network) in another building or even another country. In this instance, you could be using a UNIX terminal with a character-based display or a bitmapped display (which allows for graphics) or a PC running terminal software (which will be covered in the next section, "Logging in Remotely").

If you're running on a single-user system, you'll probably be working via a keyboard and monitor that's attached directly to the computer. A Sun SPARCstation, SCO Open Desktop, or Linux user falls into this category.

For our purposes—at least initially—it doesn't matter if you're using a multiuser or single-user system. The commands and procedures we detail will apply to both configurations.

The one area where it *will* matter occurs before you actually start computing. With UNIX, you'll need an *account* on a UNIX system. Every user must have an account, and not all accounts are equal: the *root* user—sometimes called the *superuser*—can do anything on the entire system. That includes having the power to set up an account for another user. With a multiuser system, the system administrator (the root user) must set up a user account and a password for you. When you actually login, as described later in this chapter, you'll use a name and password initially assigned by the system administrator.

If you're using a UNIX workstation and must set up your own user account, follow the documentation for your particular system regarding initial logins and setting up user accounts. Since these configurations are less frequent than large multiuser systems governed by a kind and benevolent system administrator, they won't be covered here.

Logging In

Logging in is a simple procedure that tells the UNIX system who you are; the system responds with a request for a password for verification.

The system presents you with the following:

```
login:
```

Enter your *username* (also known as the *login name* or *logname*) and hit the **Enter** key when finished.

 On many keyboards, the **Enter** key will be marked **Return**. This book will use **Enter** and **Return** interchangeably. Also, whenever there's an instruction for you to give information to the UNIX system—whether it be a username, password, or command—the assumption throughout the rest of this book is that you're to press the **Return** or **Enter** key at the end of the input.

If you make a typing error, you can move back one space by pressing the **Backspace (BkSp)** key or **Ctrl-H** if you're using System V Release 4. If you're using an earlier or different version of UNIX, try the **Delete** key (**Del**) or **#** (**Shift-3**). You can also delete an entire line by typing the **@** (**Shift-2**) character; when you do so, everything to the left of the cursor is deleted, and the cursor then appears at the beginning of the following line. Don't worry—whatever was contained on the earlier line is now part of the ether line.

After typing your login name, you'll then be presented with:

```
Password:
```

Enter your password. The terminal does not display what you type, preventing someone from stealing your password by looking over your shoulder.

These are the elements common to virtually every UNIX-based system. Depending on the UNIX vendor, you may see some slight variations of information displayed on the terminal. If you're logging onto a version of UNIX distributed by the Santa Cruz Operation (SCO), you'll be presented with a login sequence like the following:

```
Welcome to SCO System V/386
systemid!login: reichard
Password:
Welcome to SCO System V/386
  From
```

```
The Santa Cruz Operation, Inc.
```

If you're logging onto a UNIX System V Release 4 release, the sequence looks something like this:

```
login: reichard
Password:
UNIX System V Release 4.0 AT&T 3B2
systemid
Copyright (c) 1984, 1986, 1987, 1988 AT&T
All Rights Reserved
Last login: Fri Jun 12 10:45:21 on term/12
```

If you're logging onto a Sun SPARC platform, the sequence looks like the following:

```
systemid login: erc
Password:
Last login: Thu May 21 14:38:05 from nokomis
SunOS Release 4.1.1 (GENERIC) #1: Thu Oct 11 10:25:14 PDT 1990
```

In these cases, *systemid* refers to the name given to the system by the system administrator.

There are many other messages you may see after a successful login. If you're using a UNIX system running the X Window System, you'll see a screen with some windows and icons. (You'll learn more about X in Chapter 7). If you're using electronic-mail software (which we'll cover in Chapter 9), you may see the following message:

```
You have mail.
```

In addition, UNIX features a **news** system for all users. We'll cover the **news** commands later in this chapter.

If your login was unsuccessful, you'll be presented something like:

```
Login incorrect
login:
```

Logging In Remotely

In the previous example, you logged in the UNIX system from a local connection. Many UNIX systems allow you to login *remotely*—that is, over telephone lines from a location outside of your office. In this case, you'll need a computer—whether it be a UNIX workstation or PC—configured to call into a remote system with a *modem*. A modem is a piece of hardware that allows computers to communicate via telephone lines.

 Prices for modems are falling rapidly—high-quality, 28.8-Kbps modems can be found for approximately $200. When buying a modem, you should look for as much speed as possible, within your price parameters.

Your system administrator will know if you can remotely login your UNIX system from home or the road. They should also be able to recommend the appropriate software. For instance, you'll need *terminal-emulation* software to remotely login a UNIX system from a PC or compatible. There are freely available versions, as well as commercial packages; again, your system administrator will know what software you'll need, as well as what settings to use.

Settings? Yes. You'll need to make sure that your local system and the remote UNIX system are communicating with the same language, so to speak. For instance, you'll need to choose your terminal type. A popular terminal type when logging in remotely is *VT100*, which makes it a safe choice. (Once you've logged in, you may need to tell the remote UNIX system what terminal type you're using. This is done by setting the TERM variable, which you'll learn about in Chapter 4.)

After making the proper connection to the remote UNIX system, you'll be presented with a truncated login prompt, usually listing the name of the operating system and a login prompt:

```
SunOS 4.1.1

login: reichard
password
```

At this point you'll enter your own username and password.

What Can Go Wrong When Logging In

It's surprising to UNIX beginners that something as straightforward as logging in a system can be fraught with danger and suspense. But the typical UNIX system is built to maximize security—and the first step when addressing security is making sure that unauthorized users are denied access to the system. That's why UNIX can be a little vague when it denies you access to the system.

That's why a message like "login denied" doesn't tell you what was wrong with your login—the login or the password. This vagueness is designed to keep potential troublemakers at bay.

Try again. There are a few things that could be thwarting your login:

▼ **You inadvertently changed the case of a character**. With UNIX, case counts—a lesson you'll learn over and over again. Entering **Reichard** instead of **reichard** will cause the system to choke on your username. This is an area that frequently frustrates new users.

▼ **You entered a typo when typing the username or password**. Typos happen. When you're entering a username or password, you could have accidentally mistyped a character. In this case, you can use the **Backspace** (**BkSp**) key to go back and erase the offending character. Or you can be lazy and enter the incorrect information, knowing that the system will ask you to login again.

▼ **The system could be slow**. If you've entered the login information and then nothing happens, don't worry—there are times when the system will slow down to a crawl, especially when many people are performing the same task (such as logging in the system at the beginning of the work-day). If you get no immediate response from the system, don't worry. If, however, you don't get a response after several minutes, check with your system administrator to make sure the system is functioning properly.

If you've entered the correct information and are still told that the login information is incorrect, check with your system administrator or check your system's documentation.

Shell Games

When you login your UNIX system, you're immediately thrust into your *login shell*. Information about this shell, as well as other login information, is usually contained in the file **/etc/passwd**, as is login information for all the users on your system. (Obviously, this file is a tool for your system administrator, not for your frequent usage.) This file is organized by user, with each line containing the basic information regarding every user: name, login ID, and so on. The final field in your line lists the shell you want to run after logging in. Again, this isn't terribly important to your daily UNIX usage, but it shows that every aspect of UNIX usage is governed by a shell of some sort.

Therefore, it behooves us to go into an explanation of the shell and why it's important to you. A shell is a program like any other UNIX program. However, it's charged with a very important and unique responsibility: It serves as the intermediary between you and the UNIX system. In other words, the shell translates your instructions to the UNIX system in a way that the UNIX system can handle. It facilitates all aspects of your UNIX usage—telling the system where to find specific files, where your home directory is, and in general how to deal with your presence as a user. This information is called your UNIX *environment*—a term you'll run across repeatedly as you begin to alter and advance your UNIX usage.

Chapters 4 and 5 deal with shell management. For now, you need to know what the shell does—not necessarily how to manipulate it.

N O T E

UNIX features several shells. For the most part, you'll want to stick with the shell your system administrator has chosen, since that allows a certain level of conformity among the users. Other users on single-user workstations and PCs have a little more freedom when it comes to choosing a shell. Here's a rundown of some popular shells:

▼   **sh**, the Bourne shell. This is the shell that shipped with the original System V release of UNIX in 1979, and it has remained largely unchanged since then. It's named for its developer, Stephen Bourne.

▼   **ksh**, or the Korn shell. Developed by David Korn at Bell Labs, the Korn shell builds upon the functionality of the Bourne shell by adding useful features first introduced in the C shell (like job history and aliases). In addition, scripts and programs written for the Bourne shell can be used without alternation in the Korn shell. Because of this feature, coverage in the book of these shells will be lumped together.

▼   **csh**, the C shell. Developed by Bill Joy (a founder of Sun Microsystems, Inc.) while he was working on the release of Berkeley UNIX (also known as BSD), the C shell improves upon the Bourne shell with the introduction of job history, aliases, and other features. It's also structure much like the C programming language. C and UNIX have an important shared history—UNIX itself was developed in the C programming language, a large factor in its export to so many different hardware architectures. Most UNIX program development also takes place with the C programming language. The C shell is different enough from the Bourne and Korn shells to warrant its own coverage throughout this book.

▼ **jsh**, the job shell. An extension of the Bourne shell, the job shell features specialized tools for handling multiple jobs.

▼ **bash**, or the Bourne Again SHell. Developed by the Free Software Foundation, the Bourne Again SHell also builds upon the Bourne shell by adding useful features found in both the C shell and the Korn shell.

This isn't an extensive listing of shells; for instance, there are infrequently used shells available in the public domain, such as **wksh** (the windowing Korn shell) and **pdksh** (public-domain Korn shell). If you want more information about these shells, check with your system administrator or system documentation.

Based on this information contained in the **/etc/passwd** file, the UNIX system then launches your shell, with information contained in the **.profile** file (for C shell users, the **.login** and **.cshrc** files). As a new UNIX user, one of the most useful aspects of your shell is its flexibility. You can customize everything associated with the shell. In Chapter 4, you'll learn a lot about customizing the shell, as well as customizing your **.profile**, **.login**, or **.cshrc** files; in the meantime, you'll get a glimpse of this customization by learning about the shell prompt and how it can be changed.

System Prompts

If the login was successful, you'll be presented with something like this:

```
$
```

either on its own or within a window of some sort. This is called the *prompt*. As you might expect, the **$** prompts you for commands. If you're coming from the DOS world, the **$** is the equivalent of the **C:>** prompt.

Of course, *exactly* what you see after logging in will depend on your system and how it's configured. UNIX features two ways of interacting with users: *graphical interface* and *text-based* display. And they couldn't be more dissimilar, as you can see in Figures 1.1 and 1.2.

```
bash# ls
Info       adm        etc        info       man        share
X11        bin        g++-include interviews openwin    spool
X11R6      dict       games      lib        preserve   src
X386       doc        include    local      sbin       tmp
bash#
```

Figure 1.1 *A text-based display in action.*

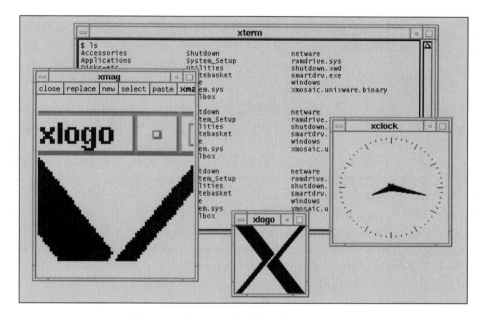

Figure 1.2 *A graphical interface in action.*

A text-based display uses the standard alphabetic characters and a few lines to interact with you. There are no windows on the screen, and essentially you're always doing one thing at a time. Older systems feature text-based displays. When you're done with a task, the screen scrolls up or clears, presenting you with a prompt, which will appear somewhere by itself on the screen (usually near the bottom of existing text).

In contrast, a graphical interface uses graphics, icons, and windows to present a more appealing face. To run a program, you double-click on an icon, or you can enter a standard UNIX command in a window. The most popular graphical interface for UNIX is the *X Window System*, a freely available interface developed at

MIT and currently administered by the X Consortium, Inc. *OSF/Motif,* a specific implementation of X developed at the Open Software Foundation, is widely used. In this instance, the prompt will appear in its own window, which is usually labeled **xterm**. (The X Window System and OSF/Motif will be covered in depth in Chapter 7.)

There's one important thing to learn about interfaces and UNIX: Under the hood, the same rules apply. For most of the commands explained throughout this book, it doesn't matter if you're using a text interface or a graphical interface. For instance, several examples in this book will be illustrated when run in an **xterm** window. The return from these commands would be the same, no matter if they're run in an **xterm** window under X or on a straight text-based terminal.

No matter which interface is featured on your UNIX system, you'll still need to know about system prompts and why they're important. In essence, the system prompt is the shell's way of saying, OK, you can enter a command whenever you're ready. The **$** prompt is used by the Korn and Bourne shells, while **%** is used by the C shell. For right now, it's important that you know that the shell in use determines your prompt.

Since the Bourne and Korn shells are so popular among UNIX users, we'll use the **$** prompt in our examples. However, we will give the C shell equivalents to commands if they differ from the Korn and Bourne shell commands. (Please note that you are not to type in the **$** or the **%** when entering commands.)

If you were the root user, your prompt would be:

```
#
```

To find out what shell you're using, you can use the following command line:

```
$ echo $SHELL
sh
```

The response should be **sh**, **csh**, **ksh**, or something else ending in *sh*. Typically, shells are stored in the **/usr/bin** directory on a UNIX system. To see what shells are available on your system, use the following command line:

```
$ ls /usr/bin/*sh
/usr/bin/csh   /usr/bin/ksh   /usr/bin/sh
```

If the response to the previous command line is:

```
*sh: No such file or directory exists
```

it means that the shell files are stored somewhere else on your UNIX system.

The shell controls almost every aspect of your UNIX usage. To show this, we'll explain how you can alter your prompt. For instance, you may want to change your prompt to appear more like the DOS prompt. In this case, you would enter the following command:

```
$ PS1="> "
```

This changes the string **$** to the string **>**, with a space at the end. The space is so that the commands you type don't abut the prompt. The quotation marks won't appear on the screen; only the characters between them will appear. (In UNIX commands, characters to be displayed on a screen are bracketed by quotation marks.) You can run the **PS1** command whenever you want; it affects only your account, so you can personalize the string to whatever extent tickles your fancy. For instance, if you have a task to perform at a specific time in the day, you could run a command like the following:

```
PS1="Call Dr. Johnson at 3 > "
```

Your prompt would be:

```
Call Dr. Johnson at 3 >
```

A C shell user would use the following command to change a prompt:

```
% set prompt = "Call Dr. Johnson at 3 > "
```

If you make an error while typing a command, you can use the **Backspace** (**BkSp**) key or **Ctrl-H** to erase the previous character—if you're using System V Release 4. Some systems use the **Delete** (**Del**) key—it all depends on your setup. If you're using an older version of UNIX, or just want to use something other than **Backspace** or **Ctrl-H**, you'll use the UNIX command **#** (**Shift-3**) to cancel the last character. Using **#** to erase a character is somewhat awkward; the character is still displayed on your terminal, and if you suffer through a lot of typing errors you must divine a command sequence containing many instances of **#**.

If you really can't figure out which key is used to delete characters (or if you don't like the system-chosen key), you can change the key used to delete characters. This is an old tradition harking back to the days when few users had compatible terminals. UNIX allows you to redefine most keys.

To change the **Delete** character key, use the **stty erase** command. You type **stty**, then a space, the word **erase**, a space, and then press the key you want, such as **Del**:

```
$ stty erase [Del]
```

In this case, [*Del*] refers to the physical act of pressing the **Delete** key.

N O T E

If you make several errors and want to erase the entire line, type the **@** character (**Shift-2**). This presents you with a new prompt:

```
$ PS1="Clla Dr. Jhohnsen at 3@
```

If you're a Korn shell user, use the **Escape (Esc)** key instead of the **@** key to erase a line:

```
$ PS1="Clla Dr. Jhohnsen at 3/
```

These failed commands will still be displayed on your screen, even though they were ignored by the computer. Why? In the old days of UNIXdom, most terminals were unable to backspace on lines—especially if the terminals were teletype or typewriter terminals that wrote everything to paper, not to a VDT screen. In UNIX, there is an almost obsessive need to maintain compatibility with older systems and mindsets, so things like backspacing characters and bitmapped graphics have been slow to gain wide acceptance.

UNIX Commands

Stty and **ls**, both used in the precious section, are examples of UNIX *commands*. In this instance, you're telling the shell to run a program called **stty**, which actually changes the information stored regarding your system prompt.

UNIX features literally hundreds of commands—too many for us to cover individually in a beginning tutorial book. Some commands are used frequently; for instance, you can use the **date** command to print out the current date and time. Some commands are specific to UNIX versions, such as the XENIX version of UNIX meant for microcomputers. If you're a System V Release 4 user, you have access to virtually every UNIX command from every UNIX version.

For instance: Depending on your version of UNIX, you may have to use UNIX commands to read news items distributed over the entire system.

If you're working on a multiuser system, a message of the day (MOTD) may follow a successful login. This is merely a text file generated by the system administrator and sent to every user, usually detailing important facts like system shutdowns for maintenance and the like. The ability to distribute information electronically to a wide range of users is a great feature of UNIX; an electronic message is certainly more efficient (and environmentally healthy) than having to distribute memos to every employee.

Some system administrators may choose not to send a message of the day and instead use UNIX's **news** command to distribute information. If this is the case in your system, you may find a message like this after you log on:

```
TYPE "news" to READ news
```

To read the news, you type:

```
$ news
```

The command **news** runs the **news** program, which displays text files containing news items. These may include notices about the computer system, or they may detail important companywide information.

With UNIX you can add *arguments* and *options* to most commands. Let's say you want to read all the news items, including those you've previously read. With UNIX, you can add an option to the **news** command, allowing you to read all news items:

```
$ news -a
```

where *-a* tells the system to display all news items. This is an option; all options are letters preceded by a minus sign. Most options are merely mnemonic shortcuts for the full names of options. In this case, we could have typed the following command and option to display all items:

```
$ news -all
```

Note that not all UNIX programs accept the same options. And those that do accept the same options (*-a*, for example) don't always mean the same thing to every command that accepts *-a*. This is one reason why UNIX has long been considered cryptic—there's a lot to memorize.

When you combine a command and any options, you're creating a *command line*. Essentially, a command line is all the information you pass after the prompt. At the least, a command line can feature only a single command; at its most complicated, it can feature several commands, each providing input and output to one another.

 In Chapter 4 you'll learn more about the command line and how it works. In the meantime, you can continue to enter the commands as presented in this chapter.

This command and option displays the current news items:

```
$ news -n
```

You'll then see a list of the current news items.

```
$ news -n
news: vacations vi
```

One-word descriptions of the news items are displayed. In this case the new news items describe changes in the company policy and changes concerning **vi**, the text editor.

To retrieve the news items about vacations, type:

```
$ news vacations
```

To stop a command, simply press the **Delete (Del)**, **Ctrl-C**, **Ctrl-D**, or **Break** keys. Your system prompt will then appear. **Ctrl-D** means end-of-file in UNIX. In UNIX, everything is a file—a fact you'll hear repeatedly in this book. Even terminal input is a file, and so to stop a command, you tell the system to end a file.

Changing Your Password

At this point you may need to use your newfound command skills immediately. If you're logging onto an account set up by a system administrator, you may have to enter a new password to replace the original password provided by the system administrator. (In fact, some system administrators *require* you to enter a new password.) This process should look like the following:

```
login: reichard
Password:
```

```
Your password has expired.
Choose a new one.
Old password:
New password:
Re-enter new password:
```

Remember that the terminal will not display the passwords for security reasons.

Changing your password is a matter of using the **passwd** command. The process is simple: After you've logged onto your system, you run a command, **passwd**, that confirms your old password and asks for the new one. (This process is shown in Figure 1.3.)

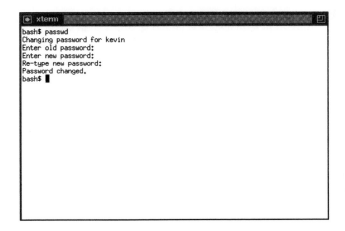

Figure 1.3 *The **passwd** command in action.*

Some UNIX systems may force you to choose new passwords every so often—the official UNIX terminology is that passwords **age** (don't we all?) and so must be replaced every so often. The system administrator sets the password time limits (some choose not to have passwords age at all). With the introduction of Release 4, you can view the status of your password by adding the -*s* command-line parameter to the **passwd** command. This is shown in Figure 1.3.

The information returned in Figure 1.3 is rather terse. Some other versions of UNIX return more information—mainly, they explain what the heck the numbers mean:

```
$ passwd -s
reichard  PW  06/15/91  10  40  7
```

```
name
passwd status
date last changed
min days between changes
max days between changes
days before user will be warned to change password
```

The final six status lines directly relate to the second line. In our example, *name* equals *reichard, passwd status* equals *PW, date last changed* equals *6/15/91, min days between changes* equals *10, max days between changes* equals *40,* and *days before user will be warned to change password* equals *7.* These parameters are set up by the system administrator, so your system may not display all six status lines.

 It's important to note that system administrators set up UNIX to prevent frequent password changes—in other words, you're stuck with a password for a certain amount of time. If you try to change your password and find that the system won't accept the change, it could be that you're prohibited from changing your password for a given amount of time.

If you're using SCO UNIX, you have the option of letting the system randomly generate a password for you. When using the **passwd** command, SCO UNIX asks you if you want the system to issue a pronounceable password.

Choosing a New Login Name and Password

This is not a perfect world, and so computer systems with more than one user must be set up with security features to prevent unauthorized usage. If you've read Clifford Stoll's excellent *The Cuckoo's Egg*, you know what havoc can be wreaked by unscrupulous users.

Now, we're not saying that every UNIX system is subject to the sort of damage Stoll outlines. But we can't overstress the importance of choosing the right password, particularly for users on large systems.

Most new users will be assigned passwords by their system administrator. This is done mainly for convenience and security reasons; when your system administrator sets up your account, it's convenient at that time to enter a secure password (in other words, it probably will appear to be total gibberish). However, there may be times when you need to choose your own password. Here are a few guidelines for login name and password selection:

▼ Your login name must be more than two characters long and normally not more than eight. It must begin with a lowercase letter (remember our lecture in the introduction about the importance of case in UNIX). In our cases, we've chosen different paths with our logins: *reichard* and *erc*. There are few Reichards in Minnesota (our home state), but Minnesota is the Land of 10,000 Johnsons and almost as many Erics. Subsequently, it was feasible to use *reichard* as Kevin's login name, and *erc* is distinctive enough to be remembered.

▼ Use a password longer than six characters. The shorter the password, the more likely it is to be divined randomly.

▼ A password should contain two alphabetic characters and one numeric or special character. It cannot contain any spaces. (Some versions of UNIX won't let you use special nonalphabetic characters in your password. These are generally older systems. Newer systems recognize the need for more distinctive passwords, which are harder for evildoers to break.)

▼ Don't use a password based on personal information. For instance, don't use your spouse's name, your middle name, your job title, or your Social Security number as a password.

▼ Don't use simple, easily guessed words like *guest, sun, hp*, or *password*.

▼ Don't use a word that can be found in a dictionary. Hackers have been known to enter words from a computer-based dictionary as passwords, hoping that a random word was selected as a password.

▼ Don't make your password too complicated. If you can't memorize your password, you'll be more likely to leave a copy on a piece of paper near your computer. Therefore, you should use a combination of easily remembered parts. Let's say your favorite book is *Valley of the Dolls*, and your favorite color is puce. You can't use *puce* as a password (too short) or *valley* (no numerals), but a password of *pucevalley1* would certainly thwart any would-be hackers.

▼ Some users try a neat technique for choosing their passwords. First, choose a word or phrase that means something to you, like *consume* (it's the American way). Then, look at the keyboard. For your real password, use the keys to the upper left of the keys for our word. For example, the first letter is *c*, and the key to the upper left of *c* is *f*. Using this technique, *consume* becomes *f0je8k4*. Use *f0je8k4* as your real password.

f0je8k4 is impossible to remember, but *consume* isn't. So you need to remember the algorithm—the method used to generate the password as well as your word, *consume*. We find this technique not only generates the special characters that are hard to guess, but makes for easy-to-remember passwords.

▼ Never display your password next to your computer terminal. You're just asking for trouble.

▼ Never send your password over electronic mail. There's no such thing as absolute privacy when it comes to e-mail, and there's always the chance—admittedly, a small chance, but a chance nevertheless—that your mail could fall into the hands of someone who could do some mischief with your password.

Make sure you remember your password. When you enter a password, it's encrypted and saved in a specific file within the UNIX system. If you forget your password, you're effectively barred from the system, as system administrators lack the ability to unencrypt this file and decipher your password. In this case the system administrator will need to create an entirely new account for you.

A Short and Sweet Security Tip

Since security is so important on so many UNIX systems, there are a variety of tools that enhance security while not impacting too heavily on users.

One such tool is the **lock** command, which is found in many, but not all, versions of UNIX. The **lock** command does only one thing: It locks your keyboard until you enter your password, as in the following:

```
$ lock
Password:
Sorry
Password:
```

If the correct password isn't entered, then the **lock** command fails to release control of the keyboard. If the correct password isn't entered in a certain number of tries, then the **lock** command logs you off of the system automatically. This isn't a tool to be used unless you're very confident of your ability to remember your password, of course, but it's a handy one to use when you're leaving your chair for a few minutes and want to make sure there's no tampering with the system done through your account.

Other Common UNIX Commands

There are many common commands you'll use regularly. This section lists some widely used commands that will illustrate some important concepts that make UNIX so unique and useful. Go ahead and type these commands into your system; they won't do any damage (even if you misuse them), and you'll certainly learn about using UNIX through them.

cal

This command displays a one-month calendar:

```
$ cal
```

The information returned by the **cal** command is shown in Figure 1.4.

Figure 1.4 *The **cal** command in action.*

If you want to see a calendar for an entire year, type:

```
$ cal 1995
```

The entire year will whip by, month by month. (It's kinda like your college graduation day, when you realize how much time you wasted over the last four years.) To stop the entire year from scrolling by, type **Ctrl-S**; to start it again, type **Ctrl-Q**. To stop the output, type **Ctrl-D**. (You can use these commands at any point in UNIX usage, to stop and start the scrolling of text.)

who

This command allows you to see who else is logged onto the system. It works as follows:

```
$ who
oper       term/10    Jun 14 12:32
reichard   term/08    Jun 14 08:12
erc        term/07    Jun 14 18:01
```

This tells you the users on the system, their terminal ID numbers, and when they logged onto the system. If you're working on a large UNIX system at a larger corporation, the results from this command can be on the voluminous side; if this information is important to you, then you'll want to learn about redirecting the output from this command, as explained in Chapter 4.

finger

In larger systems, you may get a far longer list than the one used in our **who** example, and the identities of some of the users may not be clear to you. To get more information about specific users, use the **finger** command:

```
$ finger erc
```

This gives you more information about *erc*'s identity:

```
Login name: erc                In real life: Eric F. Johnson
(612) 555-5555
Directory:/home/erc                Shell:/usr/bin/ksh
Last login Thurs Jun 11 12:14:32 on term/07
Project: X Window Programming
erc        term/07    Jun 13 18:01
```

Using the **finger** command with an argument (*erc*) gives you information about the user, no matter if they're logged onto the system. If you want to know about everyone currently logged onto the system, type:

```
$ finger
```

Again, the output from this command can be on the voluminous side for a larger corporation.

write

This command allows you to send messages to other users over the UNIX network.

Let's say you wanted to send a message to Eric over the network. After checking his status with the **who** command, you decide to initiate the message. Do so with:

```
$ write erc
```

This command causes a message to pop up on his terminal and rings his computer's bell. (Most modern UNIX systems don't really have a bell, of course, but the tradition in UNIX dictates that the sound from a speaker be referred to as the bell.) If Eric wants to participate, he sends the following:

```
$ write reader
```

where your login name is *reader*. You can then send messages back and forth over the network. When you are done sending a message, type **o-o** (over and out), and then type **Ctrl-D** or **Del** to stop the program. **Ctrl-D** is the UNIX end-of-file marker. Remember when we stated that everything in UNIX is a file? In this case, what you type using the **write** command is also treated as a file. You give the end-of-file marker (**Ctrl-D**) to terminate the file and, therefore, the **write** command.

The **Del** key and the end-of-file marker (**Ctrl-D**) can be used with almost every UNIX command.

N O T E

talk

If you're using System V Release 4 or BSD, you have an improved version of **write** available to you, called **talk**. The command **talk** allows a chat session between two users, but in an easier-to-use format. With **talk**, a screen is divided into two halves, with your messages displayed in the top half and your chat partner's messages displayed in the bottom half.

To start the **talk** command, type:

```
$ talk erc
```

Eric will see a message like the following:

```
Message from Talk_Daemon@systemid at 14:15
talk: connection requested by reader@systemid
talk: respond with: talk reader@systemid
```

where your login name is *reader* and your system's name is *systemid*. If Eric wants to chat, he can respond by typing:

```
$ talk reader@systemid
```

At this point your screen is divided into halves.

As with the **write** command, type **o-o** to signal that the conversation is over. To stop the program, press the **Del** key.

mesg

Let's say Eric is in the middle of some very important work and doesn't want to chat over the network using the **write** or **talk** commands. The **mesg** command allows him to turn away your requests for idle chatter:

```
$ mesg n
```

You'll then see the following on your terminal:

```
Permission denied
```

If Eric changes his mind and is open to receiving messages from other users, he would type:

```
$ mesg y
```

If Eric isn't sure about his status, he could type:

```
$ mesg
is y
```

This short answer tells us that Eric does allow other users to talk to him.

man

This command displays the online-manual pages associated with UNIX commands. They are the exact pages from the printed documentation. It's not quite like an online-help system; the **man** pages tend to be *very* tersely written, they apply only to commands and not to common UNIX terms or operations (for example, there's no **man** page covering the basics of electronic mail), and they tend to be technical in nature. For example, to get the **man** pages for the **man** command—sort of like help on help—type:

```
$ man man
```

A typical online-manual page is shown in Figure 1.5.

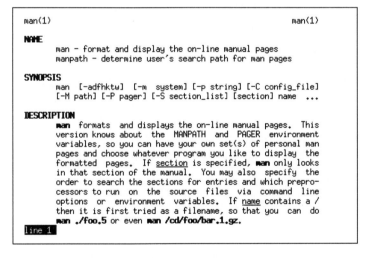

```
man(1)                                                      man(1)

NAME
       man - format and display the on-line manual pages
       manpath - determine user's search path for man pages

SYNOPSIS
       man [-adfhktw] [-m system] [-p string] [-C config_file]
       [-M path] [-P pager] [-S section_list] [section] name ...

DESCRIPTION
       man formats and displays the on-line manual pages. This
       version knows about the MANPATH and PAGER environment
       variables, so you can have your own set(s) of personal man
       pages and choose whatever program you like to display the
       formatted pages. If section is specified, man only looks
       in that section of the manual. You may also specify the
       order to search the sections for entries and which prepro-
       cessors to run on the source files via command line
       options or environment variables. If name contains a /
       then it is first tried as a filename, so that you can do
       man ./foo.5 or even man /cd/foo/bar.1.gz.
line 1
```

Figure 1.5 *The **man** command in action.*

The online-manual pages show UNIX at its best and worst simultaneously. It's great that the entire manual is online. It's terrible that the online manual is as obtuse, as you'll soon find out. Personally, we find **man** pages to be an advanced topic and of more interest to programmers looking for information about obtuse or poorly documented subjects. However, they can be handy if you're looking for the exact syntax of a command, or if you're looking for the arguments associated with a command. If you do need to know the syntax for a command, the online **man** pages can prove invaluable. But, you'll have to learn how to decipher them. Don't say you weren't warned.

Logging Out

When you're ready to leave your terminal—whether it's to go to lunch or to leave at the end of the day—it's a good idea to log off the system. Why? Security, mainly. If you leave your terminal and are still logged in, someone else could come in and tamper with your information, like deleting or reading your private files. In many large, multiuser sites, security must be on the minds of every user.

Logging off the system is also a better idea than merely turning off your terminal. Although most newer UNIX systems are smart enough to recognize that a powered-down terminal means to log off a user, many older systems—or those with PCs running as terminals—do not. It's a waste of system resources to keep your account active when you're not at your terminal.

To log off the system, type:

```
$ exit
login:
```

if you're a Bourne or Korn shell user. If you're a C shell user, **exit** will work, or you can type:

```
% logout
```

These commands should work on virtually every UNIX system. If they don't work in your situation, try one of the following:

```
logoff
bye
```

Some PC versions of UNIX that feature a graphical interface also feature a one-stop shutdown mechanism, tied to an icon. (The icon for Novell's UnixWare is shown in Figure 1.6.) In this case the entire system shuts down after it logs all the users off the system. When you select this icon, the system makes sure that you indeed want to shut down the entire system.

This leads us to a rule for PC UNIX users: Don't be so fast to shut down PC UNIX systems. UNIX, by and large, is geared for running continuously; you don't need to turn off the computer every time you're done with a PC UNIX computing session. It's better just to turn off the monitor and let the CPU run.

Figure 1.6 *The Shutdown icon in Novell UnixWare.*

N O T E

There may be times when you try to log off the system, but you're unable to do so. UNIX allows you to do more than one thing at a given time, and you have started a task, only to forget about it in the course of your daily computing activities. In these cases, the system will let you know that there are some unfinished tasks, using an error message like:

```
There are stopped jobs.
```

In this case you'll need to track down the job and deal with it. Chapter 6 covers these topics in some depth.

Summary

Every user on a UNIX system has an account. You start computing in your account by logging in. To do so, you enter your user name (or account name) and a password to authenticate that you are really you.

Guard your UNIX password with your life—it's the key that unlocks all the information in your account. Choose a password carefully and don't write it down by your terminal. Change your password with the **passwd** command.

Don't forget your password or you'll embarrass yourself in front of your system administrator.

You can change the command prompt, **$** or **%,** with the **PS1** command in the Bourne or Korn shells, or the **set prompt** command in the C shell.

The **who** command tells you who is logged in to your UNIX system.

The **exit** or **logout** commands log you out and end your UNIX session.

File and Directory Basics

This chapter covers:

- ▼ Filenames
- ▼ File types
- ▼ The UNIX file structure
- ▼ Pathnames
- ▼ Moving through directories with **cd**
- ▼ Listing files with the **ls** command
- ▼ File permissions
- ▼ Copying directories and files with **cp**

- ▼ Using wildcards in commands
- ▼ Combining and reading files with the **cat** command
- ▼ Printing files

Repeat the Mantra: Everything in UNIX is a File

Everything in the UNIX operating system can be represented by a file. A letter you write, a program, your computer, a disk drive—all of these physical entities can be represented by the abstract file.

We find that for a true beginning computer user the idea of files is not quite as simple or as clear-cut as computer veterans think. We also find that some veteran computer users don't know as much about files as they think they do—especially in a discussion of UNIX file basics. Finally, we find that we don't know as much about file as we think we do, and that something as simple as permissions trips us up more often than it should.

This chapter will cover the basics of UNIX files, how they are stored, and where you can find them. In many ways this could be the most important chapter in this book if you're a true UNIX beginner. Working directly with files is one of the great strengths of the UNIX operating system; however, to harness the extensive power, you must be thoroughly grounded in file basics.

What is a File?

In the UNIX operating system everything is represented by a file—and we mean *everything*. Your documents, software, floppy and hard disks, monitor, and keyboard are all represented by a file. Let's say you create a report for your boss. You'd use a text editor (itself comprising several files) to create a document, which is stored on your hard disk as a file. When you print that report, you're printing it on a printer that is also represented within the operating system by a file.

Simply put, a file is a computer structure to store information. This information is stored in the electronic format that a computer can use—in *bits*. A bit is either 0 or 1; when strung together, these bits comprise the characters that you and I recognize. There are eight bits in a byte, 1,024 bytes in a kilobyte, and 1,048,576 bytes in a megabyte. It's from this basic level of computing that we get much of the truly bad humor flowing through the computer world (puns on byte, etc.).

Of course, you don't need to keep track of all 1,048,576 bytes in your one-megabyte document—that's what UNIX is for. You merely need to create the file using a UNIX command (like **cat**) or an application (a word processor, a spreadsheet, a database manager, a desktop-publishing program, etc.) and then name it.

Every file has a *filename*. A filename is up to 14 characters in length (generally speaking, anyway; System V Release 4 allows unlimited length of filenames, but if the first 14 characters in two separate files match, Release 4 considers them as having the same filename). Other versions of UNIX, such as BSD, allows for much longer filenames—as many as 256 characters. If you're used to working with DOS or Macintosh computers, there are some similarities between them and UNIX when it comes to filenames, but there are also some important differences.

Some Rules Regarding Filenames

Here are a few UNIX rules and guidelines concerning filenames:

▼ A filename can be only one word, as opposed to the multiple words that comprise Macintosh and *Windows* 95 filenames. You can use periods (.) or underscores (_) to connect multiple words in a filename. Using our earlier example of creating a report for your boss, you could properly call the name of your report:

```
boss_report
```

However, the following filename is improper and will be rejected by UNIX:

```
boss report
```

If you're a DOS user, you're used to working with a filename of eight characters followed by a three-character suffix, known as a file extension (unless you're a *Windows* 95 user, which allows long filenames on the surface, but writes short filenames to disk—a most confusing and unfortunate circumstance). In this case the period denotes the end of the filename. You can follow the same model in UNIX, if you're so inclined, but with a major difference—you can place the period at any point in a UNIX filename, because the period is merely another character and doesn't denote the end of a filename. For this same reason you could place multiple periods in a filename.

For instance, you're creating many reports for your boss. You could end all their filenames with a .report suffix: **boss.report**, **daily.report**, **weekly.report**, **monthly.report**, etc. Or you could put a date at the end of a filename: **report.61292**, **report.61392**, etc. You could go a step further and insert multiple periods in a filename: **Erc.memo.612**, **Erc.mail.614**, etc. These touches allow you to keep better track of filenames; the more descriptive the filename, the less likely you are to lose a file containing important information.

▼ As you've already been told several times in this book, case counts in UNIX. You can use uppercase letters and lowercase letters in a UNIX filename (as opposed to DOS, which doesn't distinguish case in a filename). **Boss_report**, **Boss_Report**, and **boss_report** would be three different filenames in the UNIX operating system. There are times when this case sensitivity becomes a pain, particularly if you plan on tackling programming later in your computer usage.

▼ There are some characters you shouldn't use in a UNIX filename:

! @ # $ % ^ & ( ) [ ] ' " ? | ; < > ` + - . ..

Technically, you *could* use these characters in a filename, but more likely than not you will run into some problems if you use them. (You'll see this later in this chapter, when you learn that the hyphen has a special meaning as far as the shell is concerned.) In addition, you should not use spaces or tabs in a filename.

▼ There are some conventions when naming files on a UNIX system. Though they aren't necessary in UNIX, the three-character extensions forced by DOS have become an unofficial standard in the UNIX world for denoting the contents of files. Table 2.1 lists some common filename extensions and what they mean. When possible, use these extensions on your own files.

Table 2.1 *Common filename extensions and their meanings.*

Text Files

Extension	Meaning
.txt	Text file, generated (probably) by a text editor like **vi** or **emacs**. (ASCII files will be covered in the following section, "File Types.")
.mm	Text files formatted with the Memorandum Macros, a text processor covered in Chapter 11.

.ms   Text files formatted with the **ms** macros package, a text processor.

.xx *or* **.tex**   Text files formatted with TeX, a text processor.

Compressed/Archived/Encoded Files

Extension	Meaning
.gz	File(s) archived with the **gzip** command (a compression program from the Free Software Foundation not found with every version of UNIX).
.tar	File(s) archived with the UNIX **tar** command.
.uu	Files encoded with the **uuencode** command.
.z	File(s) archived with the UNIX **pack** command.
.Z	File(s) archived with the UNIX **compress** command.

Graphics Files

Extension	Meaning
.gif	File formatted in Graphics Information Format (GIF).
.jpg	File stored in the JPEG file format.
.ps	File formatted in the PostScript page-description language.

Programming Files

Extension	Meaning
.a	Library file, like a DOS **.lib** file.
.c	C-language source code.
.h	Header file.
.o	Object files.

Shell Scripts

Extension	Meaning
.csh	C-shell script.
.sh	Bourne or Korn script.

Miscellaneous Files

.tmp   Temporary files.

Throughout the course of this book, you'll learn about most of the packages and commands listed in Table 2.1, such as the **mm** macros, PostScript files, and archived files.

At the end of Table 2.1 is a listing for files ending with *.tmp*. Some UNIX applications need to temporarily store data somewhere on the filesystem, and so they store them in *temporary files* (which are usually erased by the originating application after they have served their purpose). These files usually end in *tmp* or else have *tmp* somewhere in the filename. Generally speaking, you shouldn't mess with these files if you find them in your home directory.

As an end user, you won't directly create many files within the operating system, unless you use a command like **cat** that stores keyboard input to a file. This chore usually falls to application programs, like text editors, spreadsheets, and database managers. The operations detailed in the chapter relate to the actual manipulation of files and directories; how the application creates files depends on the application.

File Types

Files can be one of several types:

▾ Ordinary files

▾ Directories

▾ Links

▾ Special device files

We've mentioned each type of file so far in this chapter (except symbolic links), though not explicitly by name.

Ordinary Files

An *ordinary file* is, well, fairly ordinary. Most of the files that you create and edit using applications are ordinary files. There are several kinds of ordinary files:

▾ Text files (sometimes called English files) contain ASCII characters. ASCII characters are numerical representations of regular letters and numerals. They are not tied to any specific operating system or computer type, so an ASCII file created in a UNIX text editor could be read by a PC or Macintosh word processor. These are the most ordinary of ordinary files.

▼ Data files are a step up from text files; in addition to ASCII characters, data files will usually contain instructions on how those characters are to be treated by an application. For instance, a letter created in a text-processing application will contain not only the characters in the text of the letter but instructions about how the characters are arranged on the page (margins, etc.), the typefaces of the characters, and other miscellaneous information.

▼ Command text files are ASCII files used to provide commands to your shell. We'll cover these files, also known as shell scripts, when we discuss shells.

▼ Executable files are programs; they are written in binary code and are created by programmers.

Directories

We've already mentioned *directories*; these are files that contain all pertinent information regarding a directory: a listing of files and subdirectories, file type, and more. You'll learn more about directories later in this chapter, in the section "A Directories Primer."

Special Device Files

Special device files represent physical aspects of a computer system. You can't read these files, nor can you change them; they're used by the operating system to communicate with your hardware, such as printers and terminals.

You won't directly use these special device files very often, and in some ways it's better to put them out of your mind. We come back to that nasty topic of abstraction again, and a special device file is perhaps the ultimate in abstractions, that is, an electronic file that represents a physical device like a printer. When you want to print a file, you should think through the process directly—to print a file, you must send the file to the printer—and leave it at that, unless you're truly into abstractions. (As many computer people are, we should hasten to add.) Your knowledge of special device files need extend only to knowing what files represent the cool laser printer down the hall.

Links

Finally, we have *links*. A link is actually a second name for an existing file. Why have two names? Remember that UNIX is a multiuser operating system, which means that it supports more than one user. Often more than one user will want access to the same file. Instead of creating two files (with separate changes from separate users—the start of a logistical nightmare), UNIX allows two users to share one file, and changes made by either user are reflected in the one file. (An added bonus is that only one file need be present on the hard disk, freeing valuable disk space.)

BSD UNIX and System V Release 4 go a step further with the introduction of *symbolic links*, files that contain the name of another file. Symbolic links address some of the limitations inherent in linked files, such as the inability to link files on different but networked computers.

 Links are best left to system administrators and programmers, whose business it is to set up these links. As a user, you should consider links to be an evil topic to be avoided, for the most part. (However, because this book is devoted to full disclosure of the UNIX operating system, there will be an extended discussion of links and the **ln** command later in this chapter.)

A Directories Primer

The UNIX operating system oversees how files are organized and stored on electronic media of some sort, which can be floppy disks, hard disks (sometimes called hard drives or fixed disks), CD-ROM drives, or tape drives. The operating system takes care of the dirty details, such as where the parts of a file are physically stored on a disk. While you don't need to know where each individual bit is stored on a disk, you do need to know where the operating system stored the file. This leads us to the concept of *directories*.

A directory on a hard disk can be thought of as a file folder containing files. (If you're a Macintosh user, you certainly recognize the concept.) Essentially, a directory is a special file that contains the names of other files. The idea is to place similar documents into the same directory so they are easier to find; for instance, the aforementioned reports to your boss could be contained in a directory named **Reports**. Correspondence from colleagues sent via electronic mail could be stored in a directory named **Mail**. And ad nauseam.

There can also be directories within directories; these are called *subdirectories*. You can have as many subdirectories as your heart desires. In a way, *every* directory in UNIX is really a subdirectory; think of your hard disk as physically one large directory, with everything contained within organized into subdirectories. (Physical disks can also be *partitioned* into multiple virtual disks, but this isn't something you'll need to know about.) In this manner you could envision your computer's hard disk as a file cabinet, your top-level directories as drawers, the subdirectories as file folders, and the actual files as pieces of paper. (As we warned you earlier, a certain amount of abstraction is needed to tackle not only the UNIX operating system but computing in general.) The term subdirectory is relative; any directory you're working in is the current directory, and any directory under that is termed a subdirectory. In the end, everything is a subdirectory, save the root directory, which is the top of the directory hierarchy.

Organization is a hard habit to teach in a computer book, but we can't stress enough that you must take your file organization seriously. Files are like rabbits; they tend to breed quickly and in great numbers, and, unless you keep a tight control over them, they'll end up wandering away and disappearing. Throwing all your files into a single directory is a logistical nightmare; you'll be scrolling through directory lists all day and lose track of older files. (In addition, you'll make your hard disk work awfully hard to list all those files.) By creating several subdirectories to organize similar files, you'll be saving yourself time doing mundane tasks like finding files. For example, we find it handy to keep reports in a directory called **reports**, memos in a directory called **memos**, and so on.

 The rules regarding capitalization and filenames also apply to directories: **Reports**, **reports**, and **REportS** would be considered three different directory names by UNIX.

The UNIX File Structure

How UNIX organizes these files, directories, and subdirectories is relatively simple.

Flash back to your childhood when you created a family tree in elementary school. Your great-grandparents were at the top of the tree, followed by your grandparents, parents, and finally your generation at the bottom. The tree got wider as you went lower, reflecting the greater number of persons in succeeding generations.

You could think of the UNIX file structure as a family tree of sorts. Technically speaking, the UNIX file system is called a *hierarchical* file system. At the top of the tree is the *root* directory, usually represented by a slash (/). Figure 2.1 illustrates a typical UNIX file structure.

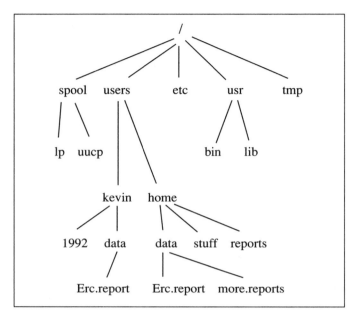

Figure 2.1 *A typical UNIX hierarchical file structure.*

There's no limit on the number of directories and subdirectories within UNIX; this figure is perhaps atypical because of the relatively small number of directories and files.

When you login your UNIX system, you'll be placed immediately by the system into your *home* directory. From there you move up, down, and through the file structure. In our example file structure, we'll use the example of **home** as a home directory.

Directory Organization

When you start looking through UNIX directory structures, you'll find that there is usually a method of the file madness, and that the same method is used in most UNIX systems. Over time many conventions have developed regarding UNIX file systems. Most UNIX systems contain the following subdirectories, usually within the root directory:

bin	This directory contains most of the standard UNIX programs and utilities. The term *bin* is short for *binary.*
dev	This directory contains device files. We discussed device files earlier in this chapter.

etc   This directory essentially contains everything but device files and program files—in short, a lot of miscellaneous files. Most system administrators use this directory to store system configurations, as well as user profiles. Most of these files are accessible only to the system administrator. You'll rarely need to modify these files.

man   Some versions of UNIX place online-manual pages (which you learned about in Chapter 1) in a separate directory.

tmp   This temporary directory is used by the system for temporary storage of working files. Many programs will temporarily store working files in this directory and then delete the files when the chore is completed. Management of the contents of this directory is best left up to system administrators.

We'd recommend that you organize your own directory in a similar fashion. It's simply easier to store programs in a **bin** directory, device files in a **dev** directory, and miscellaneous system files in an **etc** directory.

Pathnames

In our figure we've placed a number of files that have the same name in different subdirectories. But you'll recall that earlier we warned again giving files the same filenames. What gives?

When we described filenames earlier in the chapter, we weren't telling you the entire story. By including a description of the location of the file in the directory structure, you can create many files named **Erc.report**, as long as they're placed in different directories. These different **Erc.reports** are distinguished by their *pathnames*. In our example the pathnames for the two **Erc.report** files are:

```
/users/home/data/Erc.report
```

and

```
/users/kevin/data/Erc.report
```

These are called *full pathnames* because they provide an exact description of the file's location in the directory structure. These descriptions can get very long, so watch your typing carefully—it's a real drag retyping long full pathnames after you discover the system wouldn't accept your original pathname because of a typo in the middle.

How do we decipher a pathname? In our example pathname of **/users/home/data/Erc.report**, the initial slash (/) refers to the root directory, as we mentioned previously. The following slashes separate the names of subdirectories within subdirectories. The final slash denotes the actual filename. In our example, the directory **users** is a subdirectory of the root directory, **home** is a subdirectory of **users**, and **Erc.report** is a file within the **data** subdirectory.

Relative Pathnames

There are many tools within UNIX that help you avoid typing long pathnames. A *relative pathname* is just that—a pathname that's shortened in relationship to your present directory position. Since you're always entered into your home directory when you initially login your UNIX system, you can specify a pathname relative to your home directory. From your home directory location of **home**, you could specify **data/Erc.report**—which would be as valid as **/users/home/data/Erc.report**. To specify a directory from your home directory, use a tilde (~) character, for example, **~/data/Erc.report** is stored in the **data** subdirectory of your home directory.

Let's say you want to move out of your home directory and use another directory as your current directory. You may want to have your home directory contain many subdirectories, each containing different types of work data (financial reports, personnel files, etc.). We'd recommend creating a subdirectory for each type of work data (more on that later), and then using UNIX commands to navigate between the directories, according to the work being done.

If your current directory is **users**, you can use a single dot (**.**) to specify its position relative to other pathnames. If you have a subdirectory named **personnel**, and within it a subdirectory named **1992**, you could use **./personnel/1992** as its relative pathname.

If you want to specify the parent directory of the current directory, use double dots (**..**) in a relative pathname. Unless you're logged into the root directory, every directory in UNIX is actually a subdirectory of another directory.

Moving with the Cd Command

If you want to change your current directory, use the **cd** command. There are relatively few restrictions on this command. To move to the root directory, use:

```
$ cd /
```

There are two parts to this command: We're using the **cd** command to move to another directory, and the slash also denotes the root directory.

If you want to move up one level in the directory tree, to the parent directory of your current directory, use the **cd** command followed by two dots:

```
$ cd ..
```

If you want to move to another directory, you can combine the **cd** command with the pathname:

```
$ cd /users/kevin/junk
```

To move to the previous directory (if you're a Korn-shell user, anyway), use:

```
$ cd -
```

If you want to return to your home directory, use **cd** by itself:

```
$ cd
```

 Despite sharing the same name, there are some differences between the DOS **CD** command and the UNIX **cd** command. With DOS you'll get the name of the current directory when you invoke **CD** (since it's DOS shorthand for current directory):

```
C:>cd
curdir
```

where *curdir* is the current directory. In UNIX, using **cd** by itself will place you into your home directory. However, the UNIX and DOS versions of **cd** work similarly when presented with parameters like double dots (**..**) and pathnames. DOS also uses a backslash character (\), instead of the forward slash (/) that UNIX uses. In addition, DOS does not require a space after **CD**; UNIX does.

Working with Directories

As we mentioned earlier, UNIX files tend to multiply to the point of confusion. That's why a good working knowledge of directory-related commands is so important, beginning with the simple **ls** command and all related options.

The Pwd Command

When you login your UNIX system, you'll be placed automatically into your home directory. (When you first login a UNIX system, your system administrator will have set up a default home directory. You can change this default by editing your **.profile** file, an action that you probably won't want to attempt; even so, we'll cover this topic in Chapter 4.) But if you start moving between directories, it's possible to forget exactly where you are on the directory tree. To print out the current working directory, use the **pwd** (for print working directory) command:

```
$ pwd
/users/data/1992
$
```

The Ls Command

On a base level, the **ls** command combined with an argument of some sort will list the contents of your current directory. The **ls** command by itself will list the entire contents of a directory without differentiating between files and subdirectories:

```
$ ls
data       figures     misc  newdata  personnel
expenses   financials
$
```

As you can tell, the files and directories are listed in alphabetical order in columnar form.

The utility of the plain **ls** command is limited, as you don't know the difference between files and directories. Also, the **ls** command does not list any *hidden* files. In UNIX, any files beginning with a period (.) are hidden files. These files are used by the operating system for standard housekeeping tasks; the **.profile** file stores details about your particular configuration (we'll cover changing this file in Chapter 4), while other hidden files are used by programs like your electronic-mail program. This is why it's very important to know about the various useful arguments for **ls**.

If you want to view the contents of a subdirectory, use the **ls** command with the name of the subdirectory as an argument. In this instance we're asking for the contents of the subdirectory **data**:

```
$ ls data
1992.proj  Erc.report  stats
```

To determine if a given file is within your current directory, use the **ls** command with the name of the file as the argument:

```
$ ls newdata
newdata
```

If the file is not found, you'll get the following message:

```
$ ls god
god not found
```

To view hidden files (mentioned previously), use **ls** with the *-a* (for *all*) option:

```
$ ls -a
    .   ..   .mailrc   .profile   data   financials   misc   newdata
    personnel
```

The command also denotes the current (**.**) and parent (**..**) directories as well as the two hidden files (**.mailrc** and **.profile**).

Our examples so far have used as examples directories with only a few files. Most directories will contain many, many files (at least ours do), and it can be hard to find files in a long list without any logical organization. Using the *-F* option brings some order to a confusing directory:

```
$ ls -F
data/   financials/   misc/   newdata   personnel/
```

The *-F* option tells **ls** to provide us with details about each listing. This directory contains four subdirectories, as noted by the slashes (/) following the filename. Also contained is an ordinary file, **newdata**. If this directory contained symbolic file links, they would be denoted by an @ symbol following the filename. Executable files have an asterisk (*) after the filename.

If you want to display the contents of a directory in one column, use the *-1* (one, not ell) option:

```
$ ls -1
data
financials
personnel
misc
newdata
```

Your version of **ls** may not support the *-1* option.

N O T E

This command obviously works better in a directory with a relatively few contents. If you're working with a directory containing many files and directories, use the *-x* option to sort the entries in alphabetical order across the screen:

```
$ ls -x
1timer       6.21.proposal   UNIXBOOK   Notes      a1   data
financials   misc            newdata    personnel
```

As you can probably divine from this directory listing, there's a structure to the UNIX **ls -x** command: ASCII order. (Remember that everything in computing has a numerical basis, and that ASCII characters are merely representations of numerical values.) In ASCII, numerals are listed first, followed by uppercase letters and lowercase letters.

These options can be combined. For instance, you could merge entries horizontally:

```
$ ls -xF
.mailrc*   .profile*   1timer        6.21.proposal UNIXBOOK Notes
a1         data/       financials/ misc/            newdata  Personnel
```

The *-t* option to **ls** lists files in order of time (newest first) instead of alphabetically. If you forget which file you modified last, you can use **ls -t** to help find it.

Using the -R Option with Ls

You can list all the files in a directory, as well as all the files in any subdirectories, using the *-R* option:

```
$ ls -R
1timer        6.21.proposal   UNIXBOOK   Notes   a1   data
./Letters
6.21.letter   6.22.letter     letter.erc
```

This lists the contents of the current directory (**1timer**, **6.21.proposal**, **UNIX-BOOK**, **Notes**, **a1**, and **data**), as well as the contents of the subdirectory **letters** (**6.21.letter**, **6.22.letter**, and **letter.erc**).

NOTE

Again, case counts with UNIX. The *-R* option and the *-r* option do two different things when combined with the **ls** command.

Using the -t Option with Ls

The *-t* option lists files based on the last time they were updated, with the most recently changed files listed first:

```
$ ls -t
6.21.proposal  UNIXBOOK  ltimer  al  Notes  data
```

Using the -l Option with Ls

So far we've worked with the short version of the **ls** command, which provides filenames only. If we want complete information about filenames, we can use the *-l* option (short for long format) with the **ls** command.

Using this option in our home directory, we'd see a listing like the following (this has been abbreviated for space):

```
$ ls -l
total 32
-rwxrwxrwx  1  user  group1   27  Feb  2  09:20  ltimer
drwxr--r--  6  user  group1  347  Jun 21  14:41  data
-rwx------  3  user  group1  995  Dec 25  00:41  personnel
```

SunOS 4.1 users would use a slightly different command line:

```
$ ls -lg
total 32
-rwxrwxrwx  1  user  group1   27  Feb  2  09:20  ltimer
drwxr--r--  6  user  group1  347  Jun 21  14:41  data
-rwx------  3  user  group1  995  Dec 25  00:41  personnel
```

The listing starts with a summary of the disk space used by the directory, in blocks. (A block is normally 4,096 bytes, but some systems use different block sizes, depending on what type of filesystem you have.) Most of the rest of the information in this listing is self-evident, but is better explained when read right to left (backwards). The first column lists the files and directories in alphabetical order. The second column lists the date and time the entries were created. The third column lists the size (in bytes) of the entries. The fourth lists the group that the entry belongs to (we'll discuss the concept of groups in the next section), and the fifth the owner of the file (denoted by your login name, user).

The sixth column is the link count, which lists how many files are symbolically linked to the file (in the case of the personnel file, there are three linked copies), or, in the case of directories, how many subdirectories are contained within plus two (one for the directory itself, one for the parent directory; in this case there are four actual subdirectories).

In the final (but first overall) column, we see a series of seemingly illogical characters. The first character in the column lists the type of file (earlier in this chapter we covered file types, which are summarized in Table 2.2).

Table 2.2 *File types listed with the -l option.*

-	Ordinary file
b	Special block file
c	Special character file
d	Directory
l	Symbolic link
p	Named pipe special file

For our present needs, the most important file types are directory (d), symbolic link (l), and ordinary file (-). Most of the files you use regularly will fall into these three types. In our directory we used one example of each. We'll be covering named pipe files later in this book.

Permissions

The rest of this final column lists the *permissions* associated with that file or directory. In a multiuser operating system, with the needs of a potentially large number of users balanced by the diverse security needs of some users, there need to be safeguards as to who can read and write files, as well as run certain programs.

UNIX handles this elementary security through permissions. For files, there are three levels of permissions: Read permission means that you can read the file, write permission means that you can change the file, and execute permission means that you can run the file as a program.

Permissions can also be applied to directories: Read permission means that you can list the contents of a directory, write permission means that you can make or delete files and/or directories within the directory, and execute permission means that you can make that directory your current directory via the **cd** command.

Thus the final nine characters in our example first column applies different permissions to the various files and subdirectories. When reading this column (the first character denotes the file type, the final nine denote the permissions), you must divide the nine permissions characters into three clusters of three characters: The first cluster of three refers to permissions granted to the owner of the entry, the second cluster of three refers to the permissions granted to the group that the entry belongs to, and the third cluster of three refers to the permissions granted to all users.

Bear with us; permissions are better understood when illustrated by an example. Using the first file listing:

```
-rwxrwxrwx   1   user   group1   27   Feb   2   09:20   1timer
```

we can see that the permissions associated with this file are *rwxrwxrwx*. The owner can read (r), write (w), and execute (x) the file. Anyone in the group *group1* can read (r), write (w), and execute (x) the file. In fact, all users can read (r), write (w), and execute (x) the file.

Everyone on a UNIX system is assigned to a group when their accounts are set up by the system administrator, and you can belong to several groups. This normally is nothing you need to worry about; however, later in this chapter we explain how to find out what group you belong to.

However, things are different with the second listing:

```
drwxr--r--   6   user   group1   347   Jun 21   14:41   data
```

as the permissions associated with this directory are *rwxr—r—*. The owner of this directory can read (r), write (w), and execute (x) the directory. Members of the group, as well as all users, can read (r) the directory, but cannot write (-) the directory or make the directory a current directory (-). (Permissions are notated in either/or fashion; a user can either read [r] a file or not read [-] a file.)

The permissions are even more restrictive with the final personnel file

```
-rwx------   3   user   group1   995   Dec 25   00:41   personnel
```

In this instance, with such an obviously sensitive **personnel** file, the user has decided to deny access to everyone else. The user can read (r), write (w), and execute (x) the file. No one else can read (-), write (-), or execute (-) the file. This sort of restriction is common within the UNIX system and indeed forms the basic level of security.

Group? What Group?

As mentioned earlier, everyone on a UNIX system is assigned to a group, and you can be assigned to more than one group. When you login a UNIX system, you're automatically placed in your primary group, which can be found listed in the **/etc/passwd** file.

If you don't know what groups you're assigned to, you can use the **groups** command to get this information:

```
$ groups
group1
secret
```

This tells you that you're a member of the *group1* and *secret* groups. (It's always cool to belong to a *secret* group.) Information about the groups and their members can be found in the **/etc/group** file, which you can read; however, on a large system, this file can be extremely long, so you're best off using a command like **grep** (which you'll learn more about in Chapter 3) if you want to see more about the groups you belong to:

```
$ grep kevin /etc/groups
group1:114:geisha,kevin,spike
secret:446:eric,geisha,kevin,tom
```

From this, we can see the members of each group, as well as the group IDs (*114* for *group1*, *446* for *secret*). This information is important if you want to switch groups during the course of your normal work; if you're logged in as a member of *group1*, you won't have access to group permissions of the *secret* files. However, UNIX allows you to change groups at any point in your work (provided you're a member of the new group) with the **newgrp** command:

```
$ newgrp secret
```

Changing Permissions with Chmod

The method of listing permissions you've covered so far in this chapter—the *symbolic* form—is one of two ways the UNIX system tracks permissions. The other method, the *numeric* form, comes in very handy when changing permissions with the **chmod** command.

As you'd expect, the numeric form uses numerals to track permissions. This is done in a very quirky way, however, and is probably more complicated than it need be, forcing you to add up three different sets of numbers in determining who has what permissions. Note that the actual types of permissions—owners, groups, and all users having read, write, and execute permissions—have not changed; only the way of listing them has changed.

The numeric form uses *modes* to list permissions. A mode is an octal number in one of the forms listed in Table 2.3.

Table 2.3 *Modes and their meanings.*

Numeral	Meaning
400	Owner has read permission.
200	Owner has write permission.
100	Owner has execute permission.
040	Group has read permission.
020	Group has write permission.
010	Group has execute permission.
004	All users have read permission.
002	All users have write permission.
001	All users have execute permission.

You get the numeric form by adding together the numbers and then combining that number with the **chmod** command (short for *ch*ange *mode*). Let's go back to an example from earlier in this chapter:

```
drwxr--r--  6  user  group1  347  Jun 21  14:41  data
```

If we translate the above to numeric form, the result would be *744*. How did we arrive at that? Simple:

400	Owner has read permission.
200	Owner has write permission.
100	Owner has execute permission.
040	Group has execute permission.
004	All users have read permission.

744	

In essence, all you do is add the numerical values associated with each level of permission. A file that's open to the entire world (meaning they can read, write, and execute the file) would have a value of *777*; a file that's totally inaccessible would have a value of *000*.

When you want to change the permissions, you combine the numerals representing the desired permissions with the **chmod** command. To change the permissions for the aforementioned **data** file, giving the entire world permission to read, write, and execute the file, you'd use a command line like:

```
$ chmod 777 data
```

To change the permissions to where only the owner has the ability to read, write, and execute the file **data**, you'd use the following command line:

```
$ chmod 700 data
```

To change the permissions to where the owner has the ability to read, write, and execute the file, with members of the group also having the ability to read, write, and execute the file, you'd use the following command line:

```
$ chmod 770 data
```

To change the permissions where the owner has the ability to read, write, and execute the file, with members of the group and the world having the ability to read the file, you'd use the following command line:

```
$ chmod 744 data
```

You can also change the permissions of the contents of an entire directory with **chmod** by using it with the *-R* option. The following command line makes the entire contents of the **letters** directory readable for only the owner of the directory:

```
$ chmod -R 700 letters
```

The *-R* option is not supported on all versions of UNIX.

Setting Permissions Symbolically

You can also use the symbolic method when setting permissions, but this method is a little trickier than using the numeric method. With the numeric method, you're setting the new permissions absolutely; it doesn't matter what the existing permissions are. With the symbolic method, you're setting the new permissions relative to the old permissions. Also, you're embarking on some slightly different terminology when it comes to permissions and the symbolic method, as you'll see by the following example of the **chmod** command used with the symbolic method:

```
$ chmod u+x data
```

This might appear to be confusing at first, but it really isn't. When using this symbolic method, **chmod** changes permissions relative to the old one, and does so through a syntax that adds or subtracts permissions for the user (who has been called the owner of the file so far in this discussion), the group, and others (the world). Breaking down the *u+x* portion of the previous command line yields the following information:

▼ The *u* refers to the user, or the owner of the file. From this we know that the permissions are being set for the owner.

▼ The **+** refers to the process of adding a permission to the current permissions. If a minus sign (-) were used here, a permission would be subtracted from the current permissions.

▼ The *x* means that the change in the permission should mean that the ability to execute the file should be added to the permissions.

You can specify multiple permissions on a command line with the **chmod** command, provided the individual permissions are separated with a comma:

```
$ chmod u+x,go-w data
```

This command line takes away (-) the ability to write (*w*) to the file from the group (*g*) and others (*o*).

You can give every user access to a file with the following command line:

```
$ chmod ugo+rwx
```

The symbols used with the **chmod** command are listed in Table 2.4.

Table 2.4 *Symbols used with the **chmod** command.*

Symbol	Meaning
u	User (or the owner of the file).
g	Group.
o	Other (or the world).
+	Adds a permission to the existing permissions.
-	Takes away a permission from the existing permissions.
r	Reads the file.
w	Writes to the file.
x	Executes the file.
t	Sets the "sticky bit" on a directory

Changing How UNIX Assigns Permissions

When you create a file or directory, default permissions are automatically assigned to the file or directory. Most of the time, the default permissions will be acceptable. However, you may find that you want to change these defaults. To do so, you use the **umask** (short for *user-mask*) command. When run without any options, the **umask** command returns the default permissions:

```
$ umask
744
```

This is a pretty expansive set of permissions (and not usually the default; this is being used purely as an example, and it's more than likely that this won't be your default). Since most of the time the **umask** command will be used to make permissions more restrictive, the following example will change the permissions to give full permission to the owner and the group, but not to the world:

```
$ umask 007
```

Wait a second—*007?* Yes. In yet another glaring inconsistency within the UNIX system, the **umask** command changes permissions relative to a baseline of 777. Therefore, your input of 007 to the **umask** command is actually subtracted from the baseline 777, yielding a final permission of 770, which gives full permissions to the owner and the group, but no permissions to the world. After running the previous command line, you can check the new permissions like this:

```
$ umask
770
```

Changing the Ownership of a File

When you create a file, you're automatically the owner of the file (unless you change that with the **umask** command, explained in the previous section). When you copy a file with the **cp** command, you become the owner of the copied file.

There are times when you'll want to change the ownership of a file; for instance, Eric may be working on a mondo report (called, appropriately enough, **mondo_report**) on the state of the accounting department, but Kevin has to take over the preparation of the report after Eric is laid off. Using the **cp** command is one way of changing the ownership, but this works only if Kevin has permission to read the file. (Eric, distrusting Kevin, has made sure this isn't so. Isn't the cutthroat world of high finance fascinating?)

In this case, the system administrator—logged in as the root user—can use the **chown** command to change the ownership of the **mondo_report** file, specifying the name of the file and the new owner:

```
$ chown kevin mondo_report
```

In fact, the root user could make Kevin the owner of *all* the files in Eric's directory by adding the -*R* option (short for *r*ecursive) to the **chown** command:

```
$ chown -R kevin Reports
```

Setting the Sticky Bit

Messing with the directory, as opposed to individual files, has always been a way for malicious computer users to get around the permissions associated with individual files. Because this has been a concern for many system administrators, System V Release adds the ability to make a directory impregnable to everyone but the owner of the directory and the root user. To do this, you set the "sticky bit" of the directory with the **chmod** command, as follows:

```
$ chmod +t letters
```

This command line refuses everyone (except the owner and the root user) the ability to move or remove files in a directory, no matter what permissions are set with individual files.

Security and the UNIX Filesystem

The theme of *security* has been pounded into your head throughout this book, and it will be a continual theme throughout the remainder of the book, too. As you can tell from the previous section, one of the prime reasons for permissions is to make sure that an unauthorized user doesn't have access to sensitive files.

But security isn't an absolute in UNIX. Indeed, there are continued assaults on security within UNIX filesystems. Some security breaches occur because a group of people wants to show how clever they are—and they do this by hacking into a supposedly secure system. Some security breaches are due to thievery; grabbing long-distance access codes and passwords is a common security concern for many larger companies Other security breaches stem from raids on information from outsiders—the computer equivalent of industrial espionage.

There are a few lessons to draw from this:

▼ **No form of security within UNIX is absolute.** Setting the proper permissions is the most basic level of security possible. But the system administrator, who is logged in as the root user or the superuser, has access to all files on the system. A resourceful intruder always attempts to login as the root user.

▼ **Never take anything for granted when it comes to security.** Even if you take other more advanced security steps (as you'll learn about when you learn about networking and communications), your data may still be vulnerable. Plan accordingly.

▼ **If there's anything ultrasensitive, don't store it on the UNIX system.** While this is a fatalistic attitude not necessarily shared amongst the greater UNIX community, it's our belief that ultrasensitive information shouldn't be stored on a UNIX system, no matter how good the security is. (This is one of the few advantages a DOS system has over UNIX: You can physically lock up a DOS system with a key, and you can keep information on your person in the form of a floppy drive or a removable tape.)

Manipulating Files

Studies show that people directly use their operating system—as opposed to applications—mostly for the daily, mundane tasks of file manipulation: moving files, copying files, renaming files, and deleting files. You will probably fall into this category, too. This section will cover these important file-related tasks; in many ways these rather rote tasks could be the most useful tips you get from this book.

Moving Files

We'll start by moving files. There are many instances where you may want to move a file from one directory to another: You may want to move older files to an archival directory, or you may want to move previous versions of existing files. And so on.

The **mv** command allows for the movement of files in UNIX. Let's say you want to move the file **1992.reports**, located in your current directory, to the **misc** subdirectory (remember, this subdirectory's full pathname is **/users/home/misc**). The following accomplishes the task:

```
$ mv 1992.reports /users/home/misc
```

The process and syntax are simple: After invoking the **mv** command, designate the file to be moved and then the destination, which can be a directory, a subdirectory in relation to the current directory (remember what we said on the subject earlier in this chapter), or another filename. When moving a file, you can also rename it. (There's no separate command for renaming a file—an unfortunate oversight on the part of UNIX designers.) If you want to rename a file and leave it in the current directory, use the **mv** command, followed by the current filename and then the new filename:

```
$ mv 1992.reports newname
```

To rename a file and move it to a new directory simultaneously, use the **mv** command, followed by the current filename, then designating the new directory and filename (in this case, **newinfo**):

```
$ mv 1992.reports /users/kevin/newinfo
```

WARNING

Make sure that there is no existing file named **newinfo** in the **/users/kevin** subdirectory. When you move a file, UNIX will not ask for a confirmation of any sort. If there's an existing file with the same name as your new file, the old file will be wiped out and replaced by the new, renamed file.

If you're using System V Release 4 or BSD UNIX, you can avoid problems like this with the *-i* option. With it, you'll be asked if you want to overwrite an existing file:

```
$ mv -i 1992.reports /users/kevin/newinfo
mv:  overwrite newinfo ?
```

If you want to overwrite **newinfo**, type **y**. If you do not want to overwrite **newinfo**, type **n** or hit any other key. Only your positive response will overwrite the file; any other response will stop the operation.

This process is very quick and is not slowed down by the size of the file (or files) being moved. Why? When you move a file, you're not actually moving the physical information contained in the record, but rather you're moving the record of the file as maintained by the operating system. In the introduction we detailed how one of the roles of the operating system was to maintain a current listing of all the directories on a hard disk. When you move a file—as well as copy or rename it—you're merely editing that listing, not manipulating the actual file. Note that if you cross disk partitions or cross hard disks, UNIX may have to copy the file contents to the new location.

To make sure that the file was actually moved, you can use the familiar **ls** command:

```
$ ls /users/home/misc/1992.reports
1992.reports
```

You can use the **mv** command to move more than one file:

```
$ mv 1992.reports 1991.reports /users/home/misc
```

This command will move both the **1992.reports** and **1991.reports** into the **misc** subdirectory. (There's another method of moving multiple files involving wildcards; we'll cover this topic in the following section.)

Problem Characters and Removing Them

Earlier in this chapter you were warned about avoiding specific characters, such as - and ?, when naming files. Now you'll learn about the reasons behind the warning—at the least the reason why you shouldn't use a hyphen (-) in a filename.

The UNIX shell uses the hyphen to tell it that the following characters are used to slightly alter the command preceding it. As you know from reading Chapter 1, this is known as an option to the command, which is why the hyphen is reserved for use by the shell. However, UNIX (to an extent, anyway) assumes that you know what you're doing, and so if you create a file whose name begins with a hyphen, such as **-letter**, the system will let you go right ahead and do it.

You will experience untold grief after doing so, however. You can't move the file using the **mv** command, as the shell assumes that **-letter** is an option to the **mv** command (like *-i*). The same thing is true of other UNIX commands covered later in this chapter.

So what do you do? There are a few ways to get around it. As you'll recall, this chapter covered pathnames, and that some pathnames include the directories above the current directory. Using this knowledge, you can trick the shell into ignoring the hyphen because it's buried in a pathname. For example, the following command line would tell the shell to stay in the current directory and then move a file named **-letter** into a new directory:

```
$ mv ./-letter /users/eric/memos
```

This method will work with any UNIX command.

Moving Directories

Finally, you can use the **mv** command to move directories and all its contents, including files and subdirectories, provided you're using System V Release 4. Let's say you want to move the **/users/home/misc** directory (with all its files and subdirectories) to the **/users/kevin** directory. Use the following:

```
$ mv /users/home/misc /users/kevin
```

Copying Files

Copying files is also a rather routine function—you may want to make a copy of a file for backup purposes, or you may want to use a copy of an existing file as the basis of a new document. These tasks are accomplished with the **cp** command, which is used very similarly to the **mv** command—you designate the file to be copied, followed by its destination:

```
$ cp 1992.report /users/kevin
```

This copies the file **1992.report** to the **/users/kevin** subdirectory. As with the **mv** command, you can use **cp** to give a new filename to the copied file:

```
$ cp 1992.report /users/kevin/1992.report.bk
```

This copies the file **1992.report** to the **/users/kevin** subdirectory and renames it **1992.report.bk** (we've used the *.bk* suffix to denote a backup file; you can use your own verbiage, obviously).

As with the **mv** command, imprudent use of the **cp** command could lead you to overwrite existing files when copying other files. For instance, in the above example, you should make sure that there is not a file named **1992.report.bk** already existing in the **/users/kevin** subdirectory; if there is, your actions would cause it to be wiped out with a copy of the file **1992.report**.

Use the *-i* option (within System V Release 4 or BSD UNIX) to make sure the copied file doesn't wipe out an existing file:

```
$ cp -i 1992.report /users/kevin/1992.report.bk
cp:  overwrite 1992.report.bk ?
```

If you do want to overwrite the existing file, type **y**. If you do not want to overwrite the existing file, type **n** or hit any other key.

The DOS **COPY** command works similarly to the UNIX **cp** command, at least on a base level. To copy a file in DOS, you'd use the following:

```
C:>COPY 1992.REP
```

In addition, you'd use the DOS **COPY** command to move files; there is no equivalent in DOS for the UNIX **mv** command. The process is a tad more complicated; first copy the file and then delete its original:

```
C:>COPY 1992.REP
1 file(s) copied
C:> DEL 1992.REP
C:>
```

Copying Directories

You can use the **cp** command to copy the entire contents of a directory, including all files and subdirectories, provided you're using System V Release 4:

```
$ cp -r /users/data /users/kevin
```

Removing Files

Unneeded files can clog up a hard disk, slowing it down and making your file-management chores unnecessarily complicated. It's good to regularly go through your subdirectories and remove unneeded files.

Do so with the **rm** (for remove) command:

```
$ rm 1992.report
```

UNIX will not confirm that a file was removed, nor will it confirm the actual operation, asking you if you do indeed want to remove the file.

If you want to remove multiple files, merely list them in the command:

```
$ rm 1992.report 1993.report
```

You can remove many files at one time by using a wildcard; we'll cover wildcards later in this chapter. If you're worried about removing the wrong files, use the *-i* option, which will confirm if you do want to delete a file:

```
$ rm-i 1992.report 1993.report
1992.report: ?
1993.report: ?
```

At each **?** prompt, type **y** to delete the file, **n** to keep the file.

Removing Directories

There are two ways to remove directories under UNIX. Both require a little planning.

The UNIX command **rmdir** will remove an empty directory, containing no files or subdirectories:

```
$ rmdir users
```

where **users** is an empty directory. If **users** contains files or subdirectories, UNIX will interrupt the operation with an error message. Also, you cannot use **rmdir** to remove your current directory; you must be in another directory to perform this action. To successfully remove a directory with the **rmdir** command, first remove all the files in the directory with the **rm** command and then remove each subdirectory with the **rmdir** command.

An alternative method—though a decidedly more dangerous method—is through the combination of **rm** with the **-r** option:

```
$ rm -r users
```

This will remove all the contents of the directory **users** (including directories and subdirectories).

SunOS users would use the following command line:

```
$ rm -rf users
```

These commands remove all the contents of the **users** directory, as well as the directory itself. Why the tinge of danger? Because any commands that can do such extensive damage should be treated with a good deal of caution.

 There are two ways to remove a file under DOS: **DELETE** (**DEL** for short) or **ERASE**:

```
C:>DEL 1992.REP
```

or

```
C:>ERASE 1992.REP
```

Like UNIX, DOS does not tell you when a file is removed, nor does it ask you to confirm a file erasure.

Like UNIX, DOS does not allow you to remove all the contents of a directory in one fell swoop. Instead, you must delete all the files in a directory:

```
C:>DEL *.*
All files in the directory will be erased! Proceed? <y/n>
```

and then remove the actual directory:

```
C:>RMDIR
```

With such convoluted processes, we can see why DOS shells are so popular.

WARNING

Beginning users frequently remove needed files or directories by accident. As a beginning UNIX user, you may scoff at the notion—after all, elementary mistakes are made by less-advanced users, right?—so no matter how often we warn you about the dangers inherent in sloppy file manipulation, you'll probably go out and have to learn a nasty lesson for yourself.

If you do accidentally delete a file, there are some steps you can take to mitigate the damage. When you use the **rm** command, you're erasing the record of the file **1992.report** by the operating system and allowing the hard-disk space previously occupied by the file for use by other files. You are not actually erasing the file contents.

Therefore, theoretically it should be possible to restore the file by restoring the record of it in the operating system. This is how utilities like The Norton Utilities for UNIX can unerase deleted files: They restore the record of the file in the operating system. However, these utilities work best if they're used immediately after a file was accidentally erased. Since the operating system is free to write the contents of a new file to the space vacated by the deleted file, it's possible that portions of the old file may not exist after some time—which means that the entire file cannot be unerased. So it's dangerous to rely on The Norton Utilities to restore deleted files.

The best way to avoid damage through inadvertently deleted files is by making frequent backups of your work. If you're working on a large UNIX system, your system administrator should be making frequent backups of the entire system. If you accidentally erase the file **1992.report**, you should be able to ask your system administrator to copy an old version of the file for present use. How frequently the system is backed up depends on the system administrator's policies.

If you're working on a UNIX workstation and are storing files locally (as opposed to the file server), you're on your own, bub. If you are sporadic in your backup efforts, you run the danger of not having a recent backup. We advocate regular backups; if you're on a network with a large file server, you can copy important files frequently to the server (and remember to remove them when they become unnecessary); if your workstation features a tape drive, you should frequently backup to tape—weekly, if possible. (We find that Friday afternoons are perfectly suited to making backups.)

We also strongly recommend that you use the *-i* option with **rm**, so that you get asked whether to delete every file you pass to **rm**.

Creating Directories

We suggest that you create many directories as a tool for file management, using the directory for storage of similar files. The process is simple:

```
$ mkdir newdirect
$ ls
newdirect
```

In this case the **mkdir** command creates a new directory, **newdirect**, as a subdirectory within the current directory. You can also use **mkdir** to create directories within directories other than the current directory:

```
$ mkdir /users/kevin/newdirect
```

This creates **newdirect** as a subdirectory within the **/users/kevin** directory, even though **/users/kevin** may not be your current directory.

You can also use **mkdir** to create multiple subdirectories within the current directory:

```
$ mkdir memos letters
```

Finally, you can use **mkdir** to create a directory and a subdirectory when using the *-p* option:

```
$ mkdir -p /memos/letters
```

 DOS uses the same command, **mkdir**, to create new directories:

```
C:>MKDIR\USERS\KEVIN\NEWDIRECT
```

Linking Files

As we noted earlier in this chapter, UNIX allows you to link files. Remember that UNIX is a multiuser operating system, which means that it supports more than one user. Often more than one user will want access to the same file—a very common occurrence within many company departmental situations, where many users may need access to a file containing addresses, for example. Instead of creating two files (with separate changes from separate users—the start of a logistical nightmare), UNIX allows two users to share one file, and changes made by either user are reflected in the one file. Also, only one file need be present on the hard disk, freeing valuable disk space.

Let's say Kevin wanted to share information with Eric. The information is contained in Kevin's home directory, **/users/kevin**, under the filename **addresses**. We want to link the file to a file created in Eric's home directory, **/users/erc**. We do so with the **ln** command, working out of Kevin's home directory:

```
$ ln addresses /users/erc/addresses
```

In other words, the syntax is:

```
$ ln originalfile targetfile
```

Even though there are two directory entries for the file addresses (in the **/users/kevin** and **/users/erc** directories), there exists only one actual file, in the **/users/kevin** directory.

Here we use addresses to denote the linked files. However, both linked files do not necessarily need to share the same name. You may want to use the suffix **.link** (as in **address.link**) to denote a linked file. If you remove this linked file later, it will not affect the original file.

 This explanation of links is done with great reluctance. Most UNIX users won't need to be creating links unless they're a system administrator of some sort. In addition, there's the potential for creating future harm if you create an ill-conceived link. Therefore, approach links with caution.

Symbolic Links

As we mentioned earlier, System V Release 4 introduces the notion of symbolic links, which can link files from other filesystems. Use the *-s* option to the **ln** command:

```
$ ln -s /othersystem/data/numbers numbers.link
```

This creates a linked file named **numbers.link** in your current subdirectory; the file is linked to the file **numbers** in the **/othersystem/data** directory on the other file system. In other words, the syntax is:

```
$ ln -s originalfile targetfile
```

WARNING

The previous warning about links also applies to symbolic links. Again, approach links with caution.

Wildcards

So far our discussion has centered about the manipulation of single files and directories. UNIX provides an amazingly powerful tool, called *wildcards*, that allows you to manipulate multiple files at one time, with a single command. Wildcards are a kind of shorthand that allows you to specify similar files without having to type multiple names. And wildcards allow you to search for files even if you don't remember the exact name.

There are three types of UNIX wildcards: *****, **?**, and **[...]**. We'll cover each of them.

In every instance in this chapter where we've used single filenames you could use a wildcard. Let's go back to the **ls** command. Let's say you want to find all files in your directory ending with the string *report*. You could use the **ls** command in conjunction with a wildcard:

```
$ ls *report
1991.report      1992.report      erc.report      kevin.report
```

These four files represent the number of files in the current directory ending in the string *report*.

The asterisk wildcard is used to match any number of characters in a string (including zero characters). It can be used anywhere in the string. If you wanted to list the files beginning with the string *report*, you would use **ls** along with the following wildcard:

```
$ ls report*
report.new      report.old      reports.old      reporters.note
```

If you wanted to list the files with the string *report* somewhere in the filename, use:

```
$ ls *report*
1991.report      1992.report      erc.report      kevin.report
newreport91      newreport92      oldreport91      oldreport92
report.new       report.old       reports.old      reporters.note
```

Note that we've received a list of files that both end and begin with report, as well as the files with report in the middle of the filename. As we said, the * wildcard can be used to match any number of characters in a string. In this case the wildcard matched zero characters.

Conversely, the **?** wildcard is used to match a single character in a string:

```
$ ls report?
report1      report2      report3      report4
```

In our example the **ls** command did *not* return **report.1992** as a match. That's because there are five characters following the string *report*, and we only asked for one. As with the asterisk wildcard, the **?** wildcard can appear anywhere in a string.

You can combine the * and **?** wildcards:

```
$ ls ?report*
1report1991      2report      3report92
```

to return the filenames of all files beginning with a single character followed by the string *report* and ending with any number of characters.

The final wildcard option is denoted by brackets. Here you can ask UNIX to match specified characters:

```
$ ls report199[01]
report1990
```

This becomes especially useful when you're looking for files and you're not entirely sure of the case (remember, UNIX distinguishes between uppercase and lowercase characters):

```
$ ls report.[Ee]rc
report.Erc      report.erc
```

You can also use a hyphen to denote a range of characters between brackets:

```
$ ls report[a-d]
reporta      reportb      reportc      reportd
```

This command did *not* return the filename **reporte**, because it did not fall in the range of characters defined within the brackets.

Even though we've used the **ls** command in our examples, wildcards can be used with any UNIX command—**rm**, **mv**, **cp**, and so on.

Be careful, though, with versions of System V UNIX. With this type of UNIX system, you can ask for too many files. System V enforces a finite size for the command-line parameters to any program. Thus, you'll sometimes see a message like the following:

```
$ ls */*
Arguments too long.
```

If you see such a message, your only recourse is to create a command that takes a much smaller number of parameters. For example, you could ask for all files in directories that begin with uppercase letters:

```
$ ls [A-Z]*/*
```

Then ask for all files in directories that begin with lowercase letters:

```
$ ls [a-z]*/*
```

Whatever method you use, you must find a way to divide up the number of files passed on the command line.

The moral of this section on wildcards is simple: *Thoughtful file organization will save you tons of time in the future.* Instead of giving your files haphazard or cutesy names, take the time to think through your work and name your files accordingly. For example, if you place the string *report* or *rep* in every report file you create, it will be a lot easier to locate these files in the future thanks to wildcards.

DOS wildcards are similar to UNIX wildcards. However, DOS wildcards are surprisingly limited. Only the *** and *?* wildcards are supported, and they can be used in limited circumstances: either at the beginning or end of filenames, or only as a substitute for the entire suffix. The following would be an acceptable DOS command:

```
C:>dir *.c
```

but not the following:

```
C:>dir *.C*
```

If you're a Macintosh user, then the notion of wildcards will be as foreign as Sanskrit. One of the great failures of the Macintosh operating system is the lack of wildcards for file manipulation.

 Removing multiple files with wildcards is easy—perhaps *too* easy. Before clearing a directory, take the time to look through it and make sure that you do really want to delete the files.

WARNING

It's also very easy to make a typing error when entering a command—and in the case of wildcards and file removals, a typo can be disastrous. Let's say you want to remove all the files in your current directory ending in **1990**. The command is simple:

```
$ rm *1990
```

But if you're sloppy or inattentive, you could easily type a command that is slightly different:

```
$ rm * 1990
```

In this case UNIX will ignore the **1990** and concentrate on the wildcard when removing files—in other words, *all* your files in the current directory will be removed. You can use the *-i* option to **rm**, described above, to help limit the effects of a misformed **rm** command.

Finding Files

Even though we've lectured you about the necessity of good file organization, it's inevitable that you'll lose track of a file—and usually the more important the file the more likely you'll lose track of it.

UNIX features a powerful command, **find**, that helps you locate the wayward file (too powerful at times, as we'll see). Let's say that you've misplaced a file named **1992.data**. If you're truly masochistic, you can use the following command to find it:

```
$ find / -name 1992.data -print
```

Why do we call this a masochistic maneuver? Because UNIX does exactly as you tell it. In this case we told it to start its search from the top of the directory structure (remember, the root directory is indicated by the slash character). We told it to look for a file named **1992.data** (using the *-name* option) and then tell us the results via the *-print* option. If you don't specify the *-print* option, UNIX will search the file but fail to tell you the results. (There are valid reasons for this seeming incongruity, mostly concerning pipes. But it's nothing you need to worry about.)

In this case UNIX searches for the file **1992.data** in every directory and subdirectory in the entire system. If you're working on a large, multiuser system with hundreds of megabytes of storage space, it can take quite a while to find this file—especially given the fact that **1992.data** is not exactly a distinctive filename and that there's a very good chance another user may have appropriated the same name. Even on a single-user system with 300 or 600 megabytes of hard-disk space, the search can take too long.

It's best to use the **find** command with some limitations, such as specific directories. Let's say we know that the file **1992.data** is located somewhere in the **/users** directory. We use the following to narrow the search criteria:

```
$ find /users -name 1992.data -print
/users/home/data/1992.data
/users/kevin/data/1992/1992.data
```

Let's say you don't remember the exact name of the file; you know that you created it sometime in the 1990s but don't remember the exact year. Since you're an organized user and denote all your files with the year as a prefix, you could use a wildcard to search for all files beginning with the string *199*:

```
$ find -name "199*" -print
```

When using the *-name* option, be sure to enclose your *search* string in quotes. UNIX is rather quirky on this point and perhaps overly complex. The reason for this is that the command interpreter (called *shell* in UNIX parlance) would expand the **199*** to mean the name of every file *in the current directory* that starts with *199*—which is most definitely *not* what you intended.

Finding Files in the Background

As we mentioned earlier, it's best to use the **find** command with some constraints; after all, it takes a long time to chug through a large hard disk.

But there are times when you can't avoid searching for a file across the entire hard disk. Remember: UNIX is a multitasking operating system, which means it can perform more than one task at a time. Under these circumstances you may want to run the **find** command in the background; this allows you to perform other tasks in the foreground while UNIX looks for the file.

To search for the file **1992.report** in the background, end the command with an ampersand:

```
$ find / -name 1992.report -print &
```

This tells UNIX to search for the file **1992.report**, beginning at the top of the file structure with the root directory and moving downward, and alerting you when the file is found. The ampersand (**&**) tells UNIX to perform this task in the background. (We'll discuss running tasks in the background in Chapter 4.)

However, you may not want to be alerted when the file is found, particularly if there are potentially many instances of the file. To print the results to a file instead of to your screen, insert the > symbol as well as a filename in the command:

```
$ find / -name 1992.report -print > results &
```

This directs the output of the search to the file **results**. In general, the > command will direct the output of a command to a file; we'll use the > command many times throughout the course of this book.

Viewing Files with Cat

There are times when you may want to view the contents of a file but don't want to go to the fuss of running a text editor. UNIX provides a number of relevant commands, the simplest being **cat**.

To merely display the contents of a file containing ASCII text, use the **cat** (short for *concatenate*) command:

```
$ cat erc.memo
The proposal by Spacely Sprockets is simply
unacceptable and does not fit with our long-term
corporate interests. Nuke it.
```

In this instance, the screen is the default output for the **cat** command: This means that the results of your command are displayed on your screen, unless you specify otherwise. This refers back to the UNIX philosophy as defined at the beginning of this chapter: Everything in UNIX can be represented as a file, and in this case the unsaid assumption is that the output of the **cat** command is output to the screen.

However, this means you can direct the output of the **cat** command to other outputs, such as other files (this is also how UNIX manages to print files). For example, you can send the output of the **cat** command to another file (creating a very simple backup procedure for single files):

```
$ cat erc.memo > eric.memo.bak
```

The system creates the file **eric.memo.bak** if it doesn't exist. If it does exist, **cat** will overwrite the file with the new data—once again, we see that UNIX will trample existing files unless you, the user, take some safeguards.

Using Cat to Create a File

You can also use **cat** to create ASCII files if you're not inclined toward using a text editor. The command:

```
$ cat > spacely
```

creates a file named **spacely** and sends output from your keyboard into that file, one line at a time. When you're typing this file, there are a few rules to follow:

▼ At the end of every line, hit the **Enter** key.

▼ You can move around the current line with the **Backspace** key. However, you cannot move from line to line.

▼ When you're finished typing into the file, type **Ctrl-D**.

You can also use **cat** to add data to the end of an existing file. If you want to add information to the file **spacely**, use the following:

```
$ cat >> spacely
```

and begin typing, using the same rules outlined in the previous paragraph.

Viewing Files with Pg

The **cat** command may be adequate for viewing short files, but it is awkward for viewing long files. The **pg** command allows you to view files one page at a time. In many ways **pg** invokes a primitive text editor—not quite as advanced as something like **vi** or **emacs**, but powerful enough for rudimentary work.

Starting **pg** is simple:

```
$ pg spacely
```

This displays the first page of the file **spacely** on your screen, then prompts you for a subsequent command:

▼ To display the next page, hit the **Enter** key.

▼ To move back one page, type - (the hyphen key).

▼ To move ahead or back a given number of pages, use plus (**+**) or minus (**-**) and the number of pages to be moved.

▼ To move by lines, use plus (**+**) or minus (**-**) in combination with **l** (ell) — the command **+6l** moves the text ahead six lines.

▼ To move ahead one-half of a page, type **d**.

▼ To search for a string of text, bracket the string between slashes:

```
/eric/
```

Using More to View a File

In addition to **pg**, there's a similar command called **more**. **More** presents a page at a time of a file. Some UNIX users argue that **more** is easier to use than **pg**, and they may be right; if you find yourself needing the capability to view files often, you'll want to compare the two and make your own decision.

Using **more** is pretty simple: You press the **Spacebar** to go ahead one page, and you press **q** to quit.

```
$ more long_file
```

Heads and Tails

You many not want to scroll through an entire document to get to the end, or you may just want to quickly check out the beginning of a file. Use the **head** and **tail** commands in these instances. To view the first 10 lines of the file **data**, use the following:

```
$ head data
```

To view the last 10 lines of the file data, use the following:

```
$ tail data
```

To view a specific number of lines at the beginning or end of a file, combine **head** or **tail** with a numerical argument. The following displays the final 15 lines in the file **data**:

```
$ tail -15 data
```

Combining Files

You can also use the **cat** command to combine files. Let's say that both Eric and Kevin have been compiling lists of corporate contacts in address files named **kevin.address** and **eric.address**. You can use the **cat** command to combine these files into a third, new file named **addresses**:

```
$ cat kevin.address eric.address > addresses
```

You can merge more than two files into a combined file. Using **cat**, we could combine all the files in a directory into a final, merged file:

```
$ ls
luser            addresses       erc.address
farmers          geisha.address  kevin.address
spike.address    tom.address     uber.address
$ cat *address > many.addresses
```

In this procedure we first listed the files in the current directory. With the resulting **cat** command, we combined all filenames ending with the string *address* (**erc.address**, **geisha.address**, **kevin.address**, **spike.address**, **tom.address**, and

uber.address) into a final file named **many.addresses**. The command did not affect the files **1user**, **addresses**, and **farmers**.

You can also use the **cat** command to add the contents of a file to the end of an existing file. Using our same example, we may want to add Eric's addresses to the end of Kevin's address file. We would use the following command:

```
$ cat eric.address >> kevin.address
```

The resulting file would contain Kevin's addresses, followed by Eric's addresses.

What the Heck is in this Old File?

As you meander your merry way through your UNIX usage, you'll accumulate a lot of files. And we mean *a lot*—UNIX encourages the accumulation of these files.

When this happens, you'll discover that, despite your best organization efforts, you have a host of files sitting in various directories—and you don't have a clue as the contents of these files. You don't want to use **cat** to view these files; if the file is a binary file, **cat** will send all sorts of garbage to the terminal, with the result being a screwed-up login (some of the characters may be interpreted in strange ways by the shell). The same goes for using **vi** or another text editor to view the file.

UNIX contains a command, **file**, that looks through a file and returns information about the file. Some UNIX files contain a *magic number* that identifies the type of the file, its purpose, and its originator. The use of magic numbers isn't total in the UNIX world (check the file **/etc/magic** to see what file types your system can spot), but in most cases you'll find that the **file** command works quite well when identifying these mystery files.

To use **file**, enter it on a command line, along with the mystery file:

```
$ file mysteryfile
```

If **mysteryfile** is a binary program, **file** will return information relating to your machine (such as *sparc* if the file is compiled to run on your Sun SPARCstation), how it's compiled (*dynamically linked*), and the "pure" file type, described earlier in this chapter (in this case the file would be an *executable*). However, if the file is a program file and **file** can't figure out exactly what it contains, you'll be told that the file is *data*:

```
$ file mysteryfile
mysteryfile          data
```

If the file is text, you'll be told that:

```
$ file mysteryfile
mysteryfile          text
```

In this case you can use **head** or **tail** (as explained earlier in this chapter) to view the file.

Printing Files

Our final topic relating to files and directories concerns printing. If you're a system administrator, printing can be a complex area filled with arcane printer types and configurations. But for the user, printing documents in UNIX is a relatively simple matter that revolves around three commands: **lp**, **lpstat**, and **cancel**. We'll cover each of these commands.

Using lp

Depending on your version of UNIX, you'll use the **lp** (System V) or **lpr** (System V Release 4 and BSD UNIX) commands to print a file:

```
$ lp filename
```

or

```
$ lpr filename
```

After running the commands, the system will list the printer (sysdot) and will generate an ID number (141) should you want to check the status of the printing request at a later time.

Using wildcards, you could print several files at once:

```
$ lpr file*
```

In this instance we are printing all files that begin with the string *file*.

There may be more than one printer on a UNIX network (dot-matrix for internal user, laser for correspondence and important documents, etc.). UNIX allows for a system default, which is the printer used by the system unless specified otherwise. (You can change your default by editing your **.profile** file, a topic we'll cover in Chapter 4). Printer names may not be immediately clear to you (sometimes lazy system administrator use numbers, while others will use names like *laser1* to provide clearer information to users), so if you have access to multiple printers on your network, ask your system administrator for a complete and clear listing.

If you want to send a file to a printer that is not the default printer, use the *-d* option along with the printer's name:

```
$ lpr -d pslaser filename
```

This sends the file **filename** to the printer *pslaser*.

On a large multiuser system, there may be several users wanting access immediately to a printer. UNIX manages these multiple requests by setting up a print queue to the printer. Printer requests are handled in the order they appear. The print requests are then spooled: kept in memory by UNIX and then acted upon later.

Some Things to Note When Printing Files

How UNIX actually prints files can be a sometimes confusing notion to users—and rightfully so. When you send a file to be printed, you're not *really* sending the actual file somewhere along the network: You're sending a request for the system to print a particular file when it is ready. Since printer requests can be spooled, the system may take a few minutes or more to get ready. If you change the file and save those files to disk—by editing it, renaming it, or deleting it—the system will print the changed file or, in the case of renamed or deleted files, not be able to complete the print request.

 This isn't universally true in the UNIX world, unfortunately; BSD UNIX does it the opposite way, printing the file as it existed when you made the **lp/lpr** command.

N O T E

If you're using System V Release 4 and are planning on immediately changing a file after sending to the printer, use the *-c* (*copy*) option in your command:

```
$ lp -c filename
```

The system makes a copy of the file filename and uses that file for printing. If you need to make changes to that file, go ahead; they won't be reflected in the printed copy.

 Some systems use **lpr** for the print command, instead of **lp**. In such a case, to print out a file named **1993.report**, you'd use the following command:

N O T E
```
% lpr 1993.report
```

Using Lpstat

As mentioned, print requests may not be performed immediately. If there are many files to be printed, you may want to monitor the print requests; after all, printers do go down, and UNIX does not provide for an error messages should a printer run out of paper or suffer a paper jam.

Use the **lpstat** command to view the current status of print requests:

```
$ lpstat
sysdot-141          kevin       2121    Jun 28 10:29 on sysdot
laser1-198          erc        19002    Jun 28 10:31 on laser1
laser1-124          erc         5543    Jun 28 10:35
laser1-136          kevin       1992    Jun 28 10:36
```

Using the first line as the guide, we can divine the printer (*sysdot*), the document ID (*141*), the user ID (*kevin*), the size of the file in bytes (*2121*), the date (*June 28*), the time (*10:29*), and whether the file is printing (denoted by the on notation; if the file was not printing, there would be no on notation). We can also see from this output that there are multiple print requests from both Kevin and Eric to the laser printer, and that Kevin and Eric should both be patient because Eric has sent a large file to the laser printer.

Canceling Print Requests

A common situation occurs when you want to cancel a print request. You may have designated the wrong file for printing, or you may have decided to make changes in the printed file. You can cancel print requests with the **cancel** command:

```
$ cancel laser1-124
request "laser1-124" canceled
```

BSD UNIX users would use the **lprm** command:

```
$ lprm laser1-124
```

Summary

UNIX uses files for just about everything. Every document you create is a file. Every command you run is a program stored in a file on disk. Even the printer is a special file. Files are classes into file types: ordinary files, directories, links, and special files (like the printer). Every file has access permissions, based on user (the owner of the file), the owner's group, and everyone else, called oddly enough, world permissions (the whole world is the computer—a scary thought). These permissions include the ability to read, write, and execute the file as a command. For files, there are three levels of permissions: Read permission means that you can read the file, write permission means that you can change the file, and execute permission means that you can run the file as a program.

UNIX uses a hierarchical file system. At the top of the tree is the root directory, usually represented by a slash (/). Each user on a UNIX system is given an account, with a home directory. For a user named kevin, this home directory might be **/users/kevin**.

The **cd** command allows you to change your current working directory. The **pwd** command prints out the name of this current directory.

The **ls** command lists the files in a given directory. You can use many options with **ls** to control how much information about files you see, as well as the way **ls** formats the data.

To manipulate files, the **mv** command moves files. The **cp** command copies files and the **rm** command removes files. The **find** command helps you track down errant files. **Cat** prints a file to the screen and **lp** prints a file to the printer.

To create a directory, use **mkdir**. To get rid of a directory, use **rmdir**.

UNIX Tools

This chapter covers the following commands:

- ▼ **Grep**, **egrep**, and **fgrep**, used for searches
- ▼ **Sort**, used for sorting files
- ▼ **Cmp**, **comm**, **diff**, and **dircmp**, used for comparing files
- ▼ **Cut**, used to grab data from files
- ▼ **Paste** and **join**, used to merge files
- ▼ **Tr**, used to search and replace
- ▼ **Split**, used to split files
- ▼ **Strings** and **od**, used to view non-ASCII files

Small Tools, Large Tasks

Much of the hidden power in the UNIX operating system lies within the various utilities summoned from the command line. While these utilities may not appear to be overwhelmingly powerful individually, they do the job, and they do it well and efficiently (which is all we can expect from our computer tools). These tools can be used by themselves (as detailed in this chapter) or in conjunction with other commands (a process we'll cover in Chapter 4) to create ever more-powerful combinations.

The tools we present here are varied. Working with our tutorial theme in mind, we'll present the tools organized by subject grouping and show you specific examples of how these UNIX tools can be used to solve many of your basic computing problems.

Many of the tools presented here were designed with very specific purposes in mind. And many of them are described in UNIX parlance, accurately, as *filters*.

Looking for Love—Or Something Like It

We've all done it: needed to find a nugget of data and couldn't remember exactly where we stored it. Instead of manually searching through the hundreds of files on our system, we can invoke three UNIX tools: **grep**, **egrep**, and **fgrep**.

Grep

Grep searches for text either in a single file or in any number of files you specify. It goes through the file and returns the lines containing your specified text. The text can be a single word or a string surrounded by quotation marks.

To have **grep** search through the file **erc.memo.712** for the string *Spacely,* enter the following:

```
$ grep Spacely erc.memo.712
This proposal from Spacely Sprockets is a farce and
```

In this instance we had **grep** search for a single word. To have **grep** search for a phrase containing a space, we must enclose the phrase in quotation marks, as follows:

```
$ grep "Spacely Sprockets" erc.memo.712
This proposal from Spacely Sprockets is a farce and
```

If we can't remember the exact file containing the string *Spacely Sprockets*, we could use a wildcard to have **grep** search through some or all of the files in the current directory:

```
$ grep "Spacely Sprockets" *
erc.memo: This proposal from Spacely Sprockets is a farce and
erc.memo.712: This proposal from Spacely Sprockets is a farce and
```

As we can see, **grep** returns the names of the two files containing the string *Spacely Sprockets*, as well as the lines containing the text.

Here are some rules to remember when using **grep**:

▼ **Grep** searches one line at a time. If, in our example, *Spacely* and *Sprockets* had appeared on two different lines, **grep** would not have reported a match.

▼ **Grep** looks for strings of text and does not limit itself to whole words. A search for the string *town* could return lines containing the words *townspeople*, *downtown*, and *town*.

▼ **Grep** can be used with wildcards to search for patterns. Let's say that you want to look for all instances of *Spacely Sprockets*, but you're familiar with **grep**'s rules, and you know that if the two words appear on different lines, **grep** would ignore them. In this case, we could use a wildcard search to return all instances of words beginning with *Sp*:

```
$ grep "Sp*" *
```

In this case we used wildcards (denoted by the asterisks) to mean two different things. The first instance tells **grep** to search for any word beginning with *Sp*; the second wildcard tells **grep** to search through all the files in the current directory.

▼ **Grep** distinguishes between uppercase and lowercase characters, unless told otherwise. To tell **grep** to ignore case, use the *-i* option:

```
$ grep -i Spacely erc.memo.712
```

▼ If you don't want **grep** to list the lines of text matching your specified string, use the *-l* (ell, not one) option to list only the matching files:

```
$ grep -l "Spacely Sprockets" *
erc.memo
erc.memo.712
```

▼ You may want to search files for lines not containing a certain string. To use **grep** as an antisearcher, insert the *-v* option:

```
$ grep -v Spacely erc.memo.712
Dear Mr. King:
an insult to the intelligence of every worker here.
--Eric
```

Egrep

While **egrep** supports all the functions of **grep**, it goes a step further and allows for the searching of multiple strings. For example, we may want to search for every instance of multiple companies that have been the recipients of our correspondence. Do this by combining the names of the companies with a pipe symbol, surrounded by quotation marks:

```
$ egrep "Spacely Sprockets|Jetson Enterprises" *
erc.memo.712: This proposal from Spacely Sprockets is a farce and
erc.memo.714: As a representative of Jetson Enterprises
```

Fgrep

Fgrep (shorthand for *fast grep*) works similarly to **egrep**, but instead of using a pipe command and quotation marks to specify the text, each item must be placed on its own line:

```
$ fgrep "Spacely Sprockets
Jetson Enterprises" *
erc.memo.712: This proposal from Spacely Sprockets is a farce and
erc.memo.714: As a representative of Jetson Enterprises
```

Many systems use an **fgrep** command that acts just like **grep**, but faster and with limited options. Consult your system manuals to determine what your version of **fgrep** does.

Sorting Files

There are times when you'll want to arrange the contents of a file in a specific order. Whether it be comparing files in alphabetic order or setting up a database in numerical order, sorting a file can be a great productivity enhancer. UNIX features a particularly useful tool for sorting files, named (predictably enough) **sort**.

To use an example: Let's say we wanted to sort a list of city and state names that we entered into a file in no particular order. We discover this disorder after reading through the file using the **cat** command:

```
$ cat AL_West
Minnesota
Oakland
Texas
Chicago
Kansas City
Seattle
California
```

Let's say we're from California and didn't like the fact that Minnesota was first in the **AL_West** file. We could sort the file to make things more palatable:

```
$ sort AL_West
California
Chicago
Kansas City
Minnesota
Oakland
Seattle
Texas
```

(This is definitely a time for abstraction; California is rarely first in the A.L. West.)

The **sort** command reports only to the screen; the actual file remains unchanged. Thus in our example Minnesota remains in first place in the file **AL_West**. If we wanted to save the results of a sort in another file, we would name both the originating and destination file on the command line:

```
$ sort AL_West > AL_West.sort
```

The results of this sort are not shown on the screen because we have used the **>** to denote a destination file. Use the **cat** command to view the resulting file, **AL_West.sort**.

You cannot use this redirection (**>**) to sort a file and have it retain the same name. Instead use the *-o* option:

```
$ sort -o AL_West AL_West
```

You could use **sort** to sort and combine more than one file:

```
$ sort AL_West AL_East NL_East NL_West > Baseball
```

To compare two sorted files, use **comm**:

```
$ comm AL_West NL_East
California
                                        Chicago
Kansas City
Minnesota
                Montreal
                New York
Oakland
                Philadelphia
                Pittsburgh
Seattle
                St. Louis
Texas
```

The output arrives in three columns: Column 1 contains lines unique to the first file, Column 2 contains lines unique to the second file, and Column 3 contains lines occurring in both files.

Saving the results of **comm** is a matter of directing the output to a file:

```
$ comm AL_West NL_East > baseball.sort
```

In our example Chicago appears in both files. If we wanted to sort multiple files and eliminate such redundancies, we would sort with the *-u* option:

```
$ comm -u AL_West NL_East > baseball.sort
```

Some versions of **comm** don't support the *-u* option. If you're using UNIX System V Release 4, **comm** should support the *-u* option.

N O T E

Additional Sorts

So far we've used the default **sort** command, which arranges the lines in a file in alphabetical order. But not every sort needs to center around a straight alphabetic sorting order. Let's say you maintained a file, **debts**, with the names of all the people who owed you money and the exact amounts they owed. To sort this file by numeral, use the *-n* option:

```
$ sort -n debts
```

Why use the numerical sort? Compare these two sorts:

```
$ sort debts
1     Kevin
12    Eric
23    Geisha
3     Spike
```

and

```
$ sort -n debts
1     Kevin
3     Spike
12    Eric
23    Geisha
```

With a sort sans the numerical option, **sort** followed the standard alphabetical rules of sorting and so did not analyze the numbers. Of course, in a file full of debtors, you'd want to list the largest debts first. The *-r* option allows you to sort a file in reverse order. Here we combine it with the *-n* option:

```
$ sort -rn debts
23    Geisha
12    Eric
3     Spike
1     Kevin
```

Let's say you wanted to sort the list of debtors by name instead of debt. You accomplish this by telling **sort** to skip a column with the *+1* (one, not ell) option:

```
$ sort +1 debts
12    Eric
23    Geisha
1     Kevin
3     Spike
```

You can tell **sort** to skip as many columns as you want.

File Comparisons

We've already seen how the number of files generated by UNIX tends to increase exponentially over the course of time. We know that many new files are created during the course of updating older files. And, knowing human nature as we do, we know that you may not have been perfectly meticulous in your file-management duties. The end result may be a set of files that are similar but contain small differences as a result of editing and revisions.

UNIX contains several tools that compares files: **cmp**, **comm**, **diff**, and **dircmp**.

Cmp and Diff

The **cmp** command compares two files and tells you if the files are different; if they are, **cmp** reports the first instance of a difference. **Cmp** does not report *all* differences between the files, and it will report nothing back to you if the files are the same. After we sneak a peek at two files (using the **cat** command), we can see how **cmp** works:

```
$ cat erc.memo
Dear Boss:
This proposal from Spacely Sprockets is a farce and
an insult to the intelligence of every worker here.
This idea should be nuked.


$ cat erc.memo.712
Dear Mr. King:
This proposal from Spacely Sprockets is a farce and
an insult to the intelligence of every worker here.
--Eric
```

```
$ cmp erc.memo erc.memo.712
erc.memo erc.memo.712 differ: char 6, line 1
```

Cmp reports that the two files differ in the sixth character of the document, located in line 1. And indeed they do—the salutation has changed. Using **cmp** is the simplest and quickest way to compare two files, but you only know if the files are different. You don't know to what extent the files are different, nor do you know how they are different.

Diff, on the other hand, compares two files, tells you if the files are different, and cites each difference:

```
$ diff erc.memo erc.memo.712
1c1
< Dear Boss:
- - -
> Dear Mr. King:
4c4
< This idea should be nuked.
- - -
> --Eric
```

As you can see, **diff** reports back significantly more information than does **cmp**. Lines beginning with < are found only in the first file, while lines beginning with > are found only in the second file. The dashed line separates the two lines that appear in the same place in the differing files. The numerals indicate exactly where and how differences occur: *1c1* means that there was a change (*c*) in line 1(*1*) of the first file and line 1 (*1*) of the second file. Characters that were deleted from one version are noted by a *d*, while an *a* means that a line was appended to a file.

Plucking Data from Tables

On a very rudimentary basis, we could use the basic UNIX commands as database-management tools.

Let's say we were the manager of a small workgroup, and we wanted keep a small database of our workers. Using **vi** or **emacs** (both reviewed in Chapter 11), we have created a file that contains vital information about our employees:

```
$ cat workers
```

```
Eric      286    555-6674    erc        8
Geisha    280    555-4221    geisha    10
Kevin     279    555-1112    kevin      2
Tom       284    555-2121    spike     12
```

Our sample database is very simple: We list the name of the worker, their office telephone extension, their login names, and the number of vacation days they have remaining this year. The columns of information are separated by tabs. Databases like this are very common in UNIX, for both personal usage and system administration.

From this **workers** file we can create many other lists. Let's say we want to create a file containing just the names and phone numbers of our workers for the personnel office. We would do so using the **cut** command, specifying a file for output:

```
$ cut f1,3 workers > workers_phone
```

The structure of this command is simple. We tell the shell to cut the first and third fields in the file **workers** and to place them in the file **workers_phone**. We could have specified one field, or we could have specified all but one field. We could have specified a range of fields:

```
$ cut f1-3,5 workers > workers_phone
```

We also could have used **cut** to pluck information from a number of similarly structured files:

```
$ cut f1,3 workers.1 workers.2 > workers_phone
```

Our example file was highly structured, using tabs to separate columns. If another character was used to separate fields, we would need to specify the character using the *-d* option:

```
$ cut -d, f1,3 workers > workers_phone
```

The character must be placed directly following the *-d* option. In our case, we told **cut** that it was to use commas as the separators between fields. If we were to use a space as a separator, we would enclose it in single quotes:

```
$ cut -d' ' f1,3 workers > workers_phone
```

If we didn't, the shell would assume that the space was a normal part of our command and not related to the *-d* option.

Of course, not all UNIX files are going to be as highly structured as our example. In these cases we could use **cut** and specify a range of characters to be cut:

```
$ cut -c1-20,23-30 workers > workers_phone
```

This tells **cut** to grab the first 20 characters in a line, as well as all characters between the 23d and 30th characters.

Merging Files

There are two ways to merge files in UNIX: With the **paste** and **join** commands.

Paste joins together two or more files line by line; that is, the first line in the second file will be pasted to the first line of the first file. With text files, the output from this command would look pretty silly; with files full of columns and tables, this command can be useful. Using **paste** is simple—just specify the files to be pasted together and a file to contain the pasted data:

```
$ paste file1 file2 > file.paste
```

As with **cut**, you can specify which character was used to separate fields:

```
$ paste -d, file1 file2 > file.paste
```

The character must be placed directly following the *-d* option. In our case, we told **paste** that it was to use commas as the separators between fields.

We could combine **cut** with **paste** to form new files or rearrange existing files. Let's say we wanted to change the order of our **workers** files. Instead of retyping the entire file, we could cut the phone number column from the file, rearrange the remaining lines, and then paste the whole shebang to a new file:

```
$ cut -f1-2,4-5 > newworkers
$ cut -f3 workers > newworkers.2
$ paste newworkers newworkers.2 > workers.2
```

Our **workers.2** would look like this:

```
$ cat workers.2
Eric      286    erc       8    555-6674
Geisha    280    geisha    10   555-4221
```

```
Kevin       279    kevin     2    555-1112
Tom         284    spike    12    555-2121
```

A better way of merging files, provided that the files contain one common field, is through the **join** command. Using our continuing example of worker-based files, let's say we were maintaining two separate files of employee information and wanted to join them. The process goes as follows:

```
$ cat workers
Eric      8    555-6674
Geisha    10   555-4221
Kevin     2    555-1112
Tom       12   555-2121


$ cat workers.2
Eric      286    erc
Geisha    280    geisha
Kevin     279    kevin
Tom       284    spike


$ join workers workers.2 > workers.3
$ cat workers.3
Eric      286    erc        8    555-6674
Geisha    280    geisha    10    555-4221
Kevin     279    kevin      2    555-1112
Tom       284    spike     12    555-2121
```

By default, the **join** command will work only when the first fields of each file match and are sorted identically. You could join files based on fields other than the first in each files. The following would join two files based on the second and fourth columns:

```
$ join -j1 2 -j2 4 workers workers.2 > workers.3
```

This syntax is somewhat confusing. Here we are using the *-j* option to join the second column of the first file (*-j1 2*) to the fourth column of the second file (*-j2 4*). The files are specified *after* the command and options.

As with **cut** and **paste**, you can specify the field separators.

Global Replacements

There are times we may want to change repeating parts of a file. For example, we may want to change our **workers** file to use commas instead of tabs as column delineators.

In these cases we can call on the **tr** (translate) command. Essentially, **tr** does a search and replace on an entire file. In our case, we want to change the tabs to commas. We would do so with the following command:

```
$ tr '<TAB>' , < workers
```

Note the single quotes. If we didn't enclose the tab in single quotation marks, the shell would assume that the tab was white space. Also, notice the strange structure of the **tr** command. It is an anomaly in the UNIX world, so make sure you don't rely on normal UNIX syntax with the **tr** command.

Tr could also be used to change the case of every character in a file. Let's say that someone has given you a text file containing nothing but uppercase letters. Common sense tells us that most text files contain far more lowercase letter than uppercase letters, so it would be easier to go through the file and make characters uppercase. However, to get to this point, we'll need to change the case of every character in the file. Do so with the following:

```
$ tr '[A-Z]' '[a-z]' < file
```

Splitting Files with Split

Some text editors, such as **ed**, choke on large files, refusing to load them for editing. Other times, large files are a pain to work with, especially if the files don't necessarily need to be large. In these cases, you'll want to split up a large file so you can easily work with it.

The UNIX **split** command does exactly this: It splits an ASCII file into smaller files. It's rather easy to use:

```
$ split names
```

The **names** file will then be split into smaller, 1,000-line files. (The original remains intact, however.) The **split** command also names the new files in a logical manner, based on the original filename: The first filename is **names.aa**, the second filename is **names.ab**, and so on.

If you want files to be smaller than 1,000 lines, you can specify your own file size on the command line as an option:

```
$ split -100 names
```

 Don't use the **split** command with non-ASCII files. Other file formats store data differently, and the data contained within may rely on information found at the beginning or end of a file.

Checking Your Spelling

Even though the ability to spell doesn't seem to be a prerequisite for attaining high government office, you can use the UNIX **spell** command to help your spelling. **Spell** is intended to work with UNIX pipes and input redirection (see Chapter 4 for more on this), so **spell** sports a very primitive interface. In addition, **spell** works backwards from what you'd expect: **spell** tells you what words it thinks you misspelled, but offers no suggestions for the proper spelling. The syntax of the **spell** command is simple:

```
$ spell filename
```

Spell will then examine all the words in the given file and print out a sorted list of all the words **spell** flagged as errors. It's up to you to search for these words in the original file and make corrections, using a text editor such as **vi** or **emacs** (see Chapter 11 for more on **vi** and **emacs**).

If you're unsure of the spelling of a word, we suggest you put in as many different spellings as you can think of. Then, use a process of elimination to figure out how to spell the word correctly. For example, if you forget how to spell *potato*, you can create a temporary file with as many different possible spellings as you can think of:

```
potatoe
potato
```

If you name this file **potato.spell**, you can then spell-check the file:

```
$ spell potato.spell
potatoe
```

From this, we know that *potato* is the proper spelling. We also know that the UNIX spelling checker, limited as it may be, is better than a certain former vice-president, who shall remain nameless.

WARNING

Don't totally trust any computerized spell-checking program, even if it comes with a full-featured word processor like WordPerfect for UNIX. These programs usually use dictionaries of words, and they often make mistakes. The UNIX **spell** command, for example, will flag any word it doesn't have in its dictionary as an error. This dictionary, however, is not all-encompassing. The dictionary may be incomplete, and you might have spelled the word correctly. Use your best judgment—and a lot of common sense—when working with any computerized spell-checker.

Viewing Files with Strings and Od

You've already learned how to view the contents of a file with the **cat** command in Chapter 2.

The **cat** command, however, is limited to displaying ASCII characters. There may be times, especially if you're a beginning programmer, when you want to display non-ASCII files (usually used when you want to look for some ASCII strings in a program file). In these cases, you'll want to use the **strings** command to view the file in a format you can handle. The following command line displays the file named **program**:

```
$ strings program
```

If this is a larger file—and chances are pretty good that it will be—you'll want to redirect the output from the screen to a file:

```
$ strings program > file
```

or display the output one screen at a time with the **pg** or **more** commands:

```
$ strings program | more
```

Similarly useful is the **od** command, which displays an *octal dump* of a file to the screen. (If you don't know what an octal dump is, chances are pretty good that you won't find this command very useful.)

Summary

UNIX provides hundreds of powerful tools for working with text files and other aspects of your system. The **grep** command and its brethren **fgrep** and **egrep** search text files for words and phrases. **Grep** searches for text in either a single file or any number of files you specify. It goes through the file and returns the lines containing your specified text. The text can be a single word or a string surrounded by quotation marks. The basic syntax for **grep** is:

```
$ grep "phrase to look for" filename_to_search
```

The **sort** command sorts lines of text in a file. **Cmp**, **comm**, and **diff** compare files.

To extract data from files and insert the data into other files, you can use the commands **cut**, **paste**, and **join**. **Tr** makes global replacements of text in files.

Learning About Your Environment

This chapter covers:

- ▼ The shell, your main way of interacting with UNIX
- ▼ The login shell
- ▼ Shell variables
- ▼ Assigning, exporting, and removing variables
- ▼ Environment variables
- ▼ Command substitutions
- ▼ Standard input and standard output
- ▼ Parsing a UNIX command
- ▼ Piping commands
- ▼ Divining standard errors
- ▼ Running commands in the background

Orders, Please!

What's the fun in having an operating system if you can't order it around? To this point we've shown you various commands that you need for basic system usage and to accomplish limited tasks. At this point in our journey, however, it will become important for you to learn a little about how these commands are actually carried out by the UNIX operating system. And how these commands are actually carried out requires a little abstraction on your part (repeat the mantra: a little abstraction, a little abstraction…).

When you type **ls** and expect to see a list of your files, you're not *really* directly telling the operating system to list the files in your directory. Instead, you're asking the shell to tell the operating system to carry out your request for a listing of files in your directory. The shell is the component of the UNIX operating system that interacts directly with you, the user. As we noted in Chapter 1, there are different shells available to you: the C shell, the System V job shell, the Korn shell, and the Bourne shell. These all are used by UNIX to execute your commands.

But there's more to the shell than carrying out your commands. The shell also contains a *programming language* that you can use to automate your tasks. Don't flinch at the use of the term programming language; we're not about to turn you into programmers, but we will share a few helpful shortcuts to streamline your daily tasks.

And, perhaps more importantly, your shell allows you to modify your *environment*: information that affects your daily usage and configuration. This chapter will cover the basics of shell functionality, list the most common shell commands, explain some of the concepts surrounding shells, show how you can use the shell to change your user environment, and illuminate how shells can make your UNIX usage go more smoothly. We'll discuss shells in general; all the procedures described here will apply to any shell you may choose to use. In the next chapter we'll discuss the C and Korn shells in more detail. Plus, skipping ahead, Chapter 13 will cover shell programming basics. You don't need to program a shell in order to use it effectively; that's why we've placed shell programming in its own chapter.

The Login Shell

When you login your UNIX system, you're immediately thrust into your *login shell*. In Chapter 1, when we discussed logging in your system and setting up a password, we were detailing how you were configuring your login shell. This information is usually contained in the file **/etc/passwd**, as is login information for all the users on your system. (Obviously, this file is a tool for your system administrator, not for your frequent usage.) This file is organized by user, with each line containing the basic information regarding every user: name, login ID, and so on. The final field in your line lists the shell you want to run after logging in. Again, this isn't terribly important to your daily UNIX usage, but it shows that every aspect of UNIX usage is governed by a shell of some sort.

Based on this information, the UNIX system then launches your shell, with information contained in the **.profile** file (for C shell users, the **.login** and **.cshrc** files; for Korn shell users, the **.kshrc** file).

As you saw earlier in this book, UNIX features several shells, and you have the power to change shells when you want. However, until you become more comfortable with your UNIX usage—a process that should take, oh, 10 or 20 years—you probably don't want to be messing around with different shells. Instead, you should be focusing on how to learn more about the shell you're currently using.

As a new UNIX user, one of the most useful aspects of your shell is its flexibility, as exemplified by its extensive use of variables.

Variables

If you go back to your high school algebra, you may remember the notion of variables. In the following line:

```
z=x+y
```

x, y, and *z* are all *variables.* That is, what *x* stands for can change depending on input from another string or by the reader.

UNIX uses variables in a similar sense; it allows the user to define information with both a name and a value that may change over the course of time. Variables can be used both by the shell and by other UNIX programs. These variables are contained in the **.profile** file or the **.login** file, which we mentioned briefly earlier. This file defines what terminal you are using, what your system prompt will be if you don't like the default, as well as any applications you want to run immediately after logging in.

When you initially login a UNIX system, many of the variables (like the prompt variables and the HOME variable) have been set by the system automatically. However, many others, like the TERM variable, have not. Configuring these variables is up to you; you've already done so (in a previous chapter) by changing your prompt. The structure is simple:

```
$ VARIABLENAME=VARIABLEVALUE
```

where *VARIABLENAME* is the name of the variable and *VARIABLEVALUE* is the value of the variable. To change your TERM (terminal) variable to the very common vt100 value, for example, type the following:

```
$ TERM=vt100
```

The TERM variable will be discussed in greater detail later in this chapter, in the section "Your Terminal."

 These examples, by and large, apply to the Bourne and the Korn shells. In some ways, the C shell differs in syntax, although the basic principles are the same. In Chapter 5 we cover the C shell in more depth.

TERM is an example of an *environment* variable, one of two types of variables in UNIX. The other type of variable is a *shell* variable (sometimes called a *local* variable). The difference is clear: An environment variable applies to the entire UNIX system, while a shell variable applies to just the shell. If you change your shell or logoff the system, the shell variable will cease to be set. All of the variables in Table 4.1 are environment variables, which means they apply to the entire operating system, not to the shell.

Here we'll discuss how the shell uses variables to set up a personalized environment, and how you can change these variables. Your particular system may not contain all these variables.

Table 4.1 Useful shell variables.

Variable	Meaning
CDPATH	Assigns directories searched via the **cd** command.
DISPLAY	Used by the X Window System to identify the display used by X applications. (This will be explained more in Chapter 7.)
EDITOR	Lists your text editor. Some applications (such as mail-reading programs) automatically load a text editor in certain situations, and this variable tells the application the editor to load.

HOME   The full name of your login directory. This is the directory where your personal files are stored.

LOGNAME Your login name.

MAIL   The full name of the directory containing your electronic mail.

MANPATH The directory containing your online-manual pages (which were covered in Chapter 1).

PAGER   Defines the program used to page through files. Some applications summon a UNIX command (more than likely, **pg** or **more**) to scroll through a text file.

PATH   The directories where the shell searches for programs.

PS1   Defines your prompt, which can be changed (as explained in Chapter 1).

SHELL   Your current shell.

TERM   Your terminal type. This determines how your UNIX system interprets keyboard input and sends output to your screen.

TZ   Your current time zone, usually in terms of Universal (Greenwich) time.

USER   Your login name, like LOGNAME, above.

VISUAL   Lists your visual text editor, such as **vi**. Some applications (such as mail-reading programs) automatically load a text editor in certain situations, and this variable tells the application the editor to load.

There are a number of variables that apply to the environment and history features found in the Korn and C shells. For more information on these variables, see Chapter 5.

N O T E

Before you start messing with your variables, you probably should know a little about your current variables. To generate a list of your current shell variables, use the command **set**:

```
$ set
CDPATH=:/users/home/:/users/kevin
HOME=/users/kevin
LOGNAME=kevin
MAIL=/users/kevin/mail
PATH=/usr/bin
PS1=:
PS2=...
SHELL=/usr/bin/sh
TERM=vt100
TZ=CST6CDT
```

C shell users would use the command **setenv** or **env**:

```
% setenv
CDPATH=:/users/home/:/users/kevin
HOME=/users/kevin
LOGNAME=kevin
MAIL=/users/kevin/mail
PATH=/usr/bin
SHELL=/usr/bin/sh
TERM=vt100
TZ=CST6CDT
```

Most users will have additional variables; most mail programs set up additional variables for sorting and storing electronic-mail messages.

You have the power to change these variables. Guess what? You already have. In Chapter 1 you covered the process of changing your UNIX prompt by changing the PS1 variable. The same process can be applied to any variable returned by the **set** or **setemv** commands.

Note the syntax of the variables containing more than one item:

```
CDPATH=:/users/home/:/users/kevin
```

N O T E

In this example, colons (:) are used to distinguish between multiple options. You'll want to do the same when you set your own variables.

There are a few additional rules to remember when working with variables:

▼ As with everything else in UNIX, case counts. DATA, Data, and data would be three different variables. The first letter of a variable must be an underscore (_) or a letter (uppercase or lowercase); subsequent characters can be letters, numerals, or underscores. The shell's reserved variables are all marked by uppercase letters. It's a good idea for you to also use all-uppercase variables.

▼ To use a variable on a command line, you must preface it with a dollar sign ($). This tells the shell that you're invoking a variable; that is, you want the value held in the variable and not a command-line argument, as in this command line:

```
$ echo $HOME
/users/home
```

▼ If you want to view a specific variable at any time (as opposed to using the **set** command, which lists *all* variables), use the **echo** command along with the name of the variable:

```
$ echo $HOME
/users/home
```

Setting Your Own Shell Variables

You aren't limited to the variables defined by the system; you could set up your own variables and refer back to them. This process is called *assigning variables* in UNIX parlance. If this seems like a dubious proposition at best, think again, and think of variables not as something connected with algebra and programming, but rather as a macro of sorts, allowing you to substitute a variable for a long filename or command line.

You can assign a variable at any point in a UNIX computing session. To use an example: Let's say you're working on a giant data-research project, and you want to save all files to the directory **/users/kevin/data/research/1995stuff**. That's quite a lot to type every time you want to call or save a file. In this instance, assigning a variable to store this long pathname would definitely be a good idea. Do so by typing the following:

```
$ DATA="/users/kevin/data/research/1995stuff"
```

Any string to be saved as a variable must be enclosed in quotation marks. If we wanted to list all files in the subdirectory **/users/kevin/data/research/1995stuff**, we would type the following:

```
$ ls $DATA
```

Exporting Your Variables

When you create a variable, it's by definition a shell or local variable, which means it is available for use by the shell, not necessarily to your UNIX applications. In these instances you'll want to explicitly tell the shell to *export* its variables to all programs. Do so with the **export** command:

```
$ export DATA
```

You could export multiple variables with the same command:

```
$ export DATA VARIABLE2 VARIABLE3
```

This command makes the variable DATA available to all programs. It can be used at the same time you assign a variable:

```
$ DATA="/users/kevin/data/research/1992stuff" export DATA
```

You can also export a specific variable (or specific variables) in your **.profile** file, using the same mechanism and making sure the **export** line is at the end of the file:

```
export DATA VARIABLE2 VARIABLE3
```

If you're planning on exporting every variable you assign, you can use the **set** command with the *-a* option to tell the shell to automatically export every assigned variable:

```
$ set -a
```

The **export** command shouldn't be used by C shell users.

N O T E

Removing Variables

After a variable serves its purpose, it's a good idea to remove it, using the **unset** command. The following command removes the variable DATA:

```
$ unset DATA
```

In this instance the use of a dollar sign before the variable name would be inappropriate.

Shells and Your Environment

We began our discussion of variables in the context of setting up your environment. And so we end our discussion of variables with an explanation of the environment.

Your environment, essentially, is a collection of all your variables, as defined by your system. These variables would not include any assigned variables. To see a listing of your environment, use the **env** command:

```
$ env
EDITOR=vi
ED=vi
HOME=/users/kevin
LOGNAME=kevin
MAIL=/users/kevin/mail
PATH=/usr/bin
PS1=:
PS2=...
SHELL=/usr/bin/sh
TERM=vt100
VISUAL=vi
```

We've listed the environment variables here in alphabetical order. Your system may not necessarily do so.

Most of these variables are controlled by specific applications; for example, the **mail** command (or its equivalent) will determine the path for the MAIL variable. However, there are a few variables that you'll want to set—or at the very least be aware of, as you'll see over the next few sections.

Specifying Your Terminal

The expression *terminal* has popped up quite a bit throughout this chapter, yet it has not been explained or defined. Here's the definition.

As you learned in the introduction, UNIX systems are built around a server, which distributes information around the network. (This is generally, but not always, true. For the purposes of this discussion, it will suffice.) Each user sits at a terminal, which can be a dumb ASCII terminal, a UNIX workstation, or a PC running connectivity software.

To function properly, the server needs to know exactly what kind of terminal is attached; there's no mechanism for the UNIX system to check the terminal and make the configurations automatically. Some UNIX programs—especially programs like **vi**—also need this information, especially if they take over an entire screen. The terminal type is specified with the TERM variable.

In theory, you shouldn't need to mess with setting the TERM variable; this is something left to system administrators. However, if you're having problems with your screen after you login a system (garbled characters, etc.), the TERM variable is one of the places to check. Popular terminal types include VT100, VT220, and ANSI.

Customizing Your Terminal

Hardcore UNIX users love to fiddle with their systems, which leads to the 70 or options available just for terminal configuration alone when using the **stty** command. Some of the options are highly technical and applicable in very specific situations (such as the options for turning on and off flow control), while some have wide application.

For example, you can use the **stty** command to erase characters from the screen when you use the **Backspace** key (the default is to leave the characters on the screen):

```
$ stty echoe
```

We won't run down the remaining 69 options to **stty** here. Some will be listed in Appendix B, which lists most useful UNIX commands.

Troubleshooting the Terminal

If you are suffering through the aforementioned garbled characters, there are a few steps you can take.

Newer systems tend to deal with problems better than do older systems; as a UNIX user, you probably won't be exposed to the wide range of weird and inconsistent problems caused by flaky terminals—strange characters, blinking letters, mistyped input from you, and so on. If you do run into these problems, however, there are some things you can do.

The first thing, should you have access to a command prompt, is to merely log off the system and then login immediately again. This will usually solve the problem, but it doesn't address the whole issue of what's causing the craziness in the first place.

An alternative for BSD UNIX users is to try the following command line:

```
$ clear
```

This calls upon the **/etc/termcap** database in an attempt to solve the display problem.

System V users can use a similar command that draws upon a similar database, *terminfo*, as shown in the following command line:

```
$ tput clear
```

There's one final thing to try: using the **stty** command to pass along some tried-and-true generic values to the terminal. These **stty** settings go by the name of (appropriately enough) *sane*, as in the following command:

```
$ stty sane
```

If your terminal is really screwed up, you'll need to use **Ctrl-J** at the end of the line, instead of the **Return** or **Enter** key.

Specifying an Editor

Most thoughtful system administrators will have a text editor specified in a **.profile** file. This is because some UNIX applications call upon a text editor for input, and these applications make a call to an editor variable, rather than defining a specific editor. In the example of variables found in "Shells and Your Environment," the following lines set the variables for a text editor:

```
EDITOR=vi
ED=vi
VISUAL=vi
```

Why three lines? Because there's no standard for invoking an editor in the UNIX world. Therefore, applications are free to call upon any editor variable. Of course, an application should call upon a common editor variable, and these are the most common. If you have an application that tries to call up a text editor and then fails, the first place to look is with your editor variable.

Setting Your Path

A *path* is the series of directories that the shell searches to find a command. For example, when you use the **set** command, the shell then looks through a predefined series of directories in search of the file that makes up the **set** command. In the example found in the previous "Shells and Your Environment" section, the following PATH statement appeared:

```
PATH=/usr/bin
```

This is not an unexpected location for a PATH; after all, you learned in Chapter 2 that the **/usr/bin** directory was used to store binary (i.e., program) files.

With PATH defined like this, the shell will not go to any other directories in search of a command. For most users, this will suffice; you'll want to keep your PATH statement short and sweet, since the more directories the shell needs to go through, the more time it will take the shell to report that a command can't be found. However, the PATH statement may be the culprit when you issue a command that you *know* exists and your system reports that the accompanying file can't be found. If it's a frequently used command, go ahead and add the directory to your PATH statement, making sure that you separate the directories with a colon:

```
PATH=/usr/bin:/bin
```

Command Substitutions

A *command substitution* inserts the output of one program into your command line. In our example we'll use date both as a string for use by the **echo** command and as input for the **echo** command. Since the **echo** command merely echoes input from the command prompt, neither example does a whole lot, but it adequately illustrates the difference:

```
$ echo date
date
$ echo `date`
Sat Jul 25 12:27:48 CST 1992
```

 Note that commands used in command substitution are enclosed with accent marks, not single quotation marks. The accent mark is usually found on the leftmost part of the number line on most keyboards.

More about the Command Line

In Chapter 1 we introduced you to the command line and how to use it to run basic commands. The command line is your gateway to the shell; using the shell easily and efficiently means grasping some of the additional command-line options and concepts. We've used the term *command* rather loosely to this point, using it to refer to anything typed at a command prompt. For our purposes now, we'll distinguish between executables (programs) and also to what we type into a command line. The two, though similar, are not synonymous.

For example, the difference between the two are demonstrated adequately in a discussion of multiple commands. You aren't limited to only one command on the command line. It is possible to run more than one command as long as the commands are separated by semicolons (;). In this instance you are telling the shell to run more than one command (or, more accurately in our next example, more than one program) on the command line:

```
$ calendar; vi
```

This command tells the shell to run the programs (in this case we are referring to actual programs) **calendar** and **vi**, one after another—they don't run at the same time. (This example uses two commands, but you can place as many as you want on a command line.)

Confusing? Not really. You won't have to make these distinctions most of the time, but they do prepare you for the remainder of this chapter, as we discuss how the basic functions of the shell allow you to redirect input and output via shell commands.

Input and output? Redirection? (Repeat the mantra…)

Let's go back to the earlier days of UNIX, when computers weren't quite so powerful and interaction with the shell not as easy as plunking down a few commands at a prompt. Tasks were processed by the computer one at a time, and so programmers/users (in those days, the two were synonymous) needed a way to combine commands and tasks into a more workable order, not requiring inter-action with the computer at every step. (Otherwise, users would need to spend even *more* time at the computer than today. Scary thought, isn't it?) The notion of batch files—files that contain a series of commands executed sequentially—evolved from this period.

Creative UNIX designers took the notion of combined commands a step fur-ther, creating an infrastructure for directing the output of one program as the input of another program; this combination took place as a command on the command line. (See, we told you the distinction would be important.) And even though today's computers are overwhelmingly more powerful than the early UNIX-based computers, this redirection of input and output, along with the related notion of piping, are still very handy tools—perhaps the handiest tools your shell has to offer.

Parsing a UNIX Command

Let's begin by examining the way your shell responds to a typical command line. The shell goes through a lot of activity before actually responding to your instruc-tions. You don't need to know exactly what the shell does before it carries out your command; you merely need to know the proper methods of structuring these commands.

Analyzing these structures is called *parsing* a UNIX command. (Grammatically speaking, when we parse a sentence, we break it into its various components—noun, verb, adjective—to analyze the structure and meaning. So even though *parse* sounds like a computer-related term, it's really not.)

Let's parse an example from an earlier chapter (see Figure 4.1).

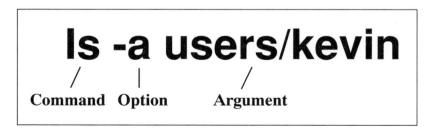

Figure 4.1 *Parsing a simple ls command.*

We discussed parameters, arguments, and options earlier; the shell uses spaces to separate these components. The shell can also use tabs or multiple spaces to distinguish between parameters. (Technically speaking, these are *inter-field separators* and can be changed by the user. We can't think of a good reason why anyone would want to use anything other than spaces or tabs to distinguish between parameters, so it's highly unlikely that you'll want to change your inter-field separators.)

The shell doesn't respond sequentially to the separate components in a command. Instead the shell runs through all aspects of the command (substituting for wildcards, examining variables, etc.). After the shell parses the command, it then executes the command.

A computer will only do what you tell it to do. Much frustration in computing occurs because users don't know how to tell the computer to do exactly what they want. With UNIX, many users experience frustration because they don't know the exact syntax or commands needed to carry out their specific wishes; the sometimes-minimalist nature of UNIX can be an impediment to effective usage. Therefore, a knowledge of the many options available on the command line is an essential tool in UNIX computing.

Let's start with the use of quotations. There are three quotations in UNIX: the prime or accent (`` ` ``), the apostrophe ('), and the quotation mark ("). Each is used in a different situation, but sometimes they can be used interchangeably—as in the case of apostrophes and quotation marks when separating parameters. Anything contained in a set of apostrophes or quotation marks is regarded by the shell as a single parameter or argument. For example, we ask for the following:

```
$ ls kevin erc
kevin erc
```

The shell provides a list of the files in the current directory that matches the parameters **kevin** and **erc**. Nothing remarkable or noteworthy about this.

If we were to use the following command:

```
$ ls "kevin erc"
```

or:

```
$ ls 'kevin erc'
```

we'd get an error message—remember, filenames can't have spaces.

Most of the time quotation marks are used to tell the shell not to do things: not to expand an asterisk (*) out to names of files on disk, not to use an exclamation mark (!) for **csh**'s history mechanism, not to use the dollar sign ($) to signify the value of a variable, and so on. For example, what happens if you accidentally create a file named **report***? (We say accidentally because you never want to use a * in a filename.) If you have a number of report files, such as **report1**, **report.1995**, **report.1994**, and so on, what do you think the following command will do?

```
$ rm report*
```

The above command *will* remove the file **report***, but it will do so by taking the Genghis Khan approach: It will also delete all files that begin with *report*, including **report1**, **report.1995**, and **report.1994**. We suspect you wouldn't want that. So, to delete a file named **report***, use quotation marks to tell the shell not to expand the * :

```
$ rm "report*"
```

The previous command tells the shell to delete only the file named **report***.

Standard Input/Output

As we can see, providing input to the shell via the command line can sometimes be complicated. We're going to increase the complexity now with a discussion of *standard input and output (I/O)*, or *redirection*, via the command line.

UNIX is unique in its treatment of virtually every aspect of the computer as a file of some sort. Here we bring the previous abstraction of previous chapters regarding computer as file (mantra time!) into a more tangible, but not necessarily less complex subject.

With standard input/output, you can take the output of one program, turn it into the input for another program, and then display or print the results of the operation—which is presented as a single command with many components. (That's why it was important for you to learn how to parse UNIX commands. There is a rhyme and reason to our approach to UNIX.)

Why is this important? Because the standard UNIX model involves input from the keyboard and output to a file. We saw it throughout our Chapter 2 examples; the **cat** program relied on input from the keyboard unless we told it otherwise. As you'll recall, the command:

```
$ cat > spacely
```

created a file named **spacely**, which consisted of input from your keyboard. Also, the command:

```
$ cat >> spacely
```

appended the file **spacely** with input from the keyboard. These both were examples of standard input. The process of standard input and output is illustrated in Figure 4.2.

Figure 4.2 *Standard input and output.*

In our illustration, standard input can come from your keyboard, another command, or a file, while output can be directed to a file, your screen, or another command. In UNIX the default output for almost every command is to print to your screen; the variance comes when you want to output to a file or to a printer. These procedures are governed by input/output commands.

Table 4.2 *Shell input/output commands.*

Symbol	Usage	Result
>	*command* > *filename*	Output of *command* is sent to *filename*.
<	*command* < *filename*	Input from *filename* is used by *command*.
>>	*command* >> *filename*	Output of *command* is appended to *filename*.
|	*command1* | *command2*	Run *command1*, then send output to *command2*.

The standard input/output commands should not look terribly new to you; we used the > symbol in Chapter 2 in our discussion of some common UNIX commands, such as **cat**, and how they are used. These commands are not limited to usage with files; you could direct output to a printer, for example. Let's use each of these input/output commands, using the by-now-familiar **ls** and **cat** commands, as shown in Table 4.3.

Table 4.3 *Shell input/output examples.*

Commands	Result
ls > *filename*	The current directory listing is sent to the file *filename*. If *filename* does not exist, the shell will create it. If *filename* does exist, the new data generated by **ls** will replace the existing data.
cat < *filename*	The **cat** program displays the file *filename* on your monitor.
ls >> *filename*	The current directory listing is appended to the file *filename*.
ls | **lp**	The current directory listing is then sent to the printer via the **lp** command.

(The | symbol is used when creating pipes. We'll cover pipes in the following section.)

N O T E

Note that the two commands:

```
$ cat < filename
```

and

```
$ cat filename
```

create the same result: a display of *filename* on your monitor. The only difference is in the process: The former is treated as a single step by the UNIX shell, while the latter is a two-step process, with **cat** taking *filename* as an argument.

The input/output tools can be used in conjunction with any commands, programs, or arguments. A particularly handy usage for standard input/output is in shell programming, which we'll cover in Chapter 13. You can also use standard input/output in the same command, using the same style:

```
$ command < infilename > outfilename
```

Note that any command employing standard input/output must begin with a command. While it would be more logical (and sequential) to use a command structure like:

```
$ infilename > command < outfilename
```

your system will choke on the above.

Pipes

The notion of *pipes* takes the notion of input/output a step further. It is also an area of particular interest to programmers, since the idea of pipes plays a large role in UNIX programming.

When you set up a pipe, you specify that the output from one command should be the input to another command. So what's the difference between a pipe and redirection? Redirection always sends output to a file, while a pipe sends output to another command. You can think of a pipe as a temporary file that holds the output of the first command in anticipation of the second command.

Usage of the pipe command is simple:

```
$ command1 | command2
```

The end result is referred to as a pipeline (naturally). In our example the shell places the output of *command1* as the input of *command2*. There are no limitations to the number of pipes on a command line.

For example, a pipe can be set up to accept input from your keyboard. Let's go back to Chapter 1's example memo, **erc.memo**:

```
The proposal by Spacely Sprockets is simply
unacceptable and does not fit with our long-term
corporate interests. Nuke it.
```

After creating the memo and storing it, Eric notices that there's no salutation on the memo. Before printing it, he wants to add his boss's name to the memo so it looks more businesslike. He could use the **cat** command to tell the shell to print the file **erc.memo** only after Eric had the chance to add a salutation—an action he can take directly from the keyboard. The command would be:

```
$ cat - erc.memo | lp
Dear Boss:
```

```
Ctrl-D
```

The pipe character is a vertical bar (|). **Ctrl-D** indicates that input from the keyboard is completed. In this case the hyphen (-) tells the shell to accept standard input from the keyboard, place it at the beginning of the file **erc.memo**, and then print the file. The printed file would appear as follows:

```
Dear Boss:
The proposal by Spacely Sprockets is simply
unacceptable and does not fit with our long-term
corporate interests. Nuke it.
```

The hyphen (-) is not accepted by all commands. An alternative is to substitute **/dev/stdin** for the hyphen:

N O T E   `$ cat /dev/stdin erc.memo | lp`

Longer Pipe Commands

As we mentioned, the shell proscribes no limits on the number of pipelines on a command line. A pipeline like the following would be acceptable:

```
$ ls *.c | grep arg | lp
```

This pipeline searches for all files ending in *.c* in the current subdirectory, searches these files for the string *arg*, and then prints out all the lines containing *arg*.

Although there are no limits to the size of a pipeline, longer pipelines can be confusing and harder for you to identify. The shell allows you to divide a long pipeline into several easier-to-read components. The previous command could be written as follows:

```
$ ls *.c |
> grep arg |
> lp
```

Are we mixing redirection commands with pipe commands? No. In this instance the > tells us that the shell is waiting for additional input from the user. The > is a secondary prompt, or PS2, as first discussed in Chapter 2. Since your initial command line ended with the pipe command, the shell correctly assumes that there's more input coming; otherwise, you'd be generating an error with the incorrect use of a pipe command. Which leads us to our next section, errors.

Errors

The shell also uses standard input and output to send you error messages; technically speaking, they are known in UNIX parlance as *standard error* (or, in a term dating from date of yore in UNIX times, *diagnostic output*). Standard error is sent to the screen by default—the most logical place for it, as you want to know immediately why a command failed. As you might expect, UNIX uses this mechanism to tell you that your commands cannot be carried out, as well as *why* they cannot be carried out. We've already seen a standard error when we searched for a file that did not exist:

```
$ ls god
ls: god not found
```

Error messages are generated under a variety of circumstances: When you try to delete a file and you only have read permission, for example, the shell tells you that you can't delete the file. Similar errors are generated if a pipe or redirection command cannot be carried out.

Since the default with most UNIX commands is sending output to your screen, it makes sense that all error messages related to commands are sent to your screen. However, this shell goes a step further and sends all error messages to the screen, even those related to file operations that don't normally generate any response. Using our previous example, let's say that you were looking for all files ending in the string *.c*, but there were no files ending in *.c* in the current directory. Instead of getting a printed page full of lines containing the string *arg*, you'd get the following:

```
$ ls *.c | grep arg | lp
ls: *.c not found
```

Without this response, you'd never know exactly why your command line failed—alternatives in the absence of such a specific response includes *grep* or the printer failing.

Redirecting Standard Error

As mentioned, the best place to display a standard error is the screen, since you'll want immediate feedback on why a command failed. However, there may be times when you'll want to redirect error messages to a file. You can do this on an as-needed basis by slightly expanding your command lines. If you're using the

Korn or Bourne shells, you'll need to add a redirection symbol to the command line—making sure to precede it with a *2*. In the following example an error message is sent to the file **kevinerror**:

```
$ ls *.c 2> kevinerror
```

Without the addition of the standard-error redirection, you'd get a response like the following on the screen:

```
$ ls *.c
ls: *.c not found
```

With the C shell, you'd use *&>* instead of *2>*:

```
% ls *.c &> kevinerror
```

Background Noise

UNIX is a multiuser, multitasking operating system. So far we've been concentrating on UNIX's multiuser capabilities, with our discussions of logging on the system and sending messages to other users. Here we'll discuss UNIX's multitasking capabilities.

Multitasking is a fancy way of saying that UNIX can do more than one thing at a time. We humans are multitasking, to a degree; most of us can walk and chew bubble gum at the same time, for example. (A notable exception was President Gerald Ford, who was incapable of walking and waving at the same time.) When you run a command in the background, the shell assigns the command a job number and prompts you for another command. In this way you can still be running multiple commands at the same time.

In Chapter 2 we ran a command in the background:

```
$ find / -name 1992.report -print &
```

This tells the shell to search for the file **1992.report**, beginning at the top of the file structure with the root directory and moving downward, and alerting us when the file is found. The ampersand (**&**) tells the shell to perform this task in the background.

Any command can be run in the background. Some tasks, such as **find** and **nroff** (used for text processing, which we'll cover in Chapter 12), should almost always be run in the background, because these commands can take a long time to execute.

What if your background command takes an exceptionally long time to execute and you want to log off the system? If you're working at the end of the day or know you'll be pulled away during your computing session, you can start a command line with the no hang up (**nohup**) command. When you log out, the command is suspended and restarted the next time you log on the system. Use it as follows:

```
$ nohup find / -name 1992.report -print > results &
```

Note that we redirected the results of the **find** command to a file. If you don't specify this output, it will go to the file **nohup.out**. Since you'll never remember to look in the file **nohup.out**, it will effectively be lost.

You can also run a series of commands in the background. As you'll recall from earlier in this chapter, the following command line was used as an example of two commands that were run sequentially from the same command line:

```
$ calendar; vi
```

In this case, the **calendar** command would be run first, followed by the **vi** command. Both of these commands would run in the foreground, tying up your machine until the command line was complete.

You can run two or more commands sequentially on the same command line in the background by adding the ampersand (&) to the command line. However, there's a trick to doing so—the commands must be enclosed in parentheses, making sure that the ampersand (&) applies to the contents of the parentheses, not just to the last command in the sequence. The resulting command line would look something like this:

```
$ (calendar; vi) &
```

There will be more information on foreground and background commands in Chapter 6.

N O T E

Summary

The shell gives you access to your basic environment under UNIX. UNIX shells, such as **sh** and **csh**, provide environment variables, also called shell variables, which you and UNIX both use to hold commonly used values. Both **sh** and **csh** set up a number of environment variables to tell other UNIX commands how your system and your personal account are configured. The TZ environment variable, for example, describes your current time zone.

You can redirect the input or output of UNIX commands using the redirection operators <, >, and >>. The < operator redirects the input for a command to come from a given file:

```
$ command < inputfile
```

The > operator redirects the output of a command to a file:

```
$ command > outputfile
```

The >> operator appends the output of a command to the end of a file:

```
$ command >> outputfile
```

The pipe symbol (|) pipes together two commands, which means that the output of the first command becomes the input of the second command:

```
$ command1 | command2
```

Use an ampersand (&) at the end of the command line to run the command in the background.

The C and Korn Shells

This chapter covers:

- ▼ The C shell
- ▼ The Korn shell
- ▼ The C shell **.login** file
- ▼ The C shell **.cshrc** file
- ▼ Variables
- ▼ Environment variables
- ▼ Toggles
- ▼ Command history
- ▼ Aliases
- ▼ The home directory
- ▼ Editing command lines
- ▼ The Korn shell and directories

119

The Shell Game

Our discussion of UNIX so far has centered around a generic discussion of shells. In many ways all the UNIX shells act similarly and react similarly to most of the basic shell commands.

In this chapter we cover two older but still widely used shells, the C shell (**csh**) and the Korn shell (**ksh**). Both offer the basic functionality found in all shells, and both improve on this functionality with such features as:

- ▼ Command history
- ▼ Command substitution
- ▼ Aliasing

Because the Korn shell builds on the C shell as well as the Bourne shell, we'd advise the Korn shell user to read this entire chapter even if you have no intention of ever using the C shell. We've organized this chapter with a discussion of the C shell, but we won't be repeating ourselves in a discussion of the Korn shell when looking at shared features.

The C Shell

The C shell's roots can be traced back to Bill Joy when he was at Berkeley and developing the Berkeley UNIX System (which we discussed in the introduction). It is still in wide usage and is only now being replaced on a large scale by other shells.

The C shell is usually found as **/bin/csh**.

When Logging In

As we discussed in Chapter 4, the C shell looks for two files, **.login** and **.cshrc**, when someone logs in a system. The **.login** file defines what terminal you are using, what your system prompt will be if you don't like the default, as well as any applications you want to run immediately after logging in. So, to an extent, does the **.cshrc** file. The difference between the **.login** and **.cshrc** files is simple: The **.login** file is read only when a user logs in the system, while the **.cshrc** file is read every time the user starts a shell or otherwise accesses a new C shell. (Note that on login, the **.cshrc** file is normally read in first, before the **.login** file. And, when you log out, **csh** executes the **.logout** file, if you have one.)

For example, you may want to place important variables in the **.cshrc** file, to make sure you or another application don't inadvertently change an important setting. The C shell accomplishes this by setting environmental variables, aliases, and other system defaults in this file through various commands.

Here are portions of our own **.login** file:

```
# Eric's .login script, ported from HP-UX

setenv PATH /bin:/usr/bin:/usr/ucb:...
setenv TERM vt100
setenv EXINIT "set autoindent"
setenv SHELL /bin/csh
set shell=/bin/csh
set ignoreeof
set nonomatch
set prompt='% '
date
```

All the important elements of a **.login** file are represented here: comment lines, environmental variables, and command.

When you start editing and changing your **.cshrc** and **.login** files, it's important that you start documenting your system usage. Do this with *comment lines*: lines that can be read by the user but are not acted upon by the shell. With the C shell, these lines begin with the # character. The following is an example of a comment line:

```
# Eric's .login script, ported from HP-UX
```

This tells us that Eric adapted his **.login** file from a similar file he used on a system running Hewlett-Packard's version of UNIX. You can include any comments you want by beginning the comment with the #; the comment can begin a line or appear at the end of a line containing a command.

Variables

In our previous shell discussion in Chapter 4, we explained variables and how useful they were. The C shell treats variables slightly differently. As you'll recall, the Bourne and Korn shells allow you to set a variable by simply using an equal sign:

```
VARIABLE=value
```

In the C shell you must precede the request with the **set** command:

```
set variable = value
```

You must also watch the following rules when working with C shell variables:

▾   C shell variables should use lowercase characters to set variables.

▾   C shell set commands allow spaces around the equal sign; other shells do not. However, the C shell does not *require* spaces around the equal sign.

▾   The C shell also contains several special variables that differ from those found in the Korn and Bourne shells.

For instance: In Chapter 4 we showed how HOME is used to set the pathname of our login directory. With the C shell, home is used to do the same thing. Other equivalents are described in Table 5.1.

Table 5.1   *C shell variables and their equivalents.*

C Shell	Korn/Bourne Shell	Result
cdpath	**CDPATH**	Sets the order of subdirectories to search when the shell looks for a file.
cwd	**pwd**	Denotes the current working directory.
path	**PATH**	Specifies the directories used by the shell to search for files.
prompt	**PS1**	Sets the command prompt. (There is no support in the C shell for a secondary prompt.)

Environment Variables

You'll notice that our **.login** file contains both **set** and **setenv** commands. **Set** is used by you to set shell variables, while environment variables, as set by **setenv**, are needed by the system to determine your configuration. Your terminal type, for example, is set as an environment variable. (See Chapter 4 for a more in-depth discussion of environment variables.)

In the C shell, setting an environment variable requires the use of the **setenv** command; with the Korn and Bourne shells, you merely need to separate the elements of the variable with an equal sign (=). Such formality is unnecessary with the C shell, since the command does the work. Here's how we set the C shell in the **.login** file:

```
setenv SHELL /bin/csh
```

You can use the **setenv** command either in the **.login** file or at the command prompt.

Toggles

In the C shell you can turn features on or off by using what's called a *toggle*. These can be set in both **.login** and **.cshrc** files (as you'll see later, we're redundant and set various toggles in both files.) For example, our **.login** file contained the following line:

```
set ignoreeof
```

This tells the shell not to log you off with the command **Ctrl-D**. As you'll recall from earlier examples, **Ctrl-D** stops a file from running and is used to quit applications as well as stopping text from scrolling in certain situations. However, if the **Ctrl-D** command were used when a program was not running, the shell would quit and you'd be logged off the system. Obviously, you don't want this to happen; hence, you should always include this line in your **.login** file.

Another useful toggle, in our experience, is the **noclobber** toggle:

```
set noclobber
```

This protects you from accidentally writing over an existing file. As we warned in previous chapters, a redirected or piped command will replace an existing file unless you take pains to avoid this situation. In the C shell you can do so by setting **noclobber**. If **noclobber** is set, you'd get the following if you tried to write over an existing *file2* with a new *file2*:

```
% cat file1 > file2
file2: file exists
```

To put the C shell in its place by telling it you really *do* want to overwrite *file2*, use the exclamation point with a redirection symbol:

```
% cat file1 >! file2
```

Here are portions of our **.cshrc** file:

```
set prompt "'hostname'% "
set history=32
set ignoreeof
set noclobber
alias   dir     ls -CF
alias   lsf     ls -CF
alias   ll      ls -l
alias   rm      rm -i
alias   mail    mailx
```

We've already covered how **set** works. New in this example file are two commands: **set history** and **alias**. We'll cover each in the following two sections.

The C Shell and Command History

The C shell will maintain a listing, or *history*, of your previous commands. (As does the Korn shell; listen up, **ksh** users.) This is useful for a number of reasons. You may have saved a file earlier in your session and now can't locate it; it's easier and quicker to use the **history** command to locate the command where you actually saved the file, as compared to using the slower **find** command to search the entire filesystem. You may repeatedly use the same command and use the **history** command to cut down on the number of your keystrokes.

To access this listing, use the following:

```
% history
ls
```

In this case we listed the current directory previously to using the **history** command. Unless we tell the system otherwise, the shell will maintain a history of only the most recent command. We tell the system otherwise by setting history in the **.cshrc** file:

```
set history=32
```

Here we are telling the shell to keep a record of the 32 most recent commands. (We do this in our **.cshrc** file and would recommend you do the same. Should you decide not to do this, you can **set history** at any point in your computing session at the command prompt.)

Here's some sample output during a typical session:

```
% history
  1 ls
  2 ls -a
  3 vi .login
  4 vi .cshrc
  5 ls
```

This output lists the five most recent commands because we've only used five commands in our session to date. If we had used hundreds of commands, we would get a listing of the 32 most recent commands.

You'll notice that the commands are numbered. We can use these numbers to set up substitute commands, first discussed in Chapter 5. For example, we may need to go back and read the **.login** file using the **vi** text editor. Using the previous history listing as an example, we could do so by either of the following:

```
% vi .login
```

or

```
% !3
```

Obviously our examples won't result in you saving enough keystrokes to avoid carpal-tunnel syndrome. However, in cases where your commands are rather long and involved (as where long pathnames are involved, or particularly complicated pipe commands), the history command can significantly cut down on your keystrokes.

To go back to the last instance of a particular command, we would use the following:

```
% !vi
vi .login
```

If you want to see a truncated list of recent command lines, you can combine the **history** command with a number:

```
% history 15
```

This command line lists the last 15 command lines.

You can rerun the previous command by using the following command line:

```
% !!
```

You can rerun a specific command line from the command history by specifying on the command line:

```
% !5
```

There is a whole command set dedicated to the editing of **history** commands. Quite honestly, most new users won't need to know about this extended command set. If you've decided to master the **history** command to its full potential, consult your system documentation or a very, *very* thick UNIX reference work. You can also look up the **csh** online manual pages via **man csh.**

Aliases

When does a command not mean what it says? When it's an *alias.* The C shell (as well as the Korn shell) allows you to define one string to do the same thing as another string. Let's review a section from our **.cshrc** file:

```
alias    dir     ls -CF
alias    lsf     ls -CF
alias    ll      ls -l
alias    rm      rm -i
alias    mail    mailx
```

Here we have shown our DOS roots: We have set up **dir** (which calls the current directory in DOS) to do the same as the **ls** command with the *-CF* option. (Shame on us!) Similarly, we have used **ll** to give us a full listing of the current directory, we have defined **rm** to conform to our most prevalent usage of that command (**rm -i**), and we have defined **mail** to mean the same at the command prompt as **mailx**.

In our example the following are equivalent:

```
dir
```

and

```
ls -CF
```

Aliases are useful in three situations: When you are moving between multiple systems and don't want to memorize multiple command sets, when you want to automate long and involved commands (or perhaps unnecessarily obscure commands—but we all know that UNIX features no unnecessarily obscure commands), and when you simply want to be lazy.

To get a list of your existing aliases, use the following:

```
% alias
dir     (ls -CF)
lsf     (ls -CF)
ll      (ls -l)
mail    mailx
rm      (rm -i)
```

You could also set up an alias for a frequently used command. For instance, we could redefine **ls** to do the same thing as **ls -CF**:

```
% alias ls ls -CF
```

WARNING Undertake an alias like this with caution. It ties you tightly to the alias. In our alias example, for instance, you could not run the normal **ls** command, nor could you run any variation of **ls** without invoking the *-CF* options. The way around this is to use the full path to the command to execute the original (**ls**) and not the alias (**ls -CF**). In our example this full command path is **/bin/ls**. Unless you're really, really sure you want to alias an existing shell command, don't. If you do and find that you want to change the setting on the fly, use the following:

```
% unalias ls
```

If you want to run the real command—as opposed to the alias—you can preface it with a backslash. For instance, the previous featured an alias of **rm** for **rm -i**. In this instance, to run the *real* **rm** command, your command line would look like this:

```
% \rm
```

Aliases and the Korn Shell

Though the Korn and C shells are very similar in their approach to aliases, there are a few areas where they differ. For instance, the C shell uses the following syntax to set an alias in a configuration file:

```
alias   dir    ls -CF
```

This syntax won't work with the Korn shell, however, which uses an equal sign as part of the command line, to denote the alias and what it stands for:

```
alias dir='ls -CF'
```

The Korn shell also requires that the original command be enclosed in single quotes, as shown above.

The Home Directory

Every user has a home directory, and the C shell (as well as the Korn shell, see below), provides a quick shorthand for the path to your home directory. The C shell allows you to use a tilde symbol (~) to replace the pathname of your home directory. Thus you could use:

```
% mv filename ~/subdirect
```

instead of:

```
% mv filename $home/subdirect
```

You could also use the tilde symbol to save files to someone else's home directory. For instance, the following would move a file to Eric's home directory, where *erc* is Eric's username:

```
% mv filename ~erc
```

Weight Watchers

Large files can choke up a UNIX system. Programmers know that a bug in a program can inadvertently create massive files, while database experts have found that the desired results of a SQL program ended up far too large to manage. In these cases, we're talking about files that end up being tens of megabytes in size.

Both the C and Korn shells allow you to create a limit on the size of files. For instance, the following C shell command would limit the size of any file to 15 megabytes:

```
$ limit filesize 15m
```

The following Korn shell command limits the size of a file to 15 megabytes:

```
$ ulimit -f 15000
```

Note the odd use of *15000* to denote the maximum size of the file. The Korn shell measures input from this command line in terms of thousands of bytes. Thus, 15,000 thousand bytes equals 15 megabytes.

The Korn Shell

We can credit David Korn of Bell Labs for the Korn shell (**ksh**). It was designed as a replacement for both the standard System V Bourne shell (**sh**) and the C shell (**csh**). Because the Korn shell is based on the Bourne shell, most Bourne shell scripts can be used without adjustment under the Korn shell.

We've used a generic description of the Bourne and Korn shells so far, and most of the discussion regarding the C shell can be applied to the Korn shell. In this rest of this chapter we'll cover a few areas that make the Korn shell unique.

When Logging In

In Chapter 4 we discussed variables and environment variables. The Korn shell supports the same environment variables as the Bourne shell, plus three important ones: ENV, HISTSIZE, and VISUAL. These are usually all defined in your **.profile** file.

ENV defines where the Korn shell can find an environment file at startup. This file is analogous to the C shell's **.cshrc** file and is usually called **ksh_env**, found in your home directory. However, the Korn shell does not assume any default position, so you must define the location in your **.profile** file. To tell the Korn shell to look for this file in your HOME directory, use:

```
$ ENV=$HOME
```

The Korn Shell and History

The Korn shell features command history in the same manner as the C shell, though there are some changes: HISTSIZE, for example, is used to maintain a history list. This is a Korn shell feature that was lifted from the C shell. Refer to earlier in this chapter for a discussion of the C shell's command history. The principles and commands behind command history in the C and Korn shells are almost identical, save some small differences. For instance, the C shell uses:

```
set history=32
```

to set the number of commands saved in the history list, while the Korn shell uses:

```
HISTSIZE=32
```

The Korn shell also adds a very handy feature, using a single letter to run the previous command:

```
$ r
```

The Korn shell also gives you a lot of flexibility with the *r* command. For instance, you can run the command line you ran five commands ago with the following command line:

```
$ r -5
```

You can also go to the last instance of a command line, but you don't need to know exactly when you ran the command or the exact command line. To rerun the last **vi** command in the history queue, you'd use the following command line:

```
$ r vi
```

Editing Command Lines

When set on, the VISUAL variable allows you to edit a command line with a vi-style text editor. (We cover **vi** in Chapter 11.) This is a very handy feature: If you make a typographical error in the middle of a long command, you can merely use a cursor to scroll back to the typo and correct the typo. Let's say you want to edit the file **chap5.doc**, but you mistakenly typed the following at the command prompt:

```
$ vi cjap5.doc
```

To correct the error, press the **Esc** key to move into editing mode. Use either your cursor key or the **vi** command (**b**) to move back one word, type over with the correct characters, and then hit the **Return** key. (The cursor can be anywhere in the command line; it doesn't have to be at the end of the line for you to hit the **Return** key.)

To set this feature in your environment file, insert the following line:

```
set -o vi
```

You can also set the VISUAL environment variable to the value *vi*:

```
VISUAL=vi
```

Borrowing from the C Shell

As we said earlier, the Korn shell borrows from the C shell. Instead of killing more trees to pad this book, we'll refer you to previous sections of this chapter for discussions of:

▼ **Ignoreeof**, used to prevent you from accidentally logging off the system by typing **Ctrl-D**. The Korn shell equivalent command is:

```
$ set -o ignoreeof
```

▼ **Noclobber**, used to prevent you from overwriting existing files by accident. The Korn shell equivalent command is:

```
$ set -o noclobber
```

One important difference between the C shell and Korn shell: Instead of using the exclamation point to override the **noclobber** command, the Korn shell uses the pipe character:

```
% cat file1 >| file2
```

The Korn Shell and Directories

The Korn shell acts like the C shell and allows you to use a tilde symbol (~) to replace the pathname of your home directory. Thus you could use:

```
$ mv filename ~/subdirect
```

instead of:

```
$ mv filename $home/subdirect
```

You could also use the tilde (~) symbol to save files to someone else's home directory. For instance, the following would move a file to Eric's home directory:

```
$ mv filename ~erc
```

Finally, the Korn shell, unlike the C shell, allows you to move between directories with the hyphen (-) option to the **cd** command:

```
$ cd -
```

This would place you in your previous directory.

Summary

Most UNIX users run under the C or Korn shells, both of which enhance the bare-bones Bourne shell. This chapter covered some of the extended features and differences offered by these two command shells.

The Korn shell, **ksh**, offers most of the extended features that the C shell, **csh**, brings to the table. Both shells allow you to set them to prevent yourself from overwriting files with the **mv**, **cp**, and other shell commands. The C shell uses the following command to set the **noclobber** mode:

```
% set noclobber
```

The Korn shell supports the same feature, but uses a different syntax:

```
$ set -o noclobber
```

Both shells support other features, such as the use of the tilde character (~) as a shorthand for your home directory.

The Korn shell extends these features with a visual command-line editing mode, where you can use commands from the **vi** or **emacs** text editors to edit your command line.

Multitasking and Processes

This chapter covers:

- ▼ Multitasking
- ▼ Processes
- ▼ Parents and children
- ▼ The **ps** command
- ▼ Killing processes
- ▼ Real-time processes
- ▼ Swapping to disk
- ▼ Virtual memory
- ▼ Paging

Forest and Trees

So far our discussion has centered around a practical approach to the UNIX operating system. We've shown you how to use UNIX's commands to automate your daily tasks. For the most part, we've avoided discussions of concepts and abstractions unless they were related directly to the task at hand. The strategy has served us well.

However, this approach takes you as a user only so far. Yes, you can perform your daily work without delving into the depths of UNIXdom. Yes, you could go along for many years without learning about processes, daemons, and signals. But this approach, while ideal for beginning computer users and those getting their feet wet in UNIX, is too limiting for the truly ambitious UNIX user. You've learned *how* things work; now we take a little side journey to cover *why* things work the way they do.

Or rather, to *introduce* why things work the way they do. Many forests have been felled in the production of books detailing the concepts underlying the UNIX operating system. (Heck, we haven't even covered some of the more esoteric and little-used UNIX commands in this book; if we were to discuss every UNIX command and concept in any detail, this book easily would be three or four times as big.) Entire academic and research careers have been devoted to conceptually advancing the UNIX operating system. Since UNIX has developed in such a seemingly haphazard fashion, different people bring different conceptual frameworks to UNIX.

Still, there are a few concepts that make UNIX what it is. Most discussions of UNIX tend to downplay or sidestep UNIX's multitasking capabilities, on the assumption that the topic is too advanced (or too esoteric) for most users. Most discussions tell you how to run commands in the background and leave it at that.

And for most UNIX beginners, however, even the concept of background tasks can be daunting. PC and Macintosh users have no experience with true multitasking; sure, *Windows* and the Macintosh operating system can load more than one application at a time and make it appear that both are running, but they don't handle multiple tasks in the same manner that UNIX does. And if you're a true beginner, the entire notion of multitasking is odd.

However, the more you know, the more efficiently you can complete your work, and multitasking is a way for you to more efficiently complete your work. Hence, this chapter and its position so soon into your introduction to the UNIX operating system.

Multitasking: Multiple Commands, One System

Multitasking is a fancy computer-speak way of saying that the operating system can do more than one thing at a time. While this may seem like a simple matter, it's really not; personal computer users have been screaming for a multitasking operating system for (seemingly) years (though, ironically, they for the most part ignore OS/2, which handles multitasking in much the same manner as UNIX).

UNIX documentation doesn't actually often use the term *multitasking* (even though the rest of the computer world uses it); instead, UNIX is said to be *multiprocessing*—the same thing described differently. When you run a UNIX command, like **ls** or **cat**, you're running a *process*. When you boot the UNIX operating system, you are actually launching a series of processes without consciously doing so. (If you use a graphical user interface like the X Window System, you're launching many, *many* processes.) On a large multiuser system, there may be literally thousands of processes running at a given time.

These processes compete with each other for computing resources. Running programs in the background, as described earlier, is a way for the UNIX user to allocate resources efficiently. Such allocation is necessary to keep the system from bogging down, especially a large multiuser system with less-than-adequate resources. If there are more processes running than can fit in your system's random-access memory (RAM), then UNIX uses a hard disk as extended RAM in a action called *swapping* to disk. However, hard disks are much slower than RAM, so swapping to disk is not the most desirable of solutions; many experts advise the purchase of UNIX systems with huge amounts of RAM. UNIX workstations with 64 megabytes of RAM are not uncommon these days, especially those systems dealing with graphics.

But we digress. As we said, it's important for the UNIX system and user to efficiently allocate resources. UNIX does this (as it does almost everything else) in hierarchical fashion: Processes beget other processes (much as directories containing subdirectories), with one process at the top of the pyramid. When a process launches another process, it uses a system call entitled a *fork*, which creates the new process.

When you boot a UNIX system, the first process (process 0) launches a program called **init**, which then launches other processes. **Init** is the mother of all UNIX processes—or, as referred to in UNIXdom, **init** is a *parent* to other processes, which in turn can act as parents to additional processes, called *child* processes. It is, ultimately, the ancestor of all processes running on the system.

When we described the shell and its importance in running programs for you, we were referring to the shell acting as the parent and managing other child processes. Unless you tell it otherwise (by issuing the **kill** command), the shell waits while you run a child and returns with a prompt after the child process is finished, or *dies*. (Telling it otherwise is accomplished through several means, background being the most common.) If a child process dies but this fact is not acknowledged by the parent, the child process becomes a *zombie*. What macabre imagery!

It's up to the operating system to keep track of these parents and children, making sure that processes don't collide. This means scheduling processes to within a fraction of a second, ensuring that all processes have access to precious CPU time. It's also up to the operating system, through the **init** program, to manage child processes that have been abandoned by their parents. These abandoned processes are called *orphans*. (Family values obviously play as important a role in the UNIX operating system as they do in the Republican Party.)

Though we have mockingly referred to the high level of abstraction associated with the UNIX operating system, using names like *parent, orphan, zombie,* and *child* to describe the various stages of processes is a very useful thing; it helps both users and programmers visualize very intangible actions.

To see what processes are running on your system, use the **ps** command:

```
$ ps
PID TTY      TIME COMMAND
 89 p1       0:01 xterm
 93 p1       0:00 csh
 95 p1       0:01 ps
```

Because we used the command on a single-user UNIX machine, our list of running processes is not very long. If you're working on a large, multiuser system and ask for the all the processes running, your list may be pages long. The third field, which covers the time the processes have run, may be of interest if there are some inordinately large numbers present. Most UNIX commands, even very complex ones, don't take tons of time to complete.

 We're using the **ps** command in its simplest form. Should you need more information than provided in the manner discussed here, use the **ps** command in the long form:

```
$ ps -1
```

or in the full form:

```
$ ps -f
```

Not all versions of UNIX support both options.

If you need to view all of the processes running on the entire system (kids, don't try this at home, unless you *really* want a lot of information, most of it of questionable value), use:

```
$ ps -e
```

To get a fuller view of the whole of the whole system (provided you're using System V Release 4), you can use:

```
$ ps -ef
```

or

```
$ ps -el
```

Depending on the size and number of users on your system, you may regret using this option.

N O T E

If your system is based on Berkeley UNIX instead of System V UNIX, the **ps** command won't accept the *-ef* option. Instead use *-aux*:

```
$ ps -aux
```

For our purposes the most important column is the first one, which lists the IDs of running processes. When the kernel launches a new process, it assigns an ID number to the process. (As we saw above, **init** is numbered *process 1.*)

This number is important because it allows you to manipulate the process via the ID number. For example, there are times when you may want to kill a process because it's using too many precious system resources or not performing in the manner that you anticipated. If the process is running in the foreground, you can press the **Delete** or **Break** keys (depending on your keyboard) to stop the process. (If **Delete** or **Break** doesn't work, try **Ctrl-C** or **Ctrl-D**.) If a process is running in the background or has been launched by another user at another terminal, however, you must **kill** the process via the kill command:

```
$ kill PID
```

using the PID returned by the **ps** or other commands. This sends a *signal* to the process, telling it to cease and desist. Most processes don't know what to do when they receive a signal, so they commit suicide. Not all processes respond to the straight **kill** command; for instance, shells ignore a **kill** command with no options. To kill a shell or other particularly stubborn processes, use **kill** with the -9 option:

```
$ kill -9 PID
```

This sends an unconditional **kill** signal to the process. If you have many processes to kill, you can wipe them all out with:

```
$ kill 0
```

This kills all of the processes in a current process group, which oversees all processes created by a common ancestor, usually the login shell.

More on the Foreground and Background

As the UNIX operating system keeps track of these many processes, it must set priorities; after all, computing resources are typically a finite resource (yes, we'd all love to have the power of a Cray for our tasks, but we make do with our underpowered multiuser systems), and some tasks are simply more important than other tasks when it comes to your attention. If a job doesn't require input from you, go ahead and run it in the background. This means that the process will run out of sight (and out of mind, too often), popping up only when the command is completed. While the command runs in the background, you're free to work on other tasks with other commands.

As you've already learned earlier in this book, running a process in the background is a matter of adding an ampersand (**&**) to the end of the command line:

```
$ command options &
```

For instance, you should run CPU-intensive commands, such as **sort**, in the background. There's no reason for you to interact with the **sort** command as it goes through large files; your role in the process is to issue the command and then stay out of the way. The **sort** command requires no input from you, and it doesn't write to the screen as it performs the sort. The same goes for programmers who need to compile programs; their damage is done when creating the source code, not when compiling said code.

The temptation, of course, is to assume that all commands can be run in the background. Yet this isn't true; as a matter of fact, there's a rather limited number of commands that you should run in the background. For instance, any command that relies on continued input from you, such as text editors and anything to do with electronic mail, shouldn't be run in the background.

Real-Time Processes

System V Release 4 contains support for real-time processes, which ensures that a given process will be executed at a given time, no matter what other processes are running. This is a radical departure from previous versions of UNIX, which used various algorithms to allocate system resources more equally. With real-time processes, the system does not interrupt a process for any reason until the process is completed.

Using real-time processes is important in many fields, including multimedia (music and sounds won't be interrupted with pauses), factory automation, and medical computing. If you're interested in learning more about real-time processes, check the System V Release 4 documentation listed in Appendix A.

Using the Job Shell

The job shell, **jsh**, may not be the most frequently used shell, but it does a credible job at allowing you tight control over multiple jobs. This is a situation where knowledge of processes is important; otherwise, the many nifty features of **jsh** would be lost on you.

For example, **jsh** allows you to get a decipherable list of current jobs:

```
$ jobs
[1]  +  Running        sort AL_West > AL &
[2]  -  Suspended      sort AL_East > AL &
```

Both of these commands are running in the background. However, job number one is currently running, while job number two is suspended.

Armed with this information, there's a lot you can do with the job shell. For instance, you could kill the job with the ever-popular **kill** command (covered earlier in this chapter). However, there's a little difference when using it in the job shell; you must combine the job number with a percentage sign (%), as in the following command line, which kills job number one:

```
$ kill %1
```

The job shell also allows you to stop (suspend) a job:

```
$ stop %1
```

The neat thing here is that you have the option of starting the command again in either the foreground or in the background. To start job number one in the foreground, use the following command line:

```
$ fg %1
```

To start job number one in the background, use the following command line:

```
$ bg %1
```

Swapping and Paging

As we mentioned above, UNIX uses hard-disk space as an extension of RAM when there's no RAM free for processes.

The mechanism is simple. When you launch a new process, the kernel attempts to fit the process in an unused portion of RAM. If there's RAM available, the kernel loads the process and begins execution. If there's not enough RAM available, the kernel looks for a loaded process that's not running at that particular moment. The process is then moved to a special area of the hard disk devoted to swaps, and the new process then takes over the RAM previously occupied by the previously running process. The kernel will then swap in the previous running process if it's activated by the user or if enough RAM becomes available.

Swapping to and from disk slows down a system tremendously; this action is called *thrashing* in UNIXdom, and it serves as a very vivid metaphor so that you can envision exactly what's happening to your hard disk(s). As we said before, a more elegant way of supporting many users would involve buying enough RAM to allow everyone's programs to be active in RAM simultaneously. It's a waste of a good UNIX system to be spending most its time accessing the hard disk.

Newer UNIX systems take the notion of swapping a step further with the implementation of *paging*, also known as *virtual memory*. Paging is very similar conceptually to swapping, but increases several efficiencies that help minimize thrashing on many systems.

If your UNIX system supports paging, all memory and programs are divided into pages, which are equally sized (usually 4,096 kilobytes). When you launch a process, the kernel searches for a page of available RAM, and into that is loaded the first page of your program. As your programs runs, it may need additional pages for data or execution space, and so the kernel looks for more free pages. If no pages are free in your system memory, then the kernel must page out to the paging area on your hard disk. Processes are not grouped contiguously, and one portion of a process may be active while another portion may be paged out. Because these processes can be split, this method of using hard-disk space as RAM requires special hardware support from the CPU.

How is paging more efficient? With swapping, entire processes were swapped to disk, including both used and unused portions of the process. With paging, small portions of different processes are paged at any given time. Many processes, in fact, use only a small portion of their memory space at a time. For example, most of the time you're using a word processor, you don't run the spell checker. Under UNIX, the memory pages used by the spell checker can be paged to disk with no ill effects. In such a case, you probably won't know the difference.

Summary

UNIX systems run multiple tasks at once, under the official rubric of multi-processing. Because of multiprocessing, UNIX supports multiple users and multiple tasks. These tasks, or processes, are started by the process called **init**. The **init** process starts the system and gets it going (although the boot process starts **init**, or starts a scheduler that starts **init**). This **init** process, process 1, then becomes the parent for a whole set of processes.

These child processes, in turn, launch other processes. Finally, your login shell is launched and becomes the parent for all the processes that you, as a UNIX user, create. To get a snapshot of all the separate processes UNIX uses, try the **ps** command:

```
$ ps
```

The **kill** command, contrary to its name, sends a message, called a signal, to a process. Since most processes don't know what to do about a signal, the processes commit suicide. Thus, in a backwards sort of way, **kill** kills processes. To kill a process, use:

```
$ kill PID
```

where *PID* is the process's ID number, which you can get from the **ps** command.

Because UNIX can run more processes than it has RAM for, UNIX systems usually support swapping or paging; both move a process (swapping) or portions of a process (paging) to disk, freeing memory for other processes. If your system is constantly paging or swapping, you'll soon see what thrashing means as your system slows to a crawl. To avoid this, you need to run less processes or buy more RAM.

The X Window System

This chapter covers:

- ▼ The X Window System
- ▼ Graphical computing
- ▼ The X server
- ▼ Open Look and Motif
- ▼ Starting X
- ▼ Setting X fonts
- ▼ Using **xterm**
- ▼ Common X command-line parameters

Going Graphical

The X Window System—even the concept—confuses most new users. Is it a UNIX shell? No. Is it the all-singing, all-dancing graphical system that will cure all your computing woes? Not yet. Is it a standard? Yes, although some vendors—most notably workstation giant Sun Microsystems—have been brought into the X fold kicking and screaming. Is it a workable business-oriented environment? Yes, but just barely.

X is complex, confusing, and bloated, but it's also a *graphical windowing system*. X provides multiple windows (run by multiple applications) on a graphics monitor—the bare bones building blocks of a graphical user interface (or GUI, to use a popular and trendy term).

X, as a graphical user interface, provides two immediate benefits for you, the UNIX user:

▼ First, X allows you to use more of your display, because you can access every dot on the monitor, instead of just 24 lines by 80 characters in text mode. Graphics monitors have dramatically dropped in price over the last few years, so that most users can take advantage of X's capabilities.

▼ Second, a graphical user interface eases your transition to UNIX and speeds up your daily work. Several studies clearly indicate that a well-designed graphical interface reduces corporate training time and increases worker productivity.

Just about every modern UNIX software package, from the **xmahjongg** game to the WYSIWYG (*what-you-see-is-what-you-get*) Asterix word processor, runs under a graphical interface. Unlike the cryptic dot commands we introduce for **troff** in Chapter 11, Asterix provides a friendly menu-driven graphical interface, as does Island Write, FrameMaker, and almost every other X-based package. All of these programs run on top of the X Window System.

X, then, provides the basics for graphical windowing in a way that is portable to most UNIX platforms. What makes X special is that this graphical interface runs on just about every UNIX platform, as well as on VMS, DOS, Windows, AmigaDOS, and the Macintosh. X is not the only modern attempt at providing a graphical user interface—Microsoft Windows and the Macintosh operating system are two very well-known graphical interfaces. So why use X? For the following reasons:

▼ ***Flexibility***. X allows you to layer any number of graphical user interfaces on top of the underlying window system. You can run Motif and Open Look programs, or programs sporting any other interface you desire. Few other windowing systems offer this flexibility.

▼ ***Portability***. X programs run on a wide variety of computer systems. If your company or university owns UNIX workstations from a number of vendors—a very common occurrence—then the knowledge you gain learning X will aid you on any of these platforms.

▼ ***Network transparency***. X programs can compute across a network. The X Window System divides computing into two parts, based on a *client-server relationship*. This relationship can be rather confusing, but it offers the ability to efficiently distribute applications over a network. (We'll cover this in more depth later.)

▼ ***Because it's there***. If you're using UNIX (which we assume you are, or you wouldn't have read this far) and run a graphical windowing system, well, you're running X. Very few non-X graphical UNIX systems survive today. Thus if you want to learn how to get the most out of your system (some of us would settle for just getting the system to run right), then it behooves you to learn X.

The X Server

The key to understanding X is grasping the confusing concept of the X server.

In the mini and micro worlds, a *server* is usually a hardware device (a VAX, an AS/400, a Novell file server) running at the center of a network, distributing data and processing power to networked workstations and terminals. Because other systems on your network have access to your display, the X server cannot be thought of in the same way as a file server on a local-area network. With X, the role of the server (sometimes called a *display server*) is reversed. The server is a program that runs on your local machine and controls and draws all output to the *display*. Your local machine, whether it's a PC running SCO Open Desktop or a Sun SPARCstation running OpenWindows, is called a display. The server draws the images on your physical monitor, tracks input via keyboard and pointing device (usually a mouse), and updates windows appropriately.

The server also acts as a traffic cop between clients running on local or remote systems and the local system. *Clients* are application programs that perform specific tasks. (In X the terms clients and applications are used interchangeably.) Because X is a networked environment, the client and the server don't necessarily compute on the same machine (although they can and do in a number of situations). That's how X features *distributed processing.* For example, a personal computer running SCO UNIX can call upon the processing power of a more-powerful Solbourne host within a network, displaying the results of the Solbourne's computations on the PC's monitor. In this case the client is actually running on the remote Solbourne, not your local machine—thus distributing the processing across the network. The idea is simple: The actual computing should take place on the machine with the most computing power on a network, not necessarily at the computer that a user happens to be using.

Most X users run a *window manager* to help control their display. A window manager is a program that defines how the interface (that is, the actual look of the programs) actually appears and acts on the screen. X does not provide a specific *look and feel* of these windows; that is, the specific arrangement of elements on a screen (scroll bars, title bars, etc.). As we noted before, X provides the building blocks for a graphical interface. The user is free to layer any look and feel on top of X.

Since the X Window System doesn't mandate a user interface, you are free to layer a particular look and feel on top of it. And indeed, most X users don't deal directly with X, but rather with vendor-supplied solutions—and that's where Motif and Open Look come in.

In this chapter we'll refer to the X Window System in a generic sense; the information will apply to whatever window manager you're running. If information does apply to a specific window manager, reference will be made to the specific window manager.

Even though you may use the terms "Motif users" and "Open Look users" in casual conversation, most users are both, because strictly speaking, there are no such things as products named Open Look and Motif. Instead, there are software products that conform to the Open Look specifications, as defined by AT&T and Sun Microsystems, or Motif specifications, as defined by the Open Software Foundation. Both Motif and Open Look provide a *style guide* with a particular look and feel. You can run both Motif and Open Look programs side-by-side and thus be a Motif and an Open Look user simultaneously, thanks to the multitasking provided by UNIX. But first and foremost, you'll be an X Window System user.

Actually Using X

While you don't need to be an X expert in order to use X, it's a good idea to be familiar with the basic X Window System.

The first step in empowerment is actually getting your hands on X. If you're a workstation user, you probably are already using X or have it available for use. Workstations from Sun, DEC, Hewlett-Packard, Silicon Graphics, and IBM all feature X as a central part of their operating environments.

If you're already working in a networked workstation environment, or work with a VAX/VMS system running DECwindows, you may be familiar with X. A way to bring the power of X to additional users, without the expense of additional workstations, is through *X terminals*. An X terminal is more than a dumb terminal, yet less than a full workstation. X terminals have enough horsepower to run a local server, but yet relies on a machine elsewhere on the network for most of its computing power.

If you do indeed have X, you can follow along with your particular installation throughout the rest of this chapter.

What X Looks Like

As stated repeatedly, X is a graphical user interface. It uses various graphical elements to represent different portions of computing.

The exact graphical elements will depend on what kind of X implementation you're using, of course; X on a PC running UnixWare will look different than X on a Hewlett-Packard workstation. (Compare Figures 7.1 and 7.2. Both show X, and both are running on personal computers.)

Though both implementations look drastically different, upon reflection you can see some commonalities, and these commonalities lie at the core of the X Window System. X uses the metaphor of windows to represent most screen elements (no surprise there, eh?). Windows, in other words, represents a program. In both figures the windows have a title at the top of the window that describes the program. Both figures show the same programs—an X logo, an **xterm**, and a clock.

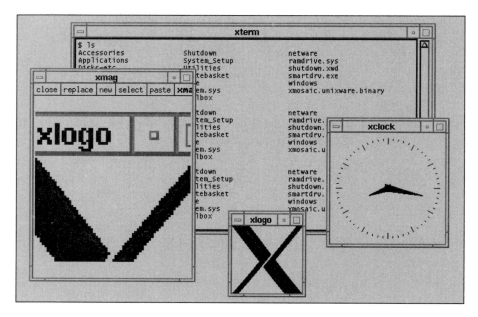

Figure 7.1 *X running as part of UnixWare.*

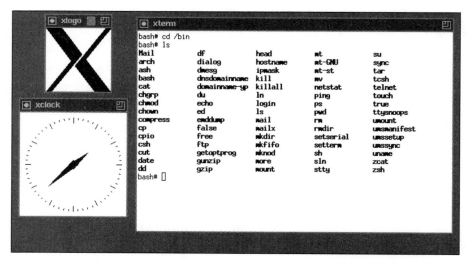

Figure 7.2 *X running as part of Linux and XFree86.*

That's where the similarities end. Though both figures are X, they are illustrating different window managers; in Figure 7.1 the UnixWare installation is running the Motif window manager, or **mwm**, and in Figure 7.2 the Tab window manager (**twm**) is running. What are you to learn from this? That no matter which window manager is running on a given UNIX implementation, at the core X is still X. **Xlogo**, no matter what window manager is running, is still **xlogo**.

Of course there's more to X Window than merely windows. X also makes extensive use of *icons* to represent screen elements. In most cases an icon represents a window that has been shrunk in order to clear up clutter on the screen (as is the case with Figure 7.3). In other cases an icon represents an application, as is the case with Figure 7.4, the icon representing the Shutdown program in UnixWare.

Figure 7.3 *The xclock application iconified.*

Figure 7.4 *The Shutdown icon from UnixWare.*

Deconstructing the Window

How do you iconify a window? That, and other window actions, can be explained by looking at the various elements of an X Window window, as shown in Figure 7.5.

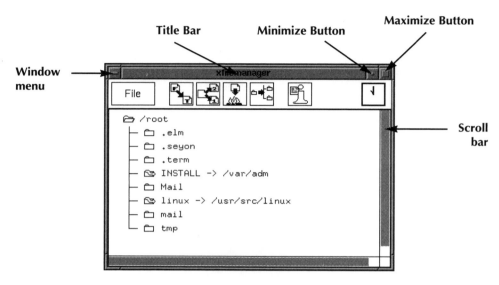

Figure 7.5 *A window deconstructed.*

The window, running under the **fvwm** window manager (which appropriates the look and feel of a window running under the Motif window manager, which in turn is based on IBM's CUA guidelines), has several tools for your use. The Window Menu, positioned at the top right of the window, yields a menu that allows you to maximize, minimize, iconify, or close a window. (An application or a user may also place additional functions on this menu.) The Title Bar, in the middle of the top of the window, is used both to label the window (in this case the ever-popular **xterm** application) and to move the window; by pressing on the left mouse button (which in turn depresses the Title Bar) and dragging, the window can be moved. (This can also be accomplished by pressing the left mouse button while the pointer is positioned on the top of any side of the window, but not the corner.) The two buttons on the top left are used to minimize (that is, turn into an icon) and maximize the window.

Finally we're left with the issue of resizing the window. As you'll learn later in this chapter, it's possible to start X with the windows in preset sizes. Should you want to change these windows sizes, however, you'll need to use the resize handles, found on all four corners of the window. By positioning the pointer over the corner and dragging, you can resize the window. How can you tell you're resizing the window and not accessing the Window Menu or the Maximize button? Because the pointer will change to an arrow against a right angle, mimicking the angle of the corner of the window.

Starting X

Before you can run any X application, though, you need to start the X server. The X server takes over control of a display: the keyboard, a pointing device (usually a mouse), and at least one video monitor—sometimes more in multiheaded systems.

An X server alone isn't worth much—all you get is a cross-hatch pattern and an X cursor. You'll also want to start a number of X applications, including a window manager, when you start up the X server. The applications are important; the X server merely provides the infrastructure.

Unfortunately, there are zillions of ways to start the X server. Many UNIX workstation vendors, in a futile attempt to add value and distract you, customize the way you start X. While these features may be considered value-*added* if you only buy workstations from one vendor (that's their point, remember), they soon become value-*subtracted* as you try to learn every system's weird customized commands. The whole point of UNIX is that it runs relatively the same on all platforms. That's also supposed to be the whole point of X. Anyway, if your system already has a method to start X, then by all means use that method. Otherwise, you can start the X server with the **xinit** or the **startx** commands.

If you're already running X, that is, if you see a graphics display in front of you, you don't need to run **xinit**, as this (or the equivalent on your system) has already been done for you.

Normally, **xinit** can run without any arguments:

```
$ xinit
```

Xinit starts the X server, a program named, appropriately enough, **X**, that's normally stored in **/usr/bin/X11**. After starting the X server, **xinit** executes the programs listed in the file **.xinitrc**, which is located in your home directory, much like the **.profile** or **.login** files used by **sh** and **csh**. This **.xinitrc** file lists the programs you want to start when you launch X. This usually includes a graphical clock, at least one **xterm**, and a window manager, such as **twm**, **olwm**, or **mwm**.

Because **.xinitrc** is a shell script, all the programs it launches, except the last, should be run in the background, with an ampersand **(&)** trailing the command. (See Chapters 5 and 9 for more on working with the various UNIX shells.)

When **.xinitrc** terminates, **xinit** kills the X server. This, in essence, is how you stop X.

If you run every program in **.xinitrc** in background, then **.xinitrc** will quickly terminate, and so will your X server. Run the last program in **.xinitrc** in the foreground, like the example **.xinitrc** file shown here:

```
xterm -geom 80x40+100+200 &
xclock -geom 120x120+900+10 &
exec twm
```

Obviously you'll choose a program that you intend to keep around for your entire X session. Like the previous example, most users end their **.xinitrc** file by running a window manager, such as **twm**.

There are two main reasons for this. First, you want a window manager running during your entire X session. Second, most window managers provide a menu choice that allows you to exit. This menu choice is an easier (and easier to remember) way to quit X than typing **Ctrl-D** in an **xterm** window, or using **kill** to terminate the X server. Using the previous example, exiting the window manager also exits X.

Whatever program you choose, this last key place holder process controls when X exits. When this process exits, X does, too.

If **xinit** fails to find a **.xinitrc** file, it merely starts the X server and one 25-line **xterm** window.

Using Startx

There's no great mystery to the **startx** command—it merely calls the **xinit** command under the hood. Most PC UNIX-based X Window implementations, such as XFree86, use **startx** to launch the X server. In every other respect, however, the process for configuring **xinit** (such as configuring the **.xinitrc** file) is the same for **startx** as it is for **xinit**.

The .xinitrc File

Let's go over our example **.xinitrc** file line by line. The **xterm** command starts an **xterm** window:

```
$ xterm -geom 80x40+100+200 &
```

Xterm is a text-based DEC VT102 terminal emulator; certainly nothing flashy. This is the most commonly used X program, in our experience, even though X is such a ballyhooed graphical environment. In this case we start an **xterm** window with a geometry of *80x40+100+200*—80 characters wide by 40 lines tall, and a location of (*100,200*), which is 100 pixels across from the left-hand side of the screen, and 200 pixels down from the top. This command is run in the background. Note that **xterm** uses a width and height in *characters* (based on the size of **xterm's** font), while most other X programs specify the width and height in *pixels*. This distinction can be confusing. The origin in *x* is the upper-left corner. Values increase in the *x* direction moving right. Values increase in the *y* direction going down. We'll cover **xterm** more later in this chapter.

The **xclock** command starts a graphical clock:

```
$ xclock -geom 120x120+900+10 &
```

Since most computer users are Type A personalities, they all want to know what time it is—all the time. There are two main X clocks: **xclock** and **oclock. Oclock** provides a rounded window on systems that support them. Both are shown in Figures 7.6 and 7.7 running under the Tab window manager.

Figure 7.6 *Xclock in action.*

Figure 7.7 *Oclock in action.*

The following command launches a window manager, **twm**, in the foreground:

```
$ exec twm
```

Window managers control the layout of windows on the screen, allowing you to move windows, iconify them, and change their sizes. Window managers also give the window title bars a certain look—such as the Motif or Open Look style. (In this case we went with a neutral player, the Tab window manager.) We use **exec** to launch **twm** because **exec** will overlay the shell process with the **twm** process, saving compute cycles, and we all know X grabs far too many cycles.

This sample **.xinitrc** file ends up displaying a screen containing two windows, like the one shown in Figure 7.8. (However, we have taken editorial license, compressing the layout of the screen to fit nicely on this page. Still, you get the idea.)

Figure 7.8 *An xterm and a clock.*

Command-Line Parameters

Most X programs accept a standard set of command-line parameters, as listed in Table 7.1. In our case we already used the *-geom* command-line parameter to set the window geometry in the example from the previous sections.

Table 7.1. *Common X command-line parameters.*

Parameter	Meaning
-background *color*	Sets window background color.
-bd *color*	Sets window border color.
-bg *color*	Sets window background color.
-bordercolor *color*	Sets window border color.
-borderwidth *border_width*	Sets window border width, in pixels.
-bw *border_width*	Sets window border width, in pixels.
-display *display_name*	Names that display (X server) to connect to.
-fg *color*	Sets foreground color.
-fn *fontname*	Sets font.
-font *fontname*	Sets font.
-foreground *color*	Sets foreground color.
-geometry *geometryspec*	Sets window size and location.
-geom *geometryspec*	
-iconic	Starts program as an icon.
-name *name*	Sets application name for grabbing resource values.
-reverse	Turns on reverse video.
-rv	Turns on reverse video.
-title *title*	Sets window title.
-xnllanguage *language[terr][.code]*	Sets language, and optionally territory and codeset for current locale.
-xrm *resource_command*	Sets the given resource, just like in a resource file.

Using the Mouse

The X Window System requires a mouse; while it is possible to do some things within X strictly from the keyboard, generally speaking you'll need the mouse to accomplish anything substantial.

The mouse allows you to directly control a *pointer* on the screen. This pointer is your agent as your move between windows, icons, dialog boxes, pull-down menus, and other screen elements. To move between the windows shown in Figure 7.9, you use a mouse.

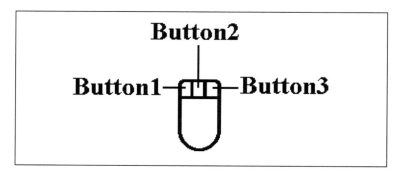

Figure 7.9 *The three mouse buttons illustrated.*

X assumes that you're using a three-button mouse, while supporting up to five buttons. (Yes, there are mice with five or more buttons, but they tend to be limited to the CAD/CAM field.) Internally, X refers to the three mouse buttons as Button1, Button2, and Button3. For the purposes of this discussion, we'll refer to the left, middle, and right mouse buttons, assuming that your mouse uses the standard X configuration (which is geared for the right-handed computer user).

Left-handed people, or users not comfortable with the default mouse configurations, can change the mouse buttons through an X client called **xmodmap**. However, this client isn't geared for the beginning computer user. If you want some more information on **xmodmap**, check in some of the more advanced X Window texts listed in Appendix A.

Using the mouse to move around the screen real estate isn't a big deal, particularly if you've already done some work on a computer running Microsoft Windows, OS/2, or the Macintosh operating system. However, if you're unused to working in a graphical environment with a mouse, there are a few things you'll need to master before you become completely at ease.

X allows you to perform many distinct acts with the mouse—probably more than you thought possible. Roughly speaking, X mouse actions can be divided into four groups:

▼ **Click**: Press a mouse button and then release it. The act should be fluid; that is, you shouldn't pause too long between pressing the mouse button and then releasing it. Two clicks in a row represents a double-click.

▼ **Drag**: Position the pointer over an on-screen object (such as a window or an icon), press the left mouse button, and then move the mouse while continuing to hold down the mouse button. As you move the mouse, the window or icon (or an outline representing the window or icon, depending on your system configuration) will move on the screen. When the window or icon reaches your desired destination point, you let go of the mouse button. The point, of course, is to be able to move windows and icons from one part of the screen to another. You also use the drag motion when you pulldown a menu and make a selection from the menu.

▼ **Press:** Simply put, you press down the mouse button. At times you'll want to release the mouse button immediately; at other times you'll want to keep the button pressed while you drag a window or choose from a menu.

▼ **Release**: Of course, this is when you let go of the mouse button.

Window Focus

As you play with the mouse and the pointer, you'll notice that not every window is always the same color on the screen, and that at times a window won't be able to accept your input.

In X, windows are said to have *focus* (or sometimes *input focus*), which is a fancy way of stating that you can type into or manipulate a window. Only one window at a time can have focus. Depending on the window manager in use, X does tell you which window has the focus; in most instances the window that has the distinctive color (or, actually, the only color) is the window with focus.

With most window managers, you need to explicitly set the focus by moving the pointer over a window and clicking on the left mouse button. If you click on a window that's partially obscured by another window, giving it the focus will move the obscured window on top of the previously obscuring window. (This sounds much more complicated than it really is. Trust us.) Don't worry if you have a window partially obscuring another; the obscured window is still fully functional and running a program.

The way the different windows work in X mimics the way UNIX manages many tasks, as explained in Chapter 6. A program running in the background in

UNIX will do the same in X, even if the program is contained in a window that doesn't have the input focus.

NOTE Some lesser-used window managers follow the model of *focus follows pointer*, which means that the window immediately underneath the pointer has the focus. (Yes, it is a tad odd to be thinking of these two-dimensional interfaces in three-dimensional terms.) In addition, your window manager can be changed to allow this. Again, this isn't something a UNIX novice should be playing around with; the X Window books listed in Appendix A outline how to implement a change in focus.

Setting Up the Proper Paths

One problem that may plague your system is not being able to find the X programs in your command path. If you get a "*command not found*" error when you run any X command, this is probably the case.

The default location for X Window binary executables is in **/usr/bin/X11**, which is a directory that isn't in your normal command path—unless your system administrator or workstation vendor took care of this detail for you. Make sure your path includes the directories where your X programs reside (see Chapters 4 and 5 for more on UNIX shells). With OpenWindows, the default location for X programs is in **/usr/openwin**.

Working with Xterm

Despite all the fuss over the X Window System's value as a graphical user interface for UNIX, we find the most frequently used X program to be **xterm**.

After all is said and done, most users still need to enter UNIX commands at a command shell prompt, mainly because X tools simply aren't advanced enough to completely hide the command prompt and obsolete the shells. Luckily, we're already well-versed on the UNIX shells. **Xterm** manages the interface to X so that all of your old text-based programs, like the **vi** text editor or the **elm** electronic mailer, as well as UNIX commands work just fine inside **xterm**, as shown in Figure 7.10.

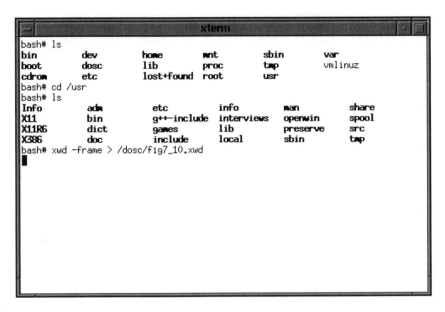

Figure 7.10 *An xterm running under the fvwm window manager.*

It seems odd to use a graphical windowing system merely for command-line windows, but **xterm** provides more than a simple command line:

▼ You can control **xterm's** window size and location, fonts (and font size), as well as the foreground and background colors.

▼ You can have multiple **xterm** windows on screen at the same time—and copy and paste between them. They can overlap or sit side-by-side.

▼ **Xterm** provides a handy scrollbar to review previous commands or the long output of complex programs. In fact, our standard X environment includes two or three very large **xterm** windows on the screen. This provides the base for a very productive software development environment on UNIX.

▼ If you like the standard 80-column by 25-line text display, then you'll like an 80-column by 46-line text display much better, particularly if you can have two of these side-by-side—a better setup than multiple 80x25 character virtual screens offered on many 386/486 systems.

Because **xterm** is such a handy way of working with both UNIX and the X Window System, we'll spend a lot of time on coverage of **xterm** in this chapter. In addition, we'll use **xterm** as a way to illustrate other X Window concepts that can be applied to almost any X Window application.

Starting Xterm

You can start an **xterm** window (normally from another **xterm**) with the following command:

```
$ xterm &
```

This will start the **xterm** in the background. You must be running the X server for this to work. Normally, you'll start the **xterm** in the background, so that you can continue to work in your current terminal. You may want to arrange your X start-up configuration to launch more than one **xterm** window—all in the background, by editing your **.xinitrc** file.

Setting X Fonts

Like most X applications, **xterm** will accept a fontname command-line parameter. Use either *-font fontname* or *-fn fontname*:

```
$ xterm -font fontname &
```

where *fontname* is the valid name of an X font installed on your system. Use **xlsfonts** to get a list of the available fonts installed on your system. If your system is fully configured, you'll see a listing of hundreds of fonts. Here's a sampling of the most common:

```
$ xlsfonts
-adobe-courier-medium-o-normal—12-120-75-75-m-70-iso8859-1
-adobe-helvetica-bold-r-normal—14-140-75-75-p-82-iso8859-1
-adobe-times-bold-i-normal—14-140-75-75-p-77-iso8859-1
-b&h-lucida-bold-r-normal—sans-14-140-75-75-p-92-iso8859-1
-bitstream-charter-bold-r-normal—19-180-75-75-p-119-iso8859-1
-jis-fixed-medium-r-normal—16-150-75-75-c-160-jisx0208.1983-0
12x24kana
6x13
9x15
9x15bold
```

```
fixed
variable
```

We find a good font for regular use is:

```
-adobe-courier-medium-r-normal—12-120-75-75-m-70-iso8859-1
```

We find this font much better looking than the small font named **fixed**, the default **xterm** font.

You must use a fixed-width font for regular usage with **xterm**. Variable-width fonts confuse **xterm**, which results in poorly displayed output.

Basic X Applications

Along with **xterm**, some other basic X applications include:

▼ the clock programs, **xclock** and **oclock**

▼ the calculator, **xcalc**

▼ the clipboard holder, **xclipboard**

▼ the text editor, **xedit**

These applications are shown in Figures 7.11, 7.12, and 7.13.

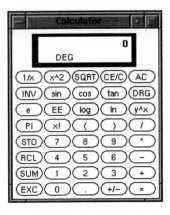

Figure 7.11 *Xcalc, the X calculator.*

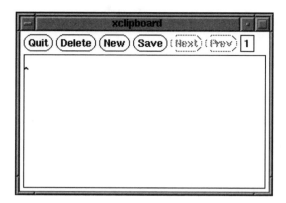

Figure 7.12 *Xclipboard, the clipboard holder.*

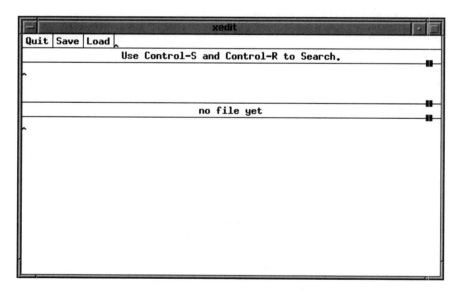

Figure 7.13 *Xedit, the X text editor.*

Many familiar UNIX clients have been adapted to also run in the X Window environment. For example, the popular **emacs** text editor now sports an X Window interface, as shown in Figure 7.14. (You'll learn more about **emacs** in Chapter 10.)

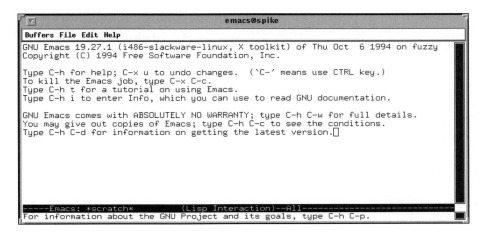

Figure 7.14 *The emacs text editor, running under X.*

In addition, users can choose their own window manager, usually from the choices of **mwm** (the Motif window manager), **twm** (the Tab window manager), and **olwm** (the Open Look window manager). Check in the **/usr/bin/X11** directory (or wherever X programs are stored on your system) for what's available.

Finally, there are a slew of other X Window applications that are quite useful, but space prevents us from delving too deeply into the subject. Check out one of the X Window books listed in Appendix A for more information on the X Window System.

Summary

The X Window System confuses most new users. Is it a UNIX shell? No. Is it the all-singing, all-dancing graphical system that will cure all your computing woes? Not yet. Is it a standard? Yes. Is it a workable business-oriented environment? Yes. X is complex, confusing, and bloated, but it's also a graphical windowing system.

X is actually a set of building blocks for others to create their own graphical interfaces. The two most popular in the UNIX world currently are Motif and Open Look.

The notion of a client and a server in X is the opposite of the norm in the PC and UNIX networking worlds: The server runs on your local machine, while clients are application programs that perform specific tasks.

Before you can run any X application, though, you need to start the X server. The X server takes over control of a display: the keyboard, a pointing device (usually a mouse), and at least one video monitor. An X server alone isn't worth much—all you get is a cross-hatch pattern and an X cursor. You'll also want to start a number of X applications, including a window manager, when you start up the X server. The applications are important; the X server merely provides the infrastructure.

One problem that may plague your system is not being able to find the X programs in your command path. If you get a *"command not found"* error when you run any X command, this is probably the case. The default location for X Window binary executables is in **/usr/bin/X11**, which is a directory that isn't in your normal command path—unless your system administrator or workstation vendor took care of this detail for you.

Like most X applications, **xterm** will accept a fontname command-line parameter. Use either *-font fontname* or *-fn fontname*:

```
$ xterm -font fontname &
```

where *fontname* is the valid name of an X font installed on your system. Use **xlsfonts** to get a list of the available fonts installed on your system.

Even though X is a graphical system, the most popular X application is **xterm**, a terminal emulator that allows you to enter commands via a command line.

Hello, Neighbor!

No user is an island in the typical UNIX configuration, since a core rationale for UNIX is the way it allows multiple users to work on the same system. In the UNIX parlance, this is called connectivity.

We've split up UNIX connectivity into three areas. Chapter 8 covers UNIX's outstanding support of electronic mail; virtually every UNIX user has electronic mail of some sort, whether it's mail for internal consumption or a full connection to the Internet. Chapter 9 covers established UNIX communications and networking tools like **uucp**, **telnet**, and **ftp**; for the most part, these tools are used to talk with other UNIX computers. Chapter 10 covers the hottest area of the computer world at the moment—the Internet, the Usenet, and the World Wide Web, allowing you to ride the trend as an enlightened and connected WWW citizen.

Electronic Mail

This chapter covers:

- ▼ UNIX and X Window mail programs
- ▼ Receiving mail messages
- ▼ Domain addressing
- ▼ Parsing a mail message
- ▼ Creating mail messages
- ▼ Mail-related commands
- ▼ Saving and deleting mail messages
- ▼ Introducing the **elm** mail program

The Paper-Filled Office

Computer cynics like to point back to several predictions made in the 1950s and 1960s regarding the office of the 1990s. Filing cabinets and typewriters would be obsolete by 1990 because the office of tomorrow would be paperless; all document delivery and storage would be done electronically.

As you can tell by looking at the pile of papers, faxes, and folders strewn across your desk, the day of the paperless office hasn't yet arrived. We still commit most of our work to paper backups (which we can consider nonvolatile storage devices), while truly important papers are never exchanged in electronic form. Indeed, the world uses more paper now than at any other time in the past.

The cynics miss the point, though: If we *truly* wanted a paperless office, we could eliminate most office paper usage in a short amount of time. Only because of factors outside the technology realm (legal reasons to maintain paper versions; cultural aversion to dependence on computers) does the business world avoid a total conversion to the paperless office. The tools are all in place, especially in the UNIX world: powerful and affordable computers that can display graphics images, networks that can shuffle huge documents and databases instantaneously, high-performance laser printers, and easy-to-use electronic mail.

The ability to send electronic messages to individuals, groups of people, or everyone in the company is not one of the flashiest features of the UNIX operating system, but it is certainly one of the most used. Other networking systems, particularly from the MS-DOS world (like Novell NetWare) lack basic electronic-mail (or e-mail) capabilities, while other operating systems featuring built-in electronic mail lack the other extensive capabilities featured in UNIX.

This chapter covers UNIX's electronic-mail capabilities. We've already covered **write** and **talk**, two primitive and limited electronic-mail functions, and we've already mentioned electronic mail in the context of the login process. Here we'll show you how to read, send, and delete an electronic-mail message. We'll also review some popular mail readers.

The **mail** program has been an important part of UNIX almost since the very beginning. As UNIX evolved, so has **mail**—to an extent. The actual electronic-mail mechanisms are similar to the original **mail** mechanisms; changes mainly concern how a user interacts with a **mail** program. The procedures described here may not appear exactly the same on your system, as there are a large number of mail programs, both UNIX- and X Window-based, that vary in how they present information to the user. Most of our examples are based on the BSD **mail** program and the SVR4 **mailx** program (which are virtually identical). Still, the commands and concepts we present here should be applicable to almost every electronic-mail situation you might encounter.

With the explosion of interest in electronic mail, there are now many electronic-mail packages available in the UNIX world. Some of these packages ship with UNIX and the X Window System, such as the **mail** command and the **xmh** application. Some are freeware and are available over the Internet and via CD-ROM in source-code form, such as **elm**, **pine**, and **mush**. Others are commercial, such as **Z-Mail**. At the end of this chapter, we'll briefly discuss some of these packages.

The thing to remember: No matter what electronic-mail package you use, the principles discussed in this chapter will apply.

Receiving Mail

As we learned in Chapter 1, UNIX informs you of incoming mail when you login the system. You'll see a message something like this:

```
You have mail.
```

Unless you read your mail at this point, this message will reappear periodically, as the shell is automatically set up to remind you of unread mail.

To view this mail, type:

```
$ mail
Mail version 4.0. Type ? for help.
2 messages:
2 kreichard@mcimail.com Sun Jul 18 2:45 11/274 "Stuff"
1 erc Thu Jul 16 21:25 11/274 "Hello"
```

The shell responds with a list of your mail messages, listed in the order that they were received by your system, newest mail first. (These messages are usually contained in the file **/usr/mail/***yourname***, /usr/spool/mail/***yourname***, or /usr/spool/mqueue/***yourname***.**) The first field lists the sender of the message, the second through fifth fields denotes the time and date the message was received, the sixth field records the number of lines in the message and the size of the message (in bytes), and the final field indicates the subject of the message.

Press **Enter** to read the first message on the list. If it's a long message, the entire message will scroll by. If you want to stop scrolling the message, type **Ctrl-S**; to start it again, type **Ctrl-Q**.

There are two types of messages waiting for us: a message from **kreichard@mcimail.com** and a message from **erc.** Your electronic mail can come from two sources: your own system and from other systems. Mail from other systems, sent on the Internet or the Usenet, has its own unique addressing scheme (more on that in the next section). Mail from your own system uses the same login names as described in Chapter 1; these names are contained in the **/etc/passwd** file.

The Internet

The Internet is the most extensive computer communications network in the world. Many corporations, universities, and research institutions send and receive mail via the Internet. Not all of the computers on the Internet run the UNIX operating system (everything from Crays to UNIX and MS-DOS-based PCs are represented), but most share two basic addressing schemes.

There will be an extended discussion of the Internet in Chapter 9.

The first and older scheme is called a *bang path*, first popularized on the Usenet, which makes up part of the Internet. Essentially you're telling the mail system the exact route it must take to send your mail. This can be a gigantic pain, especially if there are many machines a message must go through before it is delivered. Luckily this manual addressing of electronic mail is on the wane, which is why you see so few electronic-mail addresses dotted with exclamation marks.

Still, there's a need for bang paths when it comes to electronic mail. Many users now take advantage of *gateways*, which forward mail to other connected machines. If you have access to a gateway (check with your system administrator; chances are that you do if you have the ability to send and receive electronic mail from the Internet), you can just send mail to the gateway, denoting the system name and the user name:

```
$ mail uunet!concubine!kevin
```

where *uunet* is the name of the gateway (as it happens, *uunet* is a very popular gateway), the system name is *concubine*, and *kevin* is the user name. The bang character, or exclamation point (!), separates the entries. If you use the C shell, the bang character has special meaning (it is used for the list of previous commands—the command history). Thus you'll have to use the backslash character to **escape** the bangs:

```
% mail uunet\!concubine\!kevin
```

The previous command tells the C shell that you really mean to use the exclamation mark (!) and don't want **csh** to look in its record of your previous commands (see Chapter 5 for more on the C shell).

The newer addressing scheme, and one that is growing in popularity (mainly because of the growing popularity of the Internet), is called *domain addressing*. Structured as the exact opposite of a bang path, a domain address couples the name of the user with an address. This scheme grew out of the need for international standardization of electronic-mail addresses and provides a hierarchical structure to addressing. Essentially, the world is split into country domains, which are then divided into educational domains (indicated by the suffix *.edu* in the address), commercial domains (indicated by the suffix *.com* in the address), government domains (*.gov*), and more. There are hundreds and hundreds of domains, with the number growing each day.

Reading a domain address is quite simple. In the address of:

```
reichard@mr.net.com
```

reichard refers to the user, while *mr.net* refers to the domain. The user and domain names are separated by the at (@) symbol. As a user, you don't need to know the specific path a message must take, nor do you need to know the name of a gateway. With a domain address, sending a message is simple:

```
$ mail reichard@mr.net
```

The idea of the Internet is fairly amorphous and abstract (you didn't think we could make it through a chapter without a little abstraction, did you?). The Internet is technically a collection of many networks that somehow manage to talk to each other. As a user, all you need to know is a recipient's electronic-mail address; the system administrator handles the basic details of linking a system to the Internet.

If you're on the Internet, you can also receive electronic-mail from afar. To find your machine address, type *uname -n* at the prompt

```
$ uname -n
yoursystem
```

where *yoursystem* is the name of your UNIX system, also called the *hostname*. To list all the systems you can directly communicate with, type uname:

```
uname
othersystem1
othersystem2
othersystem3
```

where *othersystem* refers to the other systems.

N O T E The **uname** command doesn't support this option on all systems. If this is the case, you can look in the file **/etc/hosts** to get an understanding of the other systems your computer networks with.

In a large regional or nationwide network, the list of other systems can be quite large. If you want to find a specific system and don't want to wade through a huge list of names, use **uname** in conjunction with **grep**:

```
$ uname | grep othersystem121
othersystem121
```

If the name of the other system is returned, you can send electronic mail to someone with an account on that system. In addition, you can send messages to people on the Internet if you are connected to the Internet, provided that you know the exact address of the recipient.

Let's look at the message from *kreichard@aol.com*:

```
Sender: uu.psi.com!aolsys!kreichard
Received: from uu.psi.com by iha.compuserve.com
(5.65/5.910516)
    id AA25483; Sun, 18 Dec 94 14:08:49 -0400
Received: from aolsys.UUCP by uu.psi.com (5.65b/4.1.031792-
PSI/PSINet)
    id AA21056; Sun, 18 Dec 94 13:53:27 -0400
From: kreichard@aol.com
X-Mailer: America Online Mailer
To: 73670.3422@compuserve.com
```

```
Subject: Test
Date: Sat, 19 Dec 94 22:56:39 EDT
Message-Id: <9207182256.tn10271@aol.com>

This is a test.

-K.
```

Obviously, this was not an earth-shattering message. Even though the actual message itself was only 21 characters, the bulk of the message was other, less-important information about the route the mail took in reaching us. The information is called the *header*. With the Internet, mail may go between one or more systems on its way to you. You can't count on a direct link between systems, and because of these uncontrollable paths it make take some time for a message to reach the recipient; delivery times of 15 hours to 24 hours are not uncommon, but neither is a delivery time of 20 seconds.

The message from *erc* is considerably shorter:

```
MESSAGE 2:
from erc
Sun Dec 18 2:45 CDT 1994
Received: by odcome.apple (5.59/SMI-3.2)
        id AA00099; Sun, 18 Dec 94 02:59:48 CDT
Date: Sun, 18 Dec 94 02:59:48
From: erc
Message-ID: <9207190759.AA00099@odclone.apple)
To: kevin
Subject: Stuff
Status: R

This is a test.
```

Still, the majority of this message, too, is occupied by the header. Such is the overhead price of electronic mail.

Creating Mail

It's very easy to create mail. (*Too* easy, some would say, as they survey mailboxes full of irrelevant mail messages.) To create a short message at the keyboard, simply combine mail with the name of the recipient:

```
$ mail erc
Subject: test
This, too, is a test.
```

As always, end input from the keyboard by typing **Ctrl-D**. Some e-mail programs also accept a single period on its own line to terminate the message, instead of **Ctrl-D**. The procedure would be the same if you were sending a message to a user on a remote machine:

```
$ mail kreichard@mcimail.com
```

You can send the same message to multiple users with the *-t* option:

```
$ mail -t erc geisha spike
This, too, is a test.
```

The resulting message will contain multiple *To:* fields in the header.

Sending an existing file as the text of an electronic-mail message is almost as simple. After creating an ASCII file using **vi** or **emacs**, save the file and then redirect it as input on the command line:

```
$ mail erc < note
```

where **note** is the name of the file.

The Berkeley UNIX **mailx** program allows you to call up a text editor from within **mailx**, by using the **~v** command. You must start this command on its own line:

```
% mailx kevin
~v
```

Unless you've configured your system differently, the default text editor will be **vi**. Edit your message using the **vi** commands and then exit **vi** with the **ZZ** (save and exit) command. You'll then be back in the **mailx** program, where a single period on a line of its own ends the message.

System V Release 4 users can send binary files (such as programs) as mail messages with the *-m* option:

```
$ mail -m binaryfile erc
```

where **binaryfile** is the name of the binary file you wish to send. The resulting message will have a line in the header signifying that the file is binary.

What do I do with My Messages?

After you read a message, the shell presents you with a different prompt:

> ?

asking for a response related to the **mail** program. There are many actions that you can take at this point; the handiest options are listed in Table 8.1.

Table 8.1 *A Selection of Mail Commands*

Command	Result
RETURN	Prints next message.
-	Prints previous message.
d	Deletes current message.
dN	Deletes message number *N*.
dp	Deletes current message and goes to the next message.
dq	Deletes current message and quits.
u *N*	Undeletes message *N*.
s *filename*	Saves message to *filename*. If *filename* is not specified, message is saved to **$HOME/mbox**.
w *filename*	Saves message without header information to *filename*. If *filename* is not specified, message is saved to **$HOME/mbox**.
?	Lists mail commands.

Saving Messages

As we see in Table 8.1, saving a message is simply a matter of typing:

> ? s

If we don't specify a filename, the message is saved to **$HOME/mbox**. If you don't get many messages, it's no big deal to save them all to the same file. But if you get a lot of messages on a wide variety of topics, it's a good idea to introduce some organization to your mail habits.

Let's say you're working on a project with user *erc*, and you want to keep all of his mail messages in the same file. You do so with the *s* option at the **?** prompt:

```
? s erc
```

where *erc* is the name of the file containing his mail messages. When you do this the first time, the shell creates a file named **erc**. Subsequent uses will append mail messages to the existing **erc** file.

To read this file, use **mail** with the *-f* option:

```
$ mail -f erc
```

NOTE Don't assume your electronic-mail messages are private. Since mail messages normally appear in unencrypted text files, anyone with super user privileges, such as your system administrator, can read your mail. Even if you delete a message, the original text may have been backed up to tape. In fact, U.S. government investigators recovered deleted electronic-mail messages and used these messages against former White House officials Oliver North and John Poindexter when they were investigating the Iran-Contra scandal. (North and Poindexter used PROFS instead of UNIX mail, but the concept is the same.)

To bring the matter closer to home, few businesses have any policy at all regarding the privacy of electronic-mail communications. So, when in doubt, assume that your boss can read your mail.

Other Mail Packages

As you can tell, **mail** sports an exceedingly primitive interface. Over the years, a crop of new mail programs has appeared, some commercial software and some free, each of which has aimed at making life easier for the user. These programs include *Poste* and *Z-Mail* in the commercial realm and **mush, mh, xmh, xmail,** and **elm** among the free electronic-mail programs.

Xmh is an X Window front-end to **mh**, as shown in Figure 8.1.

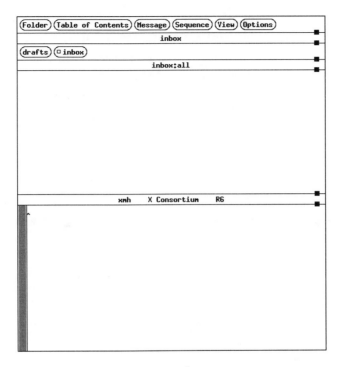

Figure 8.1 *Xmh in action.*

Pine is another popular electronic-mail program, shown in Figure 8.2.

```
PINE 3.89   MAIN MENU                              Folder: INBOX  2 Messages


        ?     HELP               - Get help using Pine

        C     COMPOSE MESSAGE    - Compose and send a message

        I     FOLDER INDEX       - View messages in current folder

        L     FOLDER LIST        - Select a folder to view

        A     ADDRESS BOOK       - Update address book

        S     SETUP              - Configure or update Pine

        Q     QUIT               - Exit the Pine program



   Copyright 1989-1993.  PINE is a trademark of the University of Washington.
                      [Folder "INBOX" opened with 2 messages]
  Help                         PrevCmd                        RelNotes
  OTHER CMDS  [ListFldrs]      NextCmd                        KBLock
```

Figure 8.2 *Pine in action.*

XMail is also an X Window mail program. Solaris OpenWindows systems come with **mailtool**, a graphical electronic-mail program.

The advantage of free software is the cost. The disadvantage is that you're responsible for maintaining the program yourself (or your system administrator is).

We've found the best electronic mail program is also free: **elm**. **Elm** stands for *el*ectronic *m*ail, and it works by providing an easy-to-use interface over the standard **mail** program.

The basic **elm** screen looks like Figure 8.3.

Figure 8.3 The elm mail program.

You can use the arrow keys on your keyboard to select a message. Pressing **Return** reads the message. **Elm** is so simple, fast, and easy that we think you'll soon be a convert. The online help, available by typing a question mark (**?**), should get you going in no time. (Like many users, we're often too busy to read the manual. In fact we've never read the **elm** manual—the program is that easy.)

There are many places to get free UNIX sources. You can buy tapes, disks, or CD-ROMs, and you can pick up the sources from a variety of places, such as the Internet, CompuServe, or other online services. See Appendix A for a listing of these sources.

Summary

Electronic mail forms a politically correct, environmentally sound, and very useful business communications tool.

The **mail** program is your standard, if primitive, means to access your electronic mail. To read your mail, just type **mail** at the shell prompt:

```
mail
```

You'll see a list of new messages.

To send mail, type **mail *username***, where ***username*** is the name of the recipient, at the shell prompt:

```
$ mail kevin
Subject: test
This, too, is a test.
```

As always, end input from the keyboard by typing **Ctrl-D**.

Extending Your Reach with Networking

This chapter covers:

- ▼ Anonymous **ftp**
- ▼ Working with the UUCP commands
- ▼ Using **uucp** to transfer files
- ▼ Downloading source code from a remote computer
- ▼ UNIX networking programs, including **rlogin** and **telnet**
- ▼ Distributed file systems
- ▼ Client/server computing

181

Reach Out and Touch Someone

The ability to link different computer systems has always been an important part of the UNIX operating system. UNIX systems have the ability to call other UNIX systems directly, and thousands of UNIX (as well as non-UNIX) systems have been linked together in loosely administered networks distributing files, news, and mail worldwide. In addition, most companies with UNIX workstations tightly connect their computers with high-speed network links, using popular networking protocols such as Ethernet or Token Ring.

You've already covered electronic mail, which is a key part of the UNIX interconnectivity. This chapter extends the discussion by explaining some of the tried-and-true UNIX tools for connectivity to remote systems, mostly centering around the UUCP commands. In the next chapter we'll cover the Usenet, the Internet, and the World Wide Web.

Informal Communications with the UUCP Commands

UNIX can use several different methods of transmitting information between systems. Originally, **UNIX**-to-**UNIX** **C**opy **P**rogram (**uucp**) was written to communicate between systems via ordinary telephone lines. The **uucp** program allows you to copy files from one system to another. Today, these connections can take place between those same telephone lines via modem (at all speeds, from 2400 bits per second to 19.2 kilobytes per second), direct wiring, a local-area network, or a wide-area network connected via dedicated phone lines. Although the connection mechanisms have changed, the basic UUCP system has not and remains mechanism-independent, which makes your life much simpler. As a user, you don't need to know the specifics of the connection mechanism; all you need to know is how to access the utilities that make communications possible.

 Dealing with **uucp** and the networking utilities on a configuration level is an advanced topic best left to system administrators and those with iron stomachs, suitable for dealing with the complex task of networking UNIX machines. Be sure and thank your system administrator for the ability to communicate with the outside world via the Usenet and Internet. If you don't have this ability, ask persistently.

There's no one, great *über*program that oversees UNIX connections to the outside world. Much like everything else in the UNIX world, the communications utilities are quite small and serve limited purposes by themselves; only when strung together do they actually make up a powerful communications system.

Why connect to the outside world? Some companies directly link far-flung offices via dedicated phone lines to ensure instantaneous communications between employees. Others connect via modem over phone lines to the UUCP Network, a series of UNIX computers that pass along electronic mail and files all around the world.

In a rather confusing situation, UUCP refers both to a specific command (**uucp**) and a series of related commands (most of which begin with *uu*). In this chapter **uucp** will refer to the specific **uucp** command, while UUCP will refer to the general command set.

To make things even more confusing, there's more than one implementation of the UUCP utilities on the market. In this chapter we'll be covering the HoneyDanBer UUCP, named for its three creators (Peter *Honey*man, *Dan A. Nowitz*, and *Brian E. Redman*). This is the most common UUCP implementation in the UNIX world, although it's sometimes referred to as the less prosaic Basic Networking Utilities, or BNU.

A UUCP Primer

At their core the UUCP commands allows machines to communicate directly via network links or telephone connections. They are limited in scope and are geared for the rudimentary purposes of sending along files, electronic mail, and (sometimes) Usenet news.

In this chapter we won't cover all of the UUCP commands; instead, we'll focus on the few you're likely to use. (If you want information about *all* of the UUCP commands, check Appendix A for a list of further reading material.) We'll also avoid configuration issues, which are best left to a system administrator.

Before you use **uucp**, you'll need to know which machines are connected to yours. The **uuname** command does just this:

```
$ uuname
geisha
spike
khan
kirk
picard
```

Why is this information important? Because you'll need to specify machine names with the **uucp** command.

Using UUCP

Basically, the **uucp** command is used to copy files from one machine to another. At first glance, in this age of Internet and the Information Superhighway, you may think that this is incredibly retro technology. And, conceptually, it is.

Realistically, however, the **uucp** command has its widest application in the corporate world, where interconnected computers are very common. In these situations the corporate systems may not be tied to the outside world, but only connected to other corporate systems. In these cases the **uucp** command is a handy way of transferring a file from your system to the corporate headquarters in Sioux City, Iowa.

The best way to understand the **uucp** command isn't to think of it as this strange and unfamiliar networking command—just think of it as an extended version of the common **cp** command, which you used earlier in this book. Instead of downloading and uploading files from a local directory, you're using **uucp** to download and upload files from another machine.

There's also one added advantage to the **uucp** command: All in all, it's a rather secure method of transferring files, when everything is set up correctly. (Ah, again, there's the issue of security popping up again.) The **uucp** command, as well as the UUCP utilities, can enact very specific guidelines on where files can be uploaded to or downloaded from.

Let's look at a typical **uucp** command line:

```
$ uucp chap9.txt spike!/usr/spool/uucppublic/chap9.txt
```

While this may seem to be an unusually long command line, a closer look will show that it's a rather simple one.

The **uucp** portion of the command line, obviously, refers to the **uucp** command. This is followed by the name of the file to be copied (**chap9.txt**).

The next portion is potentially the most confusing portion for novice users, as it represents the destination of the file by name of the machine and the directory. In this case, **spike** refers to the name of the machine; the **uucp** command knows this because the name of the machine ends with an exclamation mark (**!**). (If the exclamation mark looks familiar, it should; remember, the Usenet method of electronic-mail addressing with bang paths makes heavy use of exclamation marks.)

The exclamation mark is immediately followed by the destination directory. The **usr/spool/uucppublic** directory is a common destination for UUCP sites.

No, none of the machine names in this chapter are real. Don't use these specific examples on your own system.

N O T E

Put generically, the **uucp** command would look like:

```
$ uucp sourcefile destinationfile
```

Sharp readers will again note that the exclamation mark could prove problematic for users of the C shell; the shell will choke on an exclamation mark, as it represents a history command. To counter this, C shell users must structure their **uucp** commands differently. To tell the C shell that the exclamation mark is part of the **uucp** command, you'll need to precede it with a backslash (\):

N O T E

```
$ uucp chap9.txt spike\!/usr/spool/uucppublic/chap9.txt
```

The **uucp** command can also be used to grab files from another machine, as long as you have the proper permissions (another configuration issue that we'll duck). In this case you'll alter the **uucp** command line used earlier in this chapter. The principle is the same: Use the **uucp** command to list the source file and then its destination. In this case the remote file is the source file, and a local directory is the destination:

```
$ uucp spike!/usr/spool/uucppublic/chap9.txt\
/usr/spool/uucppublic
```

When using the **uucp** command to download a file, all you need to do is specify the destination directory; the command assumes that the filename will remain the same and that the destination directory exists on your local machine.

Potential Problems with the UUCP Command

As many frustrated users can attest, the **uucp** command, as well as the greater UUCP command set, is not foolproof.

Perhaps the greatest frustration is that the **uucp** command isn't interactive, and there's no way to monitor the status of a file transfer. You can tell **uucp** to send you a receipt via electronic mail when the file transfer is completed:

```
$ uucp -m chap9.txt spike!/usr/spool/uucppublic/chap9.txt
```

However, if you don't receive the confirming electronic mail, then you can assume that the transfer failed. Finding out why, however, isn't that easy. It is made somewhat easier, however, by the presence of a logfile that **uucp** maintains as part of the transfer process. To get at this file, use the **uulog** command:

```
$ uulog
```

This will provide a lot of output—probably too much for your troubleshooting purposes. It's probably better if you combine the **uulog** with the name of a machine:

```
$ uulog -sspike
```

Yes, *-sspike* is correct. In an oddity, the *-s* option to **uulog** must be *immediately* followed by the name of the machine (in this case, *spike*).

You'll then need to read through the arcane information and try to make some sense of it. Successful file transfers will end with *REMOTE REQUESTED* or *OK*.

What Can Go Wrong?

When a **uucp** connection fails, there can be many potential culprits. The **uulog** command can be handy to discover that a connection was denied by the remote system (something like *ACCESS DENIED* will appear in the logfile; unfortunately). In this case the login name or the password required by the remote machine may have been changed; in either case, this is a task for the system administrator to tackle.

If this isn't the case and *ACCESS DENIED* still appears in the logfile, it could be a simple case of a mistyped command line. If you type the wrong filename or directory, the connection will succeed, but the transfer will fail. Again, by a careful read of the logfile, you can determine this.

Your transfer may also be the victim of your own impatience. Not all **uucp** requests are instantaneous; many system administrators choose to queue requests and then make the transfers after hours, when long-distance rates are cheaper.

Free Software and Ftp

Depending on your version of UNIX, you may have a set of utilities that allows you to link directly to another computer using the network Transmission Control Protocol/Internet Protocol (TCP/IP) protocols. Both BSD and UNIX System V Release 4 feature these protocols, and some vendors have implemented these protocols while still supporting older versions of UNIX.

These protocols allow UNIX and non-UNIX computers to communicate efficiently, and they allow networks to be interconnected. You won't need to know how to install or configure these protocols on your own system.

The handiest use of TCP/IP is the **ftp** command, which allows you to grab files from remote machines, machines your computer is networked with. Because of UNIX's history in the public sphere, there's a lot of free software available for the taking. **Emacs**, for instance, is available from any number of machines that support downloads. Or you could acquire the entire Free Software Foundation (FSF) software collection, GNU, which includes GNU Emacs (Richard Stallman heads the FSF and wrote the original version of **emacs**), GCC (a widely used C compiler), GNU Chess (which has been ported to many different machines; we've even seen it compiled for use with PCs running Microsoft Windows!), and much more—in source-code form. Similarly, you could acquire the entire X Window System via anonymous ftp, though this is a major transfer of data.

 The ability to grab files via **ftp** is built into Internet web browsers, such as NCSA Mosaic. If you have a web browser, you can use that to grab files.

N O T E

In this section we'll guide you through an **ftp** session.

Using Ftp

The **ftp** command can be used to connect to any other computer on your network running **ftp**. If your system is connected to the Internet, you can use **ftp** to access files from other Internet computers worldwide. These machines you network with may or may not be running the UNIX operating system; this operating-system independence is what makes **ftp** so widely used.

   Ftp is interactive software, which means it asks you for information at specific times. Start it with the following:

```
$ ftp
ftp>
```

You'll be presented with the **ftp** prompt, where you enter special **ftp** commands. To get a list of available commands, type a question mark (**?**) or **help** at the prompt:

```
ftp> ?
```

or

```
ftp> help
```

The most common **ftp** commands are listed in Table 9.1.

Table 9.1 *Common ftp Commands*

Command	Result
ascii	Uses ASCII as the file-transfer type.
bell	Rings the bell when file transfer is complete.
binary	Uses binary as the file-transfer type.
bye or **quit**	Terminates **ftp** session.
cd	Changes directory on the remote machine.
close	Ends **ftp** connection to remote computer, but keeps local **ftp** program running.
delete *filename*	Deletes filename on remote computer.
get *filename*	Gets filename from the remote machine.
get *filename1 filename2*	Gets *filename1* from the remote machine and saves it locally as *filename2*.

help	Lists available commands.
mput *filename*	Copies the local *filename* to the remote machine.
pwd	Lists the current directory on the remote machine.

It's simple to download files from a remote machine with **ftp**. Let's say we want to grab some files from the machine named *mn.kevin.com*. (No, this isn't a real machine.) Assuming that this is a machine on the Internet that supports anonymous **ftp**—and our fictional machine does, of course—you would merely specify its name on the command line:

```
$ ftp mn.kevin.com
```

If the connection goes through, you'll receive a verification message, along with a login prompt. Since this is *anonymous* ftp, use *anonymous* as a login name:

```
Name: anonymous
```

You'll then be asked for a password. Most systems require you to supply your electronic-mail address, while others require *guest*. Use either. You'll then be presented with an **ftp** prompt.

The remote system has been set up to give you limited access. That means that your maneuverability is very limited, and the files you want will usually be close at hand. If you need to change to another directory, do so with the UNIX **cd** command.

Before embarking on the great file quest, you should know something about the files you're downloading. If they are straight C files in uncompressed, ASCII form, you can download them using the default file-transfer settings. Most larger files, especially binary files, are stored in compressed form so they take less time to transfer.

These compressed files end with **.Z**, **.z**, **.tgz**, or **gz**, so they are instantly recognizable. To download compressed files, you must change to binary mode, since you're downloading binary files. Do so with:

```
ftp> binary
```

Once you are placed in the correct directory containing the file to be downloaded, do so with the **get** command:

```
$ get filename
```

As you download the file, there will be no prompts on the system and you won't be able to enter any keystrokes.

After the file has been transferred successfully, you'll be told something like this:

```
Transfer complete
```

You may also be told the size of the file and/or the transfer time.

Since you're through with your file needs, close the connection with the **bye** command:

```
ftp> bye
```

What do I do with the File?

If you download an ASCII file, you can view it using any editor, including **vi** or **emacs**. If it's a source-code file, you can compile it for use on your own system; we explain the process in Chapter 14.

If you've downloaded a compressed binary file, you will have to uncompress it (and perhaps unarchive it) at the command line using **uncompress**, **unpack**, **tar**, or **gzip**. How do you know which one to use?

▼ If the file ends in *.Z*, use the **uncompress** command:

```
$ uncompress filename.Z
```

▼ If the file ends in *.z*, use the **unpack** command:

```
$ unpack filename.z
```

▼ If the file ends in *.gz* or *.tgz*, use the **gunzip** command:

```
$ gunzip filename.gz
```

▼ If the file still has a suffix of **tar** after using these commands, use the **tar** command to unarchive it:

```
$ tar xvf filename.tar
```

The **tar** command will be covered in depth in Chapter 16.

Generally speaking, these make up some good rules to follow. However, there are a few things to remember when working with compressed files.

For starters: The **gunzip** command, a companion to the **gzip** command, is not part of the standard UNIX set; it was created and maintained by the Free Software Foundation. Many free versions of UNIX, such as Linux, do include **gzip**. If your system doesn't feature **gzip**, go ahead and bug your system administrator, as it's freely available over the Internet and through books and CD-ROMs that feature UNIX freeware.

Why is **gunzip** so handy? Because it will uncompress any UNIX compressed file, even those compressed with the **compress** and **pack** commands. Conversely, **unpack** won't uncompress files compressed with the **compress** command, and the **uncompress** command won't unpack files compressed with the **unpack** command.

You don't necessarily need the **gunzip** command on your system to make use of **gzip**. The command line:

```
$ gzip -d file.gz
```

does the same thing as:

```
$ gunzip file.gz
```

Secondly, when you use the **uncompress**, **unpack**, or **gunzip** commands, the original compressed file will be replaced with an uncompressed file; *filename.gz* will be replaced by *filename*, for example. If you don't want to lose the original compressed file, make a copy of *filename.gz* in another directory for safekeeping.

Other Networking Commands

In addition to **ftp**, which is used to transfer—copy—files from system to system, there are a number of other common networking commands. These commands work to aid the connection between your computer and others on the same link.

Generally, if you work at a site with multiple UNIX computers, these computers will be networked together, usually using the TCP/IP network protocol. Your systems may also be networked with the worldwide Internet, a collection of connected networks. (Say *that* three times.)

Using the Rlogin Command

The **rlogin** command allows you to remotely login another computer on your network (remember that if you're on the Internet, you're on a worldwide network). You must, of course, have a valid user account on any machine you want to login. To use **rlogin**, you need the name of the machine to login. To login a machine named *nicollet*, you'd use a command like:

```
$ rlogin nicollet
Password:
```

At the *Password* prompt, you may need to enter in your password on machine *nicollet*, which may or may not be different than the password you use on your current machine. Once logged in, you're computing on the remote machine and can run any standard UNIX command. You also logout the same way you normally logout:

```
$ logout
Connection closed.
$
```

Note that after you logout from a remote machine, you're back to the command prompt at your original machine. This tends to get confusing, so be careful.

WARNING

The basic form of **rlogin** is:

```
$ rlogin hostname
```

where *hostname* is the name of the machine to login.

Using the Telnet Command

The **telnet** command works much the same as **rlogin**, allowing you to connect directly to a remote machine. Because the **telnet** command is considered part of the toolkit used by Internet surfer, it's actually gained in popularity over the years.

Telnet allows you to either run a command directly on a remote machine while displaying the results on your own, or to run a specific command on a remote machine (many sites that allow **telnet** put restrictions on what users can run, due to security concerns). With **telnet**, you only need to know the address of the machine you're connecting to, such as **sunsite.unc.edu**, as illustrated by the following:

```
$ telnet
telnet> open sunsite.unc.edu
Trying 198.86.40.81
Connected
************** Welcome to SunSITE.unc.edu **************
SunSITE offers several public services via login. These include:

NO MORE PUBLIC gopher login!
Use lynx the simple WWW client to access gopher and Web areas
For a simple WAIS client (over 500 databases),  login as swais
For WAIS search of political databases,       login as politics
For WAIS search of LINUX databases,           login as linux

For a FTP session, ftp to sunsite.unc.edu. Then login as anonymous

For more information about SunSITE, send mail to
info@sunsite.unc.edu

UNIX (R) System V Release 4.0 (calypso-2.oit.unc.edu)

login: swais
```

Sunsite.unc.edu offers a variety of services to the general computing public, in this case centering around WAIS databases. Other **telnet** sites may not offer such a wide variety of services; a site like **archie.rutgers.edu** offers only **archie** searches.

Archie and WAIS will be covered in Chapter 10.

N O T E

Sunsite.unc.edu is a public Internet site. If you're using **telnet** within your corporation, the rules will be slightly different. Here, **sunsite.unc.edu** offers public access; you don't need an account on **sunsite.unc.edu**, nor do you need a password. However, **sunsite.unc.edu** does put restrictions on what can be done by a visitor; for example, you can't use the standard UNIX command set, and your options are limited to the login selections. For a private system, you'll need an account on the remote system before you can login, and you may be subject to the same sorts of restrictions. Remember: security.

RFS and NFS

When using **ftp** or **rlogin**, you're logging on a remote machine after supplying the name of the remote system. The UNIX operating system features several tools that allow UNIX machines to be linked in such a way that remote machines don't appear to be remote at all.

The end result is called a *distributed file system*, and it allows all machines on a network to act as though they were really one physically large computer residing in the same location, even though they may be located miles away. For the user, the resources on a remote machine appears to be as local as the next room; no conscious effort is required on the part of the user to access a remote machine.

UNIX accomplishes this linkage through three tools: Remote File Sharing (RFS), originally developed by AT&T; Network File System (NFS), developed by Sun Microsystems; and Distributed File System (DFS), a combination of RFS and NFS implemented in UNIX System V Release 4. RFS was developed for use only with the UNIX operating system. NFS was designed for use with networks and machines running operating systems other than UNIX.

Installing and administering a distributed file system is the work of a system administrator—or, more accurately, usually several system administrators. And since the point of a distributed file system is to make the entire setup entirely transparent to the end user, there's very little in the way of commands for us to describe. However, because of the popularity of distributed file systems in the UNIX world, it's important for you to know some of the concepts behind DFS or any other tool used on your particular system. This will, of course, require a little abstraction on your part, but you should be used to that by now.

Clients and Servers

When we discuss distributed networking of almost any kind (except the X Window System), we discuss *clients* and *servers* to differentiate between the different machines on a network. The computer that supplies files and services to other computers is called the server, while the computer that accesses the files and services is called the client. Because a UNIX machine is multitasking and can perform more than one task at a time (a concept we discussed), it can be simultaneously a client and a server.

After a server advertises its file system for use by clients, the client then *mounts* the file system for its own use. For instance, Machine A may want to access files from Machine B regarding company finances, located in B's **/usr/data/finances** directory. A directory on Machine A must be specified for mounting the files; this is called the mountpoint. The files from **/usr/data/finances** will appear on Machine A just as if they were physically located on Machine A's hard-disk system.

The concept of distributed file systems fits nicely into UNIX's philosophy of modularity and expandability not requiring major change. Economics played an important role in the development of RFS. Additional storage space could be added to a UNIX system without having to install new, expensive computers; when hardware was priced much more than it is today, this was a prime concern to data-processing departments on limited budgets. Similarly, expensive peripherals like modems and printers could be shared across different systems—at least under RFS.

We're not going to cover the mounting and unmounting of distributed resources, as this is a task reserved for system administrators with superuser status. However, we will tell you how to determine exactly what resources are being shared in your system. Use the **share** command:

```
$ share
```

Summary

The UNIX operating system features a series of commands that allow you to connect directly to other UNIX systems. The most popular commands are related to UUCP, the UNIX-to-UNIX copy program. The most common of the UUCP commands is (confusingly enough) **uucp**.

The **ftp** command allows you to transfer files between networked systems; the **rlogin** and telnet commands allow you to login another system on the same network.

The UNIX operating system contains the tools necessary to link other computer systems in a way that's completely transparent to the end user. Files on one machine appear as files residing on a local machine using tools like RFS, NFS, and DFS. The end user doesn't need to know how this sharing is implemented to benefit from it.

The Usenet, the Internet, and the World Wide Web

This chapter covers:

- ▼ The Usenet
- ▼ Newsgroups
- ▼ Drawbacks to Usenet newsgroups
- ▼ Using a newsreader
- ▼ Burrowing with **gopher**
- ▼ Using **archie** to track down software
- ▼ Accessing an **archie** server via **telnet**
- ▼ An **archie** query via e-mail
- ▼ The World Wide Web
- ▼ Web browsers like Netscape and Mosaic
- ▼ URL formats

Surfing the Net

In the previous two chapters, we've covered the more mundane aspects of communicating with the outside world. In this chapter, we cover the glamorous and trendy Internet.

We saved this coverage for a separate chapter because full connectivity to the Internet is not the norm in the UNIX world. Although most UNIX systems do feature some level of connectivity to the outside world (leading to the ubiquity of electronic mail), full access to the Internet—as defined by the ability to access the World Wide Web—is available to only a minority of UNIX users. This is changing rapidly, as UNIX system administrators find that full access to the Internet can be helpful for them, as well as for employees.

As always, to see what level of Internet access your UNIX system has, check with your system administrator.

The Usenet and Newsgroups

The Internet's roots can be traced to the Usenet, a worldwide messaging system. The Usenet, while technically comprising a portion of the Internet, is know best for electronic-mail (remember the Usenet style of addressing discussed in Chapter 8?) and newsgroup distribution.

UNIX "insiders" brag of being on the *net,* but what actually constitutes the *net*—Internet or Usenet—depends on the user and their system. Though the two are linked, there are crucial differences, and more likely than not the braggart is on the Usenet, since anyone (essentially) can get on the Usenet.

Thousands of computers are linked—worldwide—in a loose network called the Usenet. The Usenet is a public network of linked UNIX and non-UNIX machines, dedicated to sending information to companies, schools, universities, the government, research laboratories, and individuals.

The Usenet performs a variety of services, but perhaps the most popular service involves *newsgroups.* A newsgroup is a discussion of various topics, ranging from computing to sociology to boomerangs to Barney the Dinosaur. In fact, there are thousands of Usenet newsgroups. Some are trivial and a waste of bandwidth, while others are of interest to only a small set of users. (Take a gander at *alt.sex.bestiality.barney,* and you'll see the validity of this point.)

These newsgroups are divided into classes, to better allow users to figure out what to read in the plethora of information arriving daily. Table 10.1 covers the major newsgroup classifications.

Table 10.1 *The major Usenet newsgroups.*

Name	Subject
alt	alternative hierarchy, not subject to other rules
biz	business-related groups
comp	computing
misc	miscellaneous subjects
news	news about the Usenet
rec	recreational activities
sci	science
soc	social issues
talk	talk

Not only is this computer-dweeb heaven, but the Usenet provides valuable information on everything from vegetarian recipes to buying a house to technical difficulties programming Macintosh computers. There are Usenet newsgroups for just about every topic you can imagine—and then some, from *rec.sport.football.college* to *soc.culture.bulgaria.* (*Alt.buddha.short.fat.guy* was definitely a surprise the first time we saw it.) In addition, there are regional newsgroups; those of us in Minnesota have access to a wide range of newsgroups that begin with *mn*, such as *mn.forsale.*

While the Usenet can be a powerful information source, you'll also find a lot of misinformed, inaccurate, biased, and generally dumb opinions, as nearly anyone can get on the Usenet. So take what you read with a grain of salt. Generally, the more technical the group, the better the information you'll get. The group *comp.compilers* (information on writing compilers for computer languages) certainly contains more unbiased information than *comp.sys.next.advocacy* (advocates—an unbiased group if there ever was one—of Next workstations).

However, there are many Usenet newsgroups that you'll find useful. Being technical types ourselves, we regularly peruse the newsgroups relating to UNIX, the X Window System, and related topics (electronic-mail packages like **elm** and **pine**, software like **emacs**).

These classifications are broken down into specific newsgroups. The syntax of a newsgroup name is simple: the name of the classification followed by a descriptive suffix. For instance, the name of the newsgroup devoted to questions concerning the UNIX operating system is *comp.unix.questions*. Note the use of periods to separate the elements. A listing of some popular newsgroups is listed in Table 10.2.

Table 10.2 *A sampling of frequently accessed Usenet newsgroups.*

Newsgroup	Topic
comp.databases	Database-management issues
comp.lang.c	C-language issues
comp.source.unix	UNIX source code
comp.text	Text-processing issues
comp.unix.questions	Questions about the UNIX operating system
misc.jobs.offered	Job openings
rec.music.gaffa	The music of Kate Bush
sci.space.shuttle	Issues associated with the NASA space shuttle

Appendix A lists some UNIX-specific newsgroups that you should check out.

NOTE

Newsgroups can also be open or moderated. Open newsgroups allow anyone to post to them, while moderated newsgroups have someone to review the postings before they're passed out to the general public. As you might surmise, moderated newsgroups are more reliable and useful.

The Usenet newsgroups are aggressively egalitarian. News can be posted by just about anyone.

WARNING

Using it as a source of information requires some skepticism on your part. On the one hand, it's a great place to find very technical, specialized information; the more technical and specialized the better. Many leading figures in the computing industry regularly post information in the newsgroups. And since there's nothing new under the sun, chances are that the problem that plagues you has already been solved by someone else in the UNIX world.

On the other hand, every opinion is not created equally, and a lot of ill-founded opinions can be found in most newsgroups. Veterans refer to the *signal-to-noise* ratio; newsgroups with a lot of ill-founded opinions and bickering are said to be filled with noise. As with any other source of information, treat what you see on the Usenet newsgroups with a healthy dose of skepticism.

Reading and Writing the News

Although all the news items are text files and in theory could be read with **vi** or **emacs**, there are so many of them in so many separate files that it's not really feasible to read each file. A full Usenet *newsfeed*, that is, all of the incoming message files from all the worldwide newsgroups, adds more than 40 megabytes of files to your disk each day. (Remember when we said earlier that UNIX files seem to propagate proportionally? Here's an example.) That's how a type of software, called *newsreaders*, evolved. These news readers help you sort out, with varying degrees of usefulness, what to read from the hundreds of new files that appear daily. The basic idea is to read those messages you're interested in and skip the rest. There's simply no way to read every incoming message, even if you spent all day in front of your computer.

We are not going to cover any of the many news readers in depth; each system, it seems, features its own news reader. We find that the most popular programs are:

- ▼ **readnews**, an older, line-oriented program with limited power
- ▼ **vnews**, a vi-like reader that displays newsgroups one item at a time
- ▼ **rn**, a reader with expanded search capabilities
- ▼ **xrn**, an X Window graphical version of **rn**
- ▼ **tin**, a threaded reader that arranges messages by topic (as shown in Figure 10.1)

```
                          Group Selection (853)                      h=help
  u    1   -  Logic
  u    2   -  alt
  u    3   -  alt.activism                       Activities for activi
  u    4   -  alt.answers                        Repository for period
  u    5   -  alt.astrology                      Twinkle, twinkle, lit
  u    6   -  alt.atheism                        Discussions of atheis
  u    7   -  alt.atheism.moderated              Atheism and related t
  u    8   -  alt.bbs                            Computer BBS systems
  u    9   -  alt.bbs.internet                   BBS systems accessibl
  u   10   -  alt.bbs.lists                      Postings of regional
  u   11   -  alt.bbs.unixbbs                    Discussion of the BBS
  u   12   -  alt.binaries
  u   13   -  alt.binaries.pictures
  u   14   -  alt.binaries.pictures.d            Discussion of posting
  u   15   -  alt.binaries.pictures.erotica      For the posting of AL
  u   16   -  alt.binaries.pictures.erotica.d    Discussion about erot

       <n>=set current to n, TAB=next unread, /=search pattern, c)atchup,
     g)oto, j=line down, k=line up, h)elp, m)ove, q)uit, r=toggle all/unread,
      s)ubscribe, S)ub pattern, u)nsubscribe, U)nsub pattern, y)ank in/out
```

Figure 10.1 *The tin newsreader.*

Responding to the news is either a function of your reader or a separate program called **postnews**. Using it is quite simple:

```
$ postnews
```

After this, you're prompted with a set of questions regarding the posting you want to respond to. You don't need to respond to a specific post, but you need to respond in a specific newsgroup.

N O T E

Not all versions of UNIX support the **postnews** command. Many use **pnews** or **nnpost**.

There's a whole set of etiquette rules for posting to Usenet newsgroups. The basic ideas are simple: be polite, don't fly off the handle, and don't post unless you have something important to add to the discussion. Also, read through all of the articles before responding. Someone else probably has already said what you are about to say.

Getting on the Usenet

Gaining access to the Usenet can be a simple process, provided you can find someone near you already on the Usenet.

There's no centralized, administrative center of the Usenet. (Indeed, that's one of its greatest strengths—as well as its major weakness.) The easiest way is to convince a local Usenet user to supply you with a feed. If you're not sure about local Usenet users, attend a meeting of your local UNIX user group or contact anyone locally who advertises UNIX-related services or supplies. In some areas the UNIX user group actually oversees local access to the Usenet, so be nice to the group members. This access should be free or close to it.

If you can't find a local feed, contact UUNET, a nonprofit firm formed by USENIX to supply low-cost access to the Usenet. Call 800/4-UUNET-4, or write 3110 Fairview Park Dr., Suite 570, Falls Church, VA 22042. Lacking that, there are several commercial firms that provide Usenet (as well as full Internet feeds), such as Netcom.

How Do I Find a File for Download?

If you're on the Usenet, you'll be surrounded by information regarding free software and how to get it. The trick is knowing where to look for it.

Some universities and corporations maintain archive sites that support anonymous FTP. These locations are referred to regularly in the newsgroup *comp.sources.*

In addition, many computer-related newsgroups will contain news items labeled FAQ, or Frequently Asked Questions. One of the frequently asked questions will (undoubtedly) concern the existence of archival sites.

And, finally, you can post a plaintive plea in a newsgroup, asking for information about a particular program. You may receive some rude comments from people who tire of answering questions from innocent beginners, but undoubtedly some kind soul will answer your request with useful information.

Gophers: Information Organizers

Another method of organizing the offerings of the Internet is through **gopher** server. Named after the mascot at the University of Minnesota (rah! rah! ski-u-mah!), where it was developed, **gopher** organizes files by menus. You can use **gopher** to retrieve files from an FTP site, for instance; the filename may be listed in a **gopher** menu, but to you it's all one big organized filesystem.

The beauty of **gopher** is that it works both in a text-based environment and in a graphical environment. In a text-based environment, the menus within a

gopher server can be selected by using the scroll keys or typing in the number of the menu. Within the graphical (i.e., X Window) environment, the menu selections can be double-clicked with a mouse.

 Gopher is rarely included in a commercial UNIX distribution. Talk with your system administrator if it's not included in your system.

NOTE

Every version of **gopher** works basically the same: You begin it by entering **gopher** on the command line:

```
$ gopher
```

or

```
$ xgopher
```

If your system is configured properly, you'll be connected to a home **gopher** server on the Internet. (This is a confusing point: The software you use locally is called **gopher**, and the servers on the Internet are also called **gophers**.) You'll see a menu like the following:

```
1. Minnesota Regional Network Gopher Hotel
2. Minnesota Regional Network
3. Object Database Management Group (gopher.odmg.org, 2073)
4. Minnesota Datametrics Corporation (gopher.mndata.com, 2074)
5. Jostens Incorporated (gopher.jostens.com, 2071)
```

 Our gopher is configured to connect to the Minnesota Regional Network **gopher**. Yours probably does not, but you'll see something similar to our preceding menu. In addition, we're treating this **gopher** session as a text-based session; if you're using an X Window version of **gopher**, you won't see the numerals on your screen; instead, you will see little file folders next to submenus and page icons next to documents.

NOTE

This menu doesn't do a whole lot for us. The next set of menus, found after we select *Minnesota Regional Network*, does:

```
1. About this Gopher and MRNet
2. MRNet User Forum
```

```
 3. Minnesota Internet Access Providers
 4. Search GopherSpace with Veronica
 5. MRNet Anonymous FTP Archives
 6. Gopher Jewels
 7. Information by Subject
 8. Other Gopher Servers
 9. Internet Dog-Eared Pages (Frequently used resources)
10. Libraries
11. IETF - RFC/FYI/STD/Drafts
12. NSFNET Info
13. NREN/NII
14. Multi User Dimension (MUD) Servers
15. Popular FTP Sites via Gopher
16. Search FTP Sites using Archie
17. Weather Forecasts
18. dialIP clients & additional Mac/DOS/Windows net software
```

The nice thing about a **gopher** server (as well as the World Wide Web, as you'll see later in this chapter) is that it can contain references to other **gopher** servers across the 'Net. For example, menu choice 9 doesn't refer to data actually stored on the Minnesota Regional Network **gopher** server. Instead, it serves as a pointer to the machine named **calypso.oit.unc.edu**. Selecting menu choice 9 facilitates a direct connection to **calypso.oit.unc.edu**, with the following information:

```
Reference Texts is the result of rambling about gopher-space
and creating links to anything that looks informative or even
just remotely useful.  We have various books on line here, as
well as WAIS indices, poetry, phone books, and of course,
standard references like dictionaries and thesari.
```

Organizing the Internet with Various Tools

As you've probably deduced from reading this chapter and the two preceding chapters, there's a cluttering of offerings on the Internet. Of course, there needs to be a way to cut through the clutter, or the Internet will collapse from its own weight.

The bright people on the Internet realize this, so there have been a series of efforts to organize the vast offerings of the Internet, centering around files stored on FTP sites.

Using Archie to Track Down Software

The best-known of these efforts is **archie**, from McGill University in Toronto, Canada. **Archie** is used to search through databases of file listings.

Archie is a flexible tool. You can connect directly to an **archie** server via **telnet**, do an **archie** search via electronic mail, or run an **archie** client on your desktop, which then connects to the **archie** server. There are **archie** servers for almost every operating system and UNIX variant.

What would you use **archie** for? Let's use an example relating to the remainder of this chapter. Later in this chapter, you'll learn about web browsers and the World Wide Web. Most UNIX systems don't come with web browsers. Therefore, it's up to you (or your system administrator) to get one—and the best place to look for it is on the Internet, via **archie**.

For this search, we'll look for **netscape**, a popular web-browser from Netscape Communications, and we'll assume that you're working with a local **archie** client. (The following two sections will cover **archie** searches via alternative means.) As mentioned earlier, **archie** can be used to search through databases. These searches can be either for exact matches or strings of text within larger listings. Since we're looking for unfamiliar software (indeed, if we knew the filename, we wouldn't really need to use **archie**, would we?), we'll just tell **archie** to look for the string *netscape*. We get back a rather long list of **ftp** sites that contain **netscape**, including the directory, the size of the file, and when the file was last changed. Armed with this information, we can connect to the **ftp** site and grab the **netscape** file.

Using Archie Via Telnet

In Chapter 9 you learned about the **telnet** command, used to connect to another computer system. The same mechanism can be used to connect to an **archie** server.

Using the command line, you'd begin a **telnet** session, specifying an archie server:

```
$ telnet archie.internix.net
```

You'd then be presented with some information about the **archie** server, followed by an **archie** prompt:

```
archie>
```

Generally speaking, this is the most inefficient way to use **archie**. Connections to **archie** servers are already overworked, and a **telnet** session exacerbates the problem.

Using Archie via Electronic Mail

Generally speaking, connecting to an **archie** server via electronic mail is the friendliest way to perform an **archie** search. Best of all, you don't need a full connection to the Internet to do it—you need only an electronic-mail connection.

You begin your e-mail message in a normal fashion, addressing it to a public **archie** server:

```
$ mail archie@archie.unl.edu
Subject: Archie Search
prog netscape
```

ending the mail message by pressing **Ctrl-D**. It should be a matter of hours before your answer arrives via e-mail.

The World Wide Web

Much of the buzz surrounding the Internet can be traced to the World Wide Web and the tools for accessing it—Mosaic, Netscape, and their ilk.

And, quite honestly, the hype is (for the most part) justified. At its best, the World Wide Web is an incredibly efficient and exciting way of distributing information. The potential of the Web has been barely scratched, and when all is said and done the Web (or, more likely, its descendants) will profoundly alter publishing as we know it.

Page Limits

Such grandiose statements, of course, are a dime a dozen in the computer world (and, to be honest, we usually scoff at such statements ourselves). But the World Wide Web is a case where the hype is warranted—both because of the makeup of the Web itself and the economics of using the Web.

It's best to look at the World Wide Web not as a computer service, but rather as a publishing medium.

At its core, the World Wide Web is actually an ingeniously simple beast. A web browser, such as Mosaic or Netscape, sends a request over the network to a web server; the request can be one of five formats (as listed in Table 10.3). The server then honors the request by sending a text file formatted in the HyperText Markup Language (HTML), which inserts "tags" in the text. The text file is then rendered by the local web browser, which matches the tags to resources on the local machine—for instance, a tag for TITLE would be rendered in a font and point size set up through the web browser.

The HTML language also allows graphics and hypertext links to be embedded in the document. Most graphics files are in the GIF and XBM file formats. The hyperlinks are noted with their own tag and are usually set off in a different color within the rendered document. For instance, under a heading titled *Other Resources*, there may be a line colored blue that says *Sun Microsystems Home Page*. To the web browser, however, there's an embedded web address (in this case, *www.sun.com*). Double-clicking on *Sun Microsystems Home Page.* initiates a request to the web server *www.sun.com.* You don't need to know the *www.sun.com* address; you only need to know how to use a mouse.

Accessing the Web

To access the World Wide Web, you'll need a *web browser.* The most famous web browser is **mosaic**, originally from the National Center for Supercomputer Applications (NCSA) at the University of Illinois.

That isn't to say that **mosaic** isn't the best web browser on the market. There are a host of competitors in the UNIX/X Window world, including:

▼ GWHIS (a commercial Mosaic implementation from Quadralay)

▼ Enhanced Mosaic (a commercial version of mosaic from a variety of resellers)

▼ Lynx (a freeware text-only browser)

▼ tkWWW (a freeware web browser written in Tcl/Tk)

▼ Viola (a freeware browser)

▼ Netscape Navigator (a browser in both commercial and freely available versions from Netscape Communications, as shown in Figure 10.2.)

 By and large, the World Wide Web is a graphical beast; most of these web browsers (the big exception is Lynx) run under the X Window System and, in most cases, OSF/Motif.

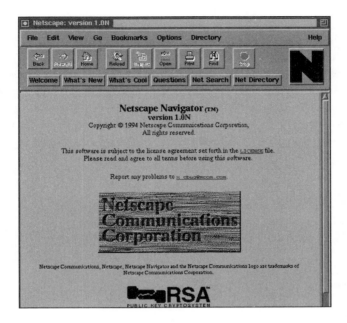

Figure 10.2 *Netscape Navigator.*

In this chapter we'll use Netscape in our examples.

To use a web browser like Netscape, your UNIX network must be properly configured to connect directly to the Internet. If you're a single user, you'll need to connect to the Internet via a dial-up account or a high-speed TCP/IP connection.

You can start Netscape with the following command in an **xterm** window:

```
$ netscape
```

When Netscape launches, it connects directly to a Netscape Communications home page (*www.mcom.com*).

By the way, this is a good way to test if Netscape is configured properly; if you or your system administrator has misinstalled Netscape, it will report that a connection to *www.mcom.com* has failed.

Chances are pretty good that you won't want to spend much time wandering around the Netscape home page. The beauty of the World Wide Web is that it allows you to jump from web site to web site, either those linked to your current page or a page totally unrelated.

A page on the World Wide Web is formatted in the HyperText Markup Language (HTML). If you were to view the document in text mode, which is possible with many web browsers, including Netscape, you'd see that the text seen in Figure 10.3 is scattered with "tags," like <H2>. There's no mentions of point sizes, colors, or the like. The beginning of the file shown in the Netscape illustration in Figure 10.3 looks like this:

```
<TITLE>Netscape Handbook: Graphical Elements</TITLE>

<A NAME="RTFToC0">
<B>
<FONT SIZE=+3>G</FONT><FONT SIZE=+2>raphical elements</FONT>
</B></A>

<ol>
<A HREF="../online-manual.html">Netscape Handbook: Table of
Contents</A>
<li><a href="graphics.html#RTFToC1">Netscape window</a>
<li><a href="graphics.html#RTFToC2">Point and click navigation</a>
<li><a href="graphics.html#RTFToC4">Content area and text fields</a>
<li><a href="graphics.html#RTFToC9">Security information</a>
<li><a href="graphics.html#RTFToC5">Window controls</a>
<li><a href="graphics.html#RTFToC3">Toolbar buttons</a>
<li><a href="graphics.html#RTFToC6">Directory buttons</a>
<li><a href="graphics.html#RTFToC7">Newsgroup list buttons</a>
<li><a href="graphics.html#RTFToC8">Newsgroup article buttons</a>
</ol>

<HR ALIGN="right"WIDTH=85%>
<A NAME="RTFToC1">
<FONT SIZE=+3>N</FONT><FONT SIZE=+1>etscape window</FONT>
</A>
<P>

This section on graphical elements describes what you see in the
Netscape window. Most of the tools and text fields that help you to
navigate the Internet are visible, though you have the option of
hiding some tools in order to give more space on the screen to the
content area.
<p>
On the page describing point and click navigation, you'll find a
description of each type of graphical element: colors/underlining,
```

status indicator, progress bar, toolbar buttons, content/text fields,
window controls, and menus. Subsequent pages go into more detail on
how toolbar buttons, text/content fields, and window controls work.
An entire section of pages is devoted to menu items, including those
that let you set important options and preferences effecting the
look, performance, and functionality of the Netscape window.
<p>
You can open multiple Netscape windows to view multiple pages of
information. The title bar of the window shows the title of currently
loaded page.

```
<P>
<HR ALIGN="right"WIDTH=85%>
<A NAME="RTFToC2">
<FONT SIZE=+3>P</FONT><FONT SIZE=+1>oint and click navigation</FONT>
</A>
<P>
```

The rendered page is shown in Figure 10.3.

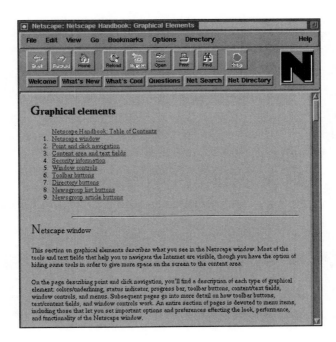

Figure 10.3 *Netscape with a rendered page.*

This is because the work of rendering the home page is done at the local level, matching local resources to the specifications of the web page. You'll notice that there are a few different point sizes and typefaces on the home page. The web document makes a reference to <TITLE>; the web page then matches a local font and point size to the text.

A graphic is also rendered locally. When the document downloads, the graphic is sent separately, in the GIF format, which makes for quicker file transfers. (Even so, some GIF documents can be *very* large and take a long time to download, even at a high-speed network link.)

URL Formats

You tell a web browser where to look by entering a Uniform Resource Locator, or URL. The WWW community has standardized on a number of URL formats, as listed in Table 10.3.

Table 10.3 *URL formats and their meanings, from the WWW FAQ.*

Format	Represents
file://wuarchive.wustl.edu/mirrors/ msdos/graphics/gifkit.zip	File at an FTP site.
ftp://wuarchive.wustl.edu/mirrors	FTP site.
http://info.cern.ch:80/default.html	WWW site.
news:alt.hypertext	Usenet newsgroup.
telnet://dra.com	**Telnet** connection to Internet-connected server.

This means that you can connect to many Internet resources via a web browser. Most web browsers have a menu selection or dialog box that allows you to enter a URL; the Netscape mechanism is shown in Figure 10.4.

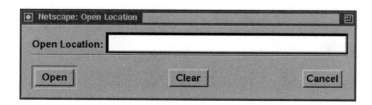

Figure 10.4 *The Netscape URL dialog box.*

Summary

The discussion of UNIX networking and communications ends with this discussion of the Usenet, the Internet, and the World Wide Web.

Each of the three tools can be useful in its own way: The Usenet for reading newsgroups, the Internet for grabbing files and useful information, and the World Wide Web for staying connected in this time of interconnectivity.

To use the resources listed in this chapter, you'll need to expand your list of UNIX tools past a newsreader (which is now generally part of a UNIX distribution) to include programs like **archie**, **gopher**, and a web browser like **netscape**, which generally are not included in most commercial UNIX distributions.

Working with UNIX Tools

Now that you've been exposed to what UNIX can do, it's time for you to put that knowledge into action.

Chapter 11 covers text editing in UNIX, which means the creation of ASCII text files with tools like **vi** and **emacs**. You can use this text for internal usage—such as programming or shell-script files—or you can send the files to text processors like **troff** for further processing. In Chapter 13 we cover shell programming basics, including changing shells and executing scripts. Chapter 14 introduces basic C programming tools; in no time at all you'll be a fully functional C programmer, whether you want to be or not. Chapter 15 covers assorted administrative topics, including system backup, setup procedures, and dealing with emergencies. Chapter 16 covers advanced and additional UNIX tools like **awk** and **perl**.

Text Editing

This chapter covers:

- ▼ An introduction to **vi**, complete with tutorial
- ▼ **Vi** command-line options
- ▼ **Vi**'s two modes: insert and edit
- ▼ Deleting and changing characters in **vi**
- ▼ Moving around the screen with cursors in **vi**
- ▼ Saving a file in **vi**
- ▼ File management in **vi**
- ▼ Cutting and pasting text in **vi**
- ▼ An introduction to **emacs**, complete with tutorial
- ▼ Accessing **emacs** commands
- ▼ **Emacs**'s help system
- ▼ Cursor commands in **emacs**
- ▼ Deleting and changing characters in **emacs**
- ▼ Searching and replacing text in **emacs**
- ▼ Saving a file in **emacs**
- ▼ Copying and moving text in **emacs**

217

From Thought to Document

Creating and editing text are probably the most common tasks you'll use in your day-to-day work. When you think about it, most of your computing needs are filled by *text editors*. Letters and memos are written with an editor. Reports are created via the editor. Lists acting as informal databases are created with an editor.

UNIX features several editors: **vi**, **ed**, and **emacs** are the most common. Their features overlap (indeed, **vi** is actually an extended version of **ed**), and the editor you decide to use regularly (and you *will* need to use one regularly) will be as much a matter of taste and availability as features and flashiness. Not every editor is available on every system: for example, **vi** is the only editor available on SCO UNIX, and **emacs**, while available for free from a variety of sources, is generally not part of a standard UNIX system. This chapter will cover the **vi** and **emacs** editors in tutorial format, guiding you through the creation and editing of a document.

There are many advanced features to **vi** and **emacs** that we won't even hint at. Our philosophy is to present you with enough information to get you going; the rest is up to you, through perusing the online manual pages or consulting other advanced books (which we'll list in Appendix A.) We'd suggest you sit down at your UNIX machine and follow along with each tutorial.

Why Ignore Ed?

Ed has been around for a long time—almost as long as UNIX. Unlike UNIX, **ed** has remained pretty much the same throughout the years. It's highly unlikely that most of you will use **ed** at all, much less as your regular text processor. **Ed** is a throwback to the days when UNIX processing was done one line at a time. (Remember: UNIX old-timers walked five miles to school in the dead of winter and processed text one line at a time.)

Quite honestly, **ed** is so retro that it's of little use when more accessible and powerful editors like **vi** and **emacs** are available. Other UNIX texts cover **ed** in detail, arguing that an introduction to **ed**'s features will serve as a suitable introduction to other UNIX functions. We differ. Most of **ed**'s useful features are incorporated in **vi**, which was designed as a full-screen successor to **ed**. Because it's so unlikely that any of you will use **ed**, we'll skip over it and move to more useful text editors.

Using Vi

Vi stands for *vi*sual editor and was considered a great leap forward when it was first introduced. (Indeed, when compared to **ed**, it *was* a great leap forward.) Virtually every UNIX system ships with **vi**, making it one of the most ubiquitous pieces of software in the UNIX world. **Vi** is used to create and edit ASCII files, which can be used in a variety of situations—creating shell scripts and mail messages, or editing UNIX system files, like the **.profile** and **.login** files.

NOTE What's an ASCII file? As you've learned from this book, what UNIX uses internally and what you'll use are often two different things. ASCII is such a thing. Since most computers actually deal with numbers on some level, ASCII is a successful attempt in the computer community to establish common ground among differing computer systems that may treat numbers different internally. When you create a file in ASCII, you're creating a file that can be shared among different computer systems. There are ASCII characters representing the entire alphabet, punctuation marks, and numerals; when you type the letter *a* in a text editor, you're actually entering an ASCII character that can be read by any computer.

If you're used to word processors in the DOS or Macintosh worlds, there are aspects to **vi** that you'll find annoying and primitive, but there are other aspects that you'll find reassuring and familiar. Like most word processors, **vi** is a full-screen editor; instead of having to edit a file one line at a time (as **ed** does), **vi** allows you to load a file and view it one screen at a time. (This capability was quite advanced for its day, so don't snicker.) **Vi** does not support any document formatting (like bold or italic), spell checking, or any views of a document as it will look when printed. On the plus side, **vi** is extremely fast when scrolling through large documents, and some of the features it lacks can be found in other standard UNIX utilities (such as the aforementioned spell checking).

Let's begin by calling **vi**. There are two ways to start **vi**—without a file loaded:

```
$ vi
```

or with a file loaded:

```
$ vi filename
```

where *filename* is the name of the file to be created or edited. If you start **vi** without a file, you'll be presented with a mostly blank screen, with a cursor in the upper-left corner and a series of tilde (~), or null, characters running down the left side of the screen. The null characters tell us that there is nothing on the page (kind of paradoxical, isn't it?), because not all typed characters are represented by an onscreen symbol—spaces and carriage returns (generated by the **Enter** or **Return** key) are invisible. As you fill a page with typing, the null characters disappear. The **vi** text editor is shown in Figure 11.1.

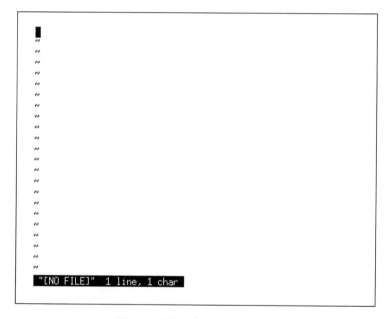

Figure 11.1 *The vi text editor.*

In our case, we'll want to start **vi** without a file loaded, so we can experience the joy of entering and editing text. Go ahead and start **vi** without a file.

(After you're more used to working with **vi**, you may need one of **vi**'s command-line options. To use one, type:

```
$ vi -option filename
```

where *-option* is the letter representing the option and *filename* refers to the file to be created or edited. Other options are listed in Table 11.1.)

Table 11.1 *Some vi command-line options*

Option	Result
-L	Starts **vi** and recovers a file lost during a system crash. Can be used in conjunction with the *-r* option, described below. (Make sure you type an uppercase *L* and not a lowercase *l* [ell]. Using *-l* would tell **vi** that it's editing a Lisp file, which would change the appearance of your ASCII text.)
-r	Recovers an open file after a crash.
-R	Reads a file, but does not allow you to change the file.

Vi's Holy Modal Rounders

Working in **vi** is a matter of working in two modes: *insert* and *command*. When you start **vi**, you're automatically placed in command mode. Here, all your keystrokes are interpreted as commands. This is the point when **vi** trips up beginners: It won't accept much in the way of keyboard input, and there's precious little feedback to the user. (Gee, we could probably use **vi** as a metaphor for UNIX's worst aspects....)

Since we have no text yet, working in command mode would be rather fruitless. (We'd also generate a series of beeps, signifying error messages.) Our first step, then, will be switching to insert mode. In this mode we can enter text and stop **vi** from sending those annoying beeps our way. Switch to insert mode by typing *i*; this places you at the beginning of the onscreen page. (Lowercase *i* is not the only way to enter insert mode—the other options are listed in Table 11.2. The other options are for entering text in an already-existing screen with text.) At this point we can begin entering text.

Table 11.2 *Other vi insert-mode options*

Command	Result
Enter	Inserts new line immediately following current character.
i	Inserts at the current character.
l	Inserts at the beginning of the current line.
a	Appends to the right of the current character.

A	Appends at the end of the current line.
o	Inserts new line immediately following current line.
O	Inserts new line immediately before current line.

Go ahead and type in the following, exactly as printed here:

```
This is a text of the Emergency UNIX system. This is a test.
We are typing this text in order to test out the
capabilities of the vi editor. If this were an actual
document, we probably would take it more seriously than we
do this flippant, unorganized memo. Really. This concludes
our text of the Emergency UNIX System.
```

You'll notice that **vi** doesn't wrap words when you get to the edge of the screen (unlike the previous example). If you want a line to end, you'll have to hit the **Enter** (or **Return**) key yourself. For our purposes, it doesn't matter one way or the other.

After typing in our text, you'll want to return to command mode; do so by hitting your **Escape** (**Esc**) key. (If at any time you're not sure if you're in command mode, go ahead and hit the **Escape** key a few times. All you'll do is generate a beep; you won't do anything to your current file.) Again, **vi** gives you no indication about what mode it is in. **Vi**, as you can tell, is a very minimalist text editor. (If you want **vi** to tell you when it's in insert mode, type:

```
:set smd
```

while in command mode. This tells **vi** to display **INSERT MODE** on the bottom-right corner of the screen when in insert mode.)

While in command mode, we can perform various, minimal, editing chores. Most of the commands in command mode are preceded by a colon (:), as we've already seen. In our case, we'll use **vi**'s search capability to find the first instance of *system*. The careful proofreaders in the audience will note that we were inconsistent in our capitalization of *System*. A handy feature of **vi** is its search capability. In command mode, type **/system**, and then hit **Enter**.

Surprise! **Vi** *does* provide some minimal feedback, as you can see at the bottom of the screen. This is called the *status line* and provides what little feedback **vi** features. (We show this in Figure 11.2.)

```
This is a test of the Emergency UNIX System. This is a test.
We are typing this text in order to test out the
capabilities of the vi editor. If this were an actual
document, we would probably take it more seriously that we
do this flippant, unorganized memo. Really. This concludes
our text of the Emergency UNIX System.
~
~
~
~
~
~
~
~
~
~
~
~
~
~
~
~
~
(wrapped)
```

Figure 11.2 *Vi with a status line at the bottom of the screen.*

A partial list of the command-mode options appears in Table 11.3.

Table 11.3 *Vi command-mode options*

Command	Result
Esc	Exits insert mode and enters command mode.
Enter	Moves the cursor to the beginning of the next line.
/string	Searches forward for the first instance of *string*.
?string	Searches backward for the first instance of *string*.

WARNING

As you can see, there is a tremendous inconsistency about commands entered in command mode: Some are preceded by colons (:), other are preceded by slashes (/), and some are preceded by nothing. It's very important to enter the commands exactly as printed here, no matter how illogical they seem.

Deleting and Changing Characters

You'll see that the cursor ended up over the *s* in system. Logically you would think that changing the *s* to *S* would be a matter of typing *S*, correct? No. The process is somewhat convoluted:

- ▼ First you must delete the current character and then insert the new character. Do this by typing *x*, which erases the character under the cursor. (To delete the character to the *left* of the cursor, type *X*. As always in UNIX—*case counts*.)
- ▼ Switch to insert mode by typing *i*.
- ▼ Type *S* to create the word *System*.

(As we said, **vi** is much better suited for scrolling and writing than it is for editing.)

Another method of changing our *s* to *S* (we'll let you decide if it's any easier) would be through the use of **vi**'s **r** command, which changes the character under a cursor to another character you specify. In our case we'll want to position the cursor over the *s* and then type **rS** to replace the current character (in this case, a lowercase *s*) with an uppercase *S*. To change case, you can also position the cursor over the letter you want to change and type the tilde (~) character in command mode. This should change an uppercase letter to a lowercase and a lowercase letter to uppercase.

Other deletion commands are listed in Table 11.4.

Table 11.4 *Vi deletion commands*

Command	Result
x	Deletes character under cursor.
dd	Deletes the current line.
D	Deletes to the end of the current line.
:x	Deletes character under cursor.
:X	Deletes character to the left of the cursor.
:D	Deletes current line.
:D$	Deletes to the end of the current line.
:U	Undoes deletion.

Any of the text-manipulation commands in this chapter—deletions, cursor movements, yankings (which we'll cover a little later), etc.—can be expanded by adding a number to the command, indicating that the command is to repeated the number of times you specify. Thus, deleting three characters can be accomplished with:

`:x3`

while deleting three lines can be done by typing:

`:D3`

Moving Around the Screen

If you considered the 1970s a really great time, you'll feel right at home in **vi** and its various ways for moving the cursor around the screen. Back then, not every keyboard featured arrow keys. (Back then, disco was trendy, too.) Because we're not enthralled with a return to the 1970s (and especially not a return to disco), we're not going to exhaustively cover all of the strange convolutions **vi** goes to in order to move the cursor around a screen without any cursor keys (or a mouse, for that matter). If your keyboard lacks cursor keys, refer to your system's documentation for a full listing of the **vi** cursor controls.

Instead, we'll present a few of the handiest cursor commands in tabular form.

▼ Cursor keys can be used in both command and insert modes.

▼ The left and right cursor keys move only to the beginning and end of current lines and will not move the cursor to the surrounding lines. To move between lines, use the up and down keys.

Other useful cursor and scrolling commands are listed in Table 11.5.

Table 11.5 *Some useful vi cursor and scrolling commands*

Command	Result
0	Moves the cursor to the beginning of the current line.
$	Moves the cursor to the end of the current line.
w	Moves the cursor to the beginning of the next word.

*n*G	Moves the cursor to the beginning of line *n* (where *n* is a numeral).
G	Moves the cursor to the last line of the file.
n|	Moves the cursor to the beginning of column *n* (where *n* is a numeral).
Ctrl-B	Scrolls the screen up one full page. (Think *b*ack.)
Ctrl-D	Scrolls the screen down one-half page. (Think *d*own.)
Ctrl-F	Scrolls the screen down one full page. (Think *f*orward.)
Ctrl-U	Scrolls the screen up one-half page. (Think *u*p.)

Saving a File

Saving a file is a simple process. We'll save our little masterpiece by going to command mode (press **Esc**) and typing:

```
:w test
```

This saves the file under the name of *test*. Our file is still on the screen; our command merely saves the file, but does not quit **vi**. If we were to continue working on this file, the original version we saved would remained unchanged on our hard disk.

For our purposes, let's save the file again and quit **vi**. Use the following:

```
ZZ
```

(Note the lack of a preceding colon.) **Vi** confirms that the file was saved by listing the name in quotation marks, along with a summary of the file's length (in lines) and size (in characters). **Vi** does not clear the screen, but you'll see that the familiar command-line prompt is now on the bottom of your screen.

Other file-saving options are listed in Table 11.6.

Table 11.6 *Options for saving a file in vi*

Command	Result
:q	Quits **vi** after a file is saved. If a file has not been saved, **vi**, quite gallantly, refuses to quit.
:q!	Quits **vi** without saving the file.

:w	Saves file. If the file has not been saved previously and you try to save without specifying a filename, **vi** will warn you.
:w *filename*	Saves file to the name *filename*. If you want to save an existing file to a new filename, use this command with a new filename. However, note that you are still editing the file under the original filename.
:x	Saves file and quits **vi**.
ZZ	Saves file and quits **vi**.
:wq	Saves file and quits **vi**, same as **ZZ**.

File Management and vi

Let's bring back our **test** file. Do so by loading **vi** with the filename specified:

```
$ vi test
```

This is a good moment to sneak in some abstraction. When we load the file, we really are loading a copy of the file into your computer's RAM (or, as referred to in UNIX parlance, the *buffer*). The original file does not change unless *you* specify a change, either through saving a newer version of the file, deleting the file or saving an entirely new file to the same filename.

What does that mean in our case? If we were to make many changes in *test* and weren't happy with the results, we could start over by quitting **vi** without saving the file and reloading the original version. If we were to accidentally make many cuts to our original file, we could discard our edited version and reload the original.

This brings us back to the oft-repeated subject of careful file management. If it's important for you to maintain copies of previous versions of files (there may be legal or administrative reasons to do so), then you need to come up with a workable file-management scheme that allows you to differentiate between these various versions of files. You may want to end each file with a suffix containing the date (*.712*, for example, would refer to July 12) and then keep all versions of the file in the same subdirectory.

Cutting and Pasting Text

Vi's editing capabilities include rudimentary cut-and-paste capabilities. It's a three-step process: Cut (or yank), position, and paste.

Going back to our test message, let's cut a word and paste it in another part of our message. Begin by placing your cursor over the word *Really*. To yank the word, type:

    y)

This tells **vi** to cut to the end of the sentence. We do this because we want to cut the entire sentence of *Really.*; if we were to use the **y** command, we would yank the word *Really* and not the following period. Other yank options are listed in Table 11.7.

Table 11.7 *A few yanking options in vi*

Command	Result
y	Yanks current character.
y*n*	Yanks *n* number of characters.
yw	Yanks current word.
yy	Yanks current line.
*n*yy	Where *n* is a number. Yanks *n* lines of text.
y$	Yanks to the end of the line.
y)	Yanks to the end of the sentence.
y}	Yanks to the end of the paragraph.
Y	Yanks the current line.

Move your cursor to the end of the first sentence; we want to paste our *Really* earlier in the text. To paste the yank to the right of the cursor, type:

    p

If we had yanked an entire line, it would have been placed directly above the cursor. To paste the yank to the left of the cursor, type:

    P

(As always, case counts.)

This ends our little tour of **vi**. As we mentioned at the beginning of the chapter, this introductory look at **vi** merely scratches the surface; we encourage you to seek out **vi**'s **man** pages or additional documentation if you want to learn more about **vi**.

Using Emacs

The Wordstar of UNIX, **emacs** is a popular, though not necessarily easy-to-use, text editor. **Emacs** does not ship with every version of UNIX; for example, it is not shipped as part of the generic System V Release 4 distribution, although several vendors have seen it fit to ship **emacs** on their UNIX systems.

The first version of **emacs** (though not for a UNIX system) was written by Richard Stallman, whom some of you might recognize as the leader of the Free Software Foundation. There are several versions of **emacs** floating around out there, including one distributed by the Free Software Foundation. We're not going to cover each version here; instead, we'll try to use a most-common-denominator approach to this discussion, and we'll use a recent version, 19.23, as our example.

This version of **emacs** is noteworthy for another reason: It's the first version that explicitly supports usage under the X Window System. As such, there are pulldown menus and support for a mouse.

The screen shots in this section will have a menu bar near the top of the screen. Your version of **emacs** may or may not have this menu bar.

If some of the keystrokes we mention here don't work on your system, don't worry—it could be that your version of **emacs** is slightly different than the ones we were using to prepare this chapter. Because we're using the most-common-denominator approach here, we would *strongly* suggest that you consult more advanced texts before relying on **emacs** as your only text editor.

In the past, we argued that **emacs** was too difficult to use for the average beginner. No more—the latest versions have convinced us that anyone can benefit from using **emacs.**

Starting Emacs

Let's begin by loading **emacs**. Do so by entering the following at the command prompt:

```
$ emacs
```

If you wanted to start **emacs** with a file loaded, you would do so by includ-ing the name of the file as an argument:

```
$ emacs filename
```

You may be presented with a startup screen containing a short intro to **emacs** and a help message, such as the one shown in Figure 11.3.

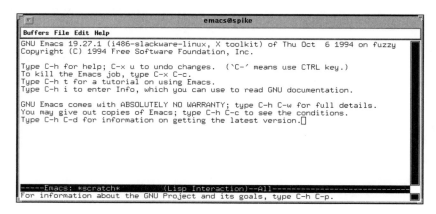

Figure 11.3 **Emacs** *at startup, without a file loaded.*

Most users will be presented with a mostly blank screen with a status line at the bottom, displaying the name of the file to be edited, information about the size of the file in lines and characters, as well as your position in the file.

Unlike **vi** or **ed**, **emacs** works in only one mode, so you don't need to worry about hitting the **Esc** key to enter a command. You can type text directly in **emacs** after starting it. Go ahead and enter our literary gem from earlier in this chapter:

```
This is a text of the Emergency UNIX system. This is a test.
We are typing this text in order to test the capabilities of
the vi editor. If this were an actual document, we probably
would take it more seriously than we do this flippant,
unorganized memo. Really. This concludes our text of the
Emergency UNIX System.
```

Emacs does not wrap text to fit text within the confines of a display (by default, although this can be changed), so you'll have to hit the **Enter** or **Return** key at the end of every line. Do so when typing in this text.

Accessing Emacs Commands

Earlier we described **emacs** as being the Wordstar of UNIX text editing. Why? Like DOS's Wordstar, **emacs** relies heavily on commands issued from the keyboard in conjunction with the **Control (Ctrl)** and **Meta** keys. Like Wordstar, **emacs** allows you to do most of your work from the keyboard; touch typists should love **emacs**. And like Wordstar, many of the commands may be obscure and hard to remember for the end user.

NOTE

We've tried to make sure that this text applies to the greatest number of UNIX systems possible, avoiding version- and vendor-specific information. In this situation we must deviate from that path when discussing **emacs** and the **Meta** key.

The **Meta** key differs from keyboard to keyboard and is used as a modifier key, performing alternate functions in conjunction with other keys. (We've been using the **Control** key as a modifier key throughout this book.) On PCs and PC-style keyboards, the **Meta** key is often labeled as the **Alt** key and located next to the Spacebar. On the Sun SPARCstation the **Meta** key is marked with a diamond shape and is located next to the spacebar; it is not the key marked **Alt**. On the Sun 3 keyboard the **Meta** keys are the **Left** or **Right** keys. On the Hewlett-Packard 9000 Series 700 and 800, the **Extend Char** key performs this function. On an Apple Macintosh keyboard (both versions), it is the **Command** key (marked with an apple outline and pretzel shape, supposedly derivative of some strange Swedish symbol).

To make matters worse, some systems respond to **Meta** commands entered with either the **Alt** key or the **Esc** key. If you try to end some of the following commands using the **Alt** key and get no response, try the command using the **Esc** key. Here's an example: When testing this chapter out on different platforms, we found that Freemacs, a version of **emacs** ported to the MS-DOS operating system, used the **Alt** key as the **Meta** key with some commands (like **Meta-G**) and used the **Esc** key as the **Meta** key with other commands (**Meta->**). In a perfect world these aberrations wouldn't exist, but we must make do with what we have—and so it's incumbent on you to test the various **Meta** commands on your own system.

Cursor Commands

Like **vi**, **emacs** features a ton of commands designed to navigate you around the screen, a throwback to the days when many users did not have cursor keys on their keyboards. As with our discussion of **vi**, we're not going to discuss all of the available obscure cursor commands. Instead, we'll list the more useful cursor commands in Table 11.8. Execution of these commands can sometimes be inconsistent, as outlined in the previous section. These commands should be tried only if your regular navigational commands, like **Page Up**, **Page Down**, and the various cursor keys, don't respond.

***Table 11.8** Useful emacs cursor commands*

Command	Result
Ctrl-L	Moves current cursor line to the middle of the screen.
Ctrl-V	Moves forward one screen.
Meta-V	Moves backward one screen.
Meta-<	Moves to the beginning of the file.
Meta->	Moves to the end of the file.

Deleting and Changing Characters

Most users can use their keyboard **Backspace** (**BkSp** or ←) and **Delete** keys to delete text. **Emacs** does provide for keyboard equivalents should your system not support **Backspace** or **Delete** keys, yet with **emacs**, you can map any function to any key you'd like, although this process should only be attempted by advanced users. Other deletion commands are listed in Table 11.9.

***Table 11.9** Emacs deletion commands*

Command	Result
Delete	Deletes the character to the left of the cursor.
Ctrl-D	Deletes character under the cursor.
Ctrl-K	Deletes all characters to the end of the line.
Meta-D	Deletes forward to the end of the next word.
Meta-Delete	Deletes backward to the beginning of the previous word.

Searching and Replacing

To search for a specific string within **emacs**, use the command:

```
Ctrl-S
```

to invoke **emacs**' search command. Appearing at the bottom of the screen is the prompt:

```
Search for:
```

Enter the search text; when done, press **Return**. Instead of the above prompt, you might see a prompt more like the following:

```
I-search:
```

If you're at the end of a file and want to search backwards, use the command:

```
Ctrl-R
```

Note that this provides an incremental search. That is, as you type in the word or phrase to search for, **emacs** is already looking.

Going back to our tutorial: Since we input text, our cursor should be at the end of the file. Let's use the search command to look for the string *Really*. Do this by typing **Ctrl-R** and respond to the subsequent prompt as follows:

```
Search for: Really
```

Emacs places the cursor at the end of the string.

Saving a File

Saving a file in **emacs** is a simple process. Save our test file by typing:

```
Ctrl-x Ctrl-s
```

Emacs will ask you for the name of the file. Let's use the name **Test**.

Since we want to continue working with this file, we won't **quit emacs**. However, if we did want to save a file and quit **emacs** simultaneously, we would use the following command sequence:

```
Ctrl-x Ctrl-c
```

Copying and Moving Text

If you plan on copying and moving a lot of text, you'll find that **emacs**' capabilities in this area are more advanced than **vi**'s. **Emacs** allows you to mark a section of text (though, in true UNIX fashion, **emacs** doesn't necessarily highlight the text you mark) for copying and deleting purposes.

To mark a section of text, move your cursor to the beginning of the section and enter the following:

```
Ctrl-@
```

(The **@** is usually contained on the same key as the number 2 on PC-style keyboards. In this instance you don't need to play Twister with your fingers in trying to press the **Ctrl**, **Shift**, and **@** keys simultaneously. You merely need to press the **Ctrl** and **2/@** keys simultaneously.) Move your cursor to the end of the section you want to mark. Applying this routine to our example, let's say we wanted to move the line:

```
We are typing this text in order to test the capabilities of the vi editor.
```

Begin by moving your cursor directly over the *W* in We. Type **Ctrl-@** and then move your cursor to the space following the period at the end of the sentence. What follows next requires a short explanation.

Emacs maintains sections of memory devoted to storage of deleted text, called a *kill buffer.* You don't need to set up a kill buffer, and you don't need to really do anything at all to the kill buffer, except to know that it exists. In our example of cutting and pasting, we are deleting a marked section of text and placing it in the kill buffer. Do so by typing the following:

```
Ctrl-w
```

The text between the mark (where you typed **Ctrl-@**) and the current cursor position disappears, and we'll want to paste it before the sentence beginning with *Really.* To retrieve it from the kill buffer, we position our cursor over the *R* in *Really* and type:

```
Ctrl-Y
```

After all of our changes, our little text file should look like this:

```
This is a test of the Emergency UNIX system. This is a test. If this
were an actual document, we probably would take it more seriously than
we do this flippant, unorganized memo. We are typing this test in order
to test the capabilities of the vi editor. Really. This concludes our
test of the Emergency UNIX System.
```

Help in Emacs

Emacs, amazingly enough, contains a primitive help system that may or may not be of use to you. (We are amazed because help features—other than man pages—are extremely rare in the UNIX world.) It's worth a try if you get stuck, anyway.

Depending on your version of **emacs**, you'll type one of the following commands to summon help:

```
Ctrl-H
F1
Esc-?
Meta-?
Meta-x
```

Unfortunately, we've found that different versions of **emacs** treat the help system differently, although **Ctrl-H** is the most common means to enter help. To get a topic of all the help subjects, we find that the following is a pretty safe bet:

```
Meta-x a
```

In addition to all these commands, you can do literally anything in **emacs**. Since **emacs** includes a built-in LISP interpreter, you can write short programs in LISP to customize **emacs** to your heart's content. Many people have extended **emacs** so that you can use it as a shell, read your electronic mail and Internet/Usenet news, and play the game **go**, all from within one interface (one interface to rule them all and in the darkness bind them). Programming with **emacs** is an advanced topic, and we just wanted to let you know that it is possible. If you want to do this, check out an **emacs** manual.

Other Text-Editing Tools

Vi, **emacs**, and **ed** aren't the only tools used to edit and create text on UNIX systems. In this section we'll cover a few tools you may or may not find useful.

Using Spell

Unless your spelling is perfect, you could benefit from a spelling checker. (We shudder when thinking about our writing careers before spelling checkers.) The UNIX operating system ships with a spelling checker built in, accessed by (surprise!) the **spell** command. Like everything in the UNIX operating system, the **spell** command is deceptively simple, but requires a little bit of work to be truly useful. To use **spell**, type the following at the command prompt:

```
$ spell filename
```

where *filename* is the name of the file to be checked.

Let's check the spelling of our **test** file. Do so with:

```
$ spell test
```

Nothing happens, as there are no misspelled words in the file. However, we did give you some experience using the **spell** command in real life. If there were some misspelled words, they would have been listed one word at a time after the command prompt:

```
$ spell test
misspelling1
misspelling2
misspelling3
misspelling4
$
```

If there are only a few misspelled words in a file, printing them to your screen isn't a big deal. However, with larger files chockfull of potential errors, you'll need smoother mechanisms for dealing with the errors. That's why we generally send the output of **spell** to a file or directly to a printer. To send the errors to a file, use the following:

```
$ spell test > errors
```

(We chose **errors** for its descriptive quality. You can choose whatever filename your heart desires.) Use **cat** to view the file:

```
$ cat errors
```

Even handier is sending the output directly to the printer. Use the following:

```
$ spell test | lp
```

Spell does not change the original test file; it's up to you to use **vi** or **emacs** and correct the misspellings on your own—which is why we find the printed output so handy.

WARNING

Many beginning computer users make the mistake of relying on their spelling checker to ferret out all errors in a file. A spelling checker will find the obviously misspelled words, but it won't find all the errors in a file. For example, **spell** won't tell you to use *hear* instead of *here* in the following sentence: "It was hard to here the band." It will always trip on proper names, since they are not usually found in the dictionary. Since the dictionary is rather small by spelling-checker standards—about 30,000 words in the last version we examined extensively— **spell** trips on properly spelled, yet justifiably obscure words. And even though **spell** finds misspelled words, it doesn't suggest correct spellings.

Using Wc to Count Words

You may want to know how many words are contained in a file. Use the following:

```
$ wc filename
21    99     489 filename
$
```

where *filename* refers to a file to be checked. The word-count (**wc**) command then tells us how many lines (21), words (99), and characters (489) are in the file *filename*. We could use wc to check more than one file:

```
$ wc file1 file2 file3
21    99     489 file1
 4    21      88 file2
69   201     998 file3
94   321    1575 total
```

Summary

UNIX uses text files for just about everything, including most system configurations. To edit these text files, we cover the two most commonly used text editors under UNIX: **vi** and **emacs**. These editors allow you to create, modify, and view text files. **Vi** was hot technology in the 1970s but shows its age today. Yet, as a new user, you'll have more luck with **vi** than with **emacs**.

Emacs, while free, is not available on as many systems as is **vi**. Known as the all-singing, all-dancing text editor, you can program **emacs** with its built-in LISP interpreter to do just about anything. This, of course, requires some experience.

Also covered were two handy commands related to text editing: **spell** (which checks the spelling of a file) and **wc** (which provides a word count of the file).

Text Processing

This chapter covers:

- ▼ An introduction to **troff**
- ▼ Distinctions between **nroff**, **troff**, and **ditroff**
- ▼ Creating a **troff** document
- ▼ **Troff** formatting commands
- ▼ **Troff** and PostScript
- ▼ The memorandum macros
- ▼ Typesetting equations
- ▼ Commercial text-processing packages

Text Editing Versus Text Processing

In the last chapter we covered the basics of text editing. In this chapter we'll extend the concept by discussing text processing and manipulation, with the powerful tool **troff**.

The traditional UNIX world makes a distinction between *text editors* and *text processors*. On a base level, both appear to do the same thing: create and print text files. The similarity ends there, however, as a text editor is geared more for internal use (creating script files, program files, electronic-mail messages), while a text processor introduces formatting features that spiff up documents intended for the outside world. A text editor allows you to designate characters as bold or italics (depending the capabilities of your printer), but a text processor actually carries out these commands.

Troff: What You See isn't Quite What You Get

Once the most popular publishing software in the world, **troff** and its predecessors are essential tools for any UNIX user who wants to create professional-looking documents and don't want to shell extra for a professional package like Island Write or FrameMaker. These tools come with most versions of UNIX, although sometimes they're split out into a package called the Documenter's Workbench.

To understand **troff**, it's important to review its history. (It's also a fairly common UNIX story: the work of one adapted to evolving needs.) The product we call **troff** began life in 1964 as **runoff** and ported to UNIX in the form of **roff**, used to supply simple formatting to documents printed on a line printer. **Roff** was revised in 1973, as **nroff** was created to add more formatting capabilities. **Nroff** didn't have a long life as the latest and greatest; it was extended that same year to support a typesetting machine and renamed **troff**. Finally, **troff** was revised to support virtually every printer and renamed **ditroff** (for *d*evice-*i*ndependent *troff*). Today, we refer to **troff** almost exclusively, even though it's most likely we're actually using **ditroff**.

In this day of graphical-user interfaces and WYSIWYG (what-you-see-is-what-you-get) computing, **troff** is a throwback to the days of Wordstar and more abstract (a-ha!) computing tools, when you had to visualize your final output and provide commands to the system on how to achieve this final output. Today we can highlight text and change its formatting from bold to italic through a simple menu choice, if we're using a word processor that supports a WYSIWYG mode.

With **troff**, though, we must visualize the change in our head, insert the commands that initiate this change, and wait for our printed page to see if these changes were implemented correctly.

To dwell on **troff**'s shortcomings, though, is counterproductive—you dance with those who brung you, and if you're not working with the X Window System, your document-formatting tools are pretty much limited to **troff**. If you're working on a UNIX system and need to create user documentation for your firm's software project, **troff** can be a useful and powerful tool. Larger organizations that needed UNIX's multiuser, multitasking capabilities (like book- and magazine-publishing firms) benefited greatly from **troff** and still can be found using it.

In this chapter we'll discuss **troff** almost exclusively, or refer to it exclusively, anyway. Your specific tool—whether it be **nroff**, **troff**, or **ditroff**—may vary. Both **troff** and **ditroff** build on **nroff**; **nroff** is generally limited for use with line printers, **troff** can be used with laser printers or typesetters, and **ditroff** can be used with just about any output device. There's also a specialized program called **psroff** that supports only PostScript printers. But these rules aren't written in stone—most systems, we find, feature **ditroff** under the **troff** name. If you're working on a larger system, you can bet that someone has probably already determined whether **nroff** or **troff** is available on your system.

Creating a Troff Document

Troff is not an island; it's not like a word processor where you can input text and then manipulate it. In the true UNIX tradition of dividing processing tasks to free the user from too much interactivity with the system, you create a text document in a text editor like **vi** or **emacs** (both explained in depth in the previous chapter), insert the proper formatting commands there, and then run your formatted document through **troff**.

The best way to explain **troff** is to look at before-and-after examples, as shown in Figures 12.1 and 12.2. Go ahead and enter the text in Figure 12.1 in your system using **vi** or **emacs**. Save the file as **trofftest**.

```
.ce1
ANDROMEDA CHALLENGE

\s10Our main competitor in the software-development field,
Andromeda Systems, has come out with a new X Window word
processor named \fIAlphaBet\fR. It poses several problems
for us:
.in 5
* Andromeda will certainly price this product \fBvery\fR
competitively. We will more than likely be forced to follow
suit. There go the year-end bonuses.
* Its packaging will be slicker than ours.
* Quite honestly, it's a better product than anything we
have on the market. To make up this market gap, we recommend
putting much more money into marketing and away from basic
research.

by Kevin and Eric, marketing.
```

Figure 12.1 *A vi document containing troff formatting commands.*

THE ANDROMEDA CHALLENGE

Our main competitor in the software-development field, Andromeda Systems, has come out with a new X Window word processor named *AlphaBet*. It poses several problems for us:

> * Andromeda will certainly price this product **very** competitively. We will more than likely be forced to follow suit. There go the holiday bonuses.
>
> * Its packaging will be slicker than ours.
>
> * Quite honestly, it's a better product than anything we have on the market. To make up this market gap, we recommend putting much more money into marketing and away from basic research.

Prepared by Kevin and Eric, marketing.

Figure 12.2 *Our document as it looks after a run through troff.*

Our originating **vi** or **emacs** document, as delineated in Figure 12.1, is a standard memo, with several formatting commands that begin with a backslash (\) or a period (.). **Troff** then interprets these commands to something the output device (laser printer, typesetting machine) can understand; the end result looks like Figure 12.2. A listing of the most useful **troff** commands are contained in Table 12.1.

The next step is to run our example file, test, through **troff**. As with any UNIX program, when you run **troff** you must specify the destination of its output; without such specification, the default output is the screen:

```
$ troff test
```

Or, better yet, go ahead and redirect the output of **troff** to a file:

```
$ troff test > test.tr
```

We can read the formatted file using **cat**:

```
$ cat test.tr
```

(With longer files, the text will scream by you, of course. To stop the text from scrolling by, type **Ctrl-S**; to start the scrolling, type **Ctrl-Q**.)

If your system has a printer connected, go ahead and print the result of the **troff** command. Use **troff** and then redirect the output to the printer:

```
$ troff -printer test | lp
```

In some cases you may need to specify the printer. This specification will depend on your particular hardware configuration; for more information, talk to your system administrator or call the online-manual page for **troff**:

```
$ man troff
```

You'll note several things about our example:

▼ The text is spaced to fill to the right margin. **Troff** will fill as many words as it can on a line, no matter if you insert character returns between characters. If you want **troff** to recognize the character returns, use **.nf**, which stands for *no fill.*

▼ The text is justified; that is, the spaces between words are increased to allow the text to be stretched across the entire line. We usually prefer that our text be ragged right, spacing the words equally and eliminating any stretched lines. To accomplish this, use the **.ad** command.

▼ We changed some characters to italic and bold using the \f command. Text to be changed must be framed with \f commands. If not, all characters after the \fB command would be bold; it was up to us to insert the \fR command to change the text back to regular (or, in the typesetting/graphics term, roman).

▼ We changed the size of several characters to 12 point, 10 point, and 8 point using the \s command. (Point size refers to the height of characters, as measured in points. It's a measurement used in the typesetting and graphics worlds. Most typewriters, for instance, feature characters that are either 12 point or 10 point.)

▼ Dot commands must be on their own line, but backslashed commands can appear anywhere in the text.

Table 12.1 *Useful troff commands.*

Command	Result
.ad	Turn off text justification.
.bp	Page break.
.ce *n*	Center next *n* lines. If no number is specified, only the following line will be centered.
.fi	Tells **troff** to fill the lines of text.
.ft *n*	Change font to *n*.
\f*n*	Change font to *n*.
.in *n*	Indent the following lines by *n* spaces.
.ls *n*	Sets the line spacing on a document; **.ls 2** would change the spacing to double-spaced. The default is single-spaced.
.na	Turn on text justification.
.nf	Tells **troff** not to fill the lines of text.
.pl *n*	Sets the number of lines on the page to *n*. The default is 66 lines to a page. Note that laser printers usually have a smaller number of lines per page.
.po *n*i	Sets the left margin; **.po 1l** would set the left margin to 1 inch. It's essential that you set this, because the default has text appearing all the way to the left of the page. (In this instance, we use inch for our example; centimeters could be specified by using **c** instead of **i**.)

.ps *n*	Change the point size to *n*.
\S*n*	Change the point size to *n*.
.sp *n*	Sets the number of lines to skip by *n*. To skip a specific amount, use *n***i** for inches or *n***c** for centimeters.
.ti *n*	Indent the first line of the following paragraph *n* spaces.
.un *n*	Underline entire following line. If a number is specified, then *n* lines will be underlined. Must be used with entire lines.

Troff and PostScript

The PostScript page-description language is becoming more extensively used these days, as many computer firms are now selling PostScript-based printers with their systems. PostScript files, whether they be graphics or text-based documents, are exceptionally portable (they can be read by virtually every kind of computer), and PostScript printers are common business tools.

Printing a **troff** document on a PostScript printer is a somewhat involved process; it concerns running a document first through **troff** and then through **dpost**, which translates **troff**'s output to PostScript. (Your system may use a program like **psroff** instead.) You can do both in the same command line. For instance, let's say we wanted to run our earlier test program through **troff**, with the final destination a PostScript printer. The command line would look something like:

```
$ troff -Tpost test | dpost | lp
```

 Note the -*Tpost* argument. As we noted above, you must specify a printer; in this case, we are specifying a PostScript printer, even though we are running the **dpost** utility.

The Memorandum Macros

All of this is well and good. However, most UNIX users don't want to turn into typesetters (trust us; we've experienced the pleasure). Nor do most of us want to go to the trouble of providing specifics to an output device every time we create a document—especially if the document is 500 pages long and serves as the main reference manual for your company's software product. And we certainly don't want to be forced to remember the 80 or so **troff** commands possible.

Luckily, someone went to the trouble of creating *memorandum macros* **(mm)** that automate the **troff** text-creating process somewhat. These macros differ greatly in capabilities and can be used to create stylized business letters, resumés, and reports. We won't go into great detail about these macros, as not every system will contain them—AT&T treats memorandum macros as a separate part of its Documenter's Workbench, Apple includes the memorandum macros as a standard part of AU/X, and other UNIX versions eliminate them completely.

To see if your system supports the memorandum macros, type **mm** at the command prompt:

```
$ mm
```

If your system supports the memorandum macros, you'll see a short message explaining all the options available with the memorandum macros. If your system does not support the memorandum macros, you'll see something like the following:

```
$ mm
mm: not found
```

If your system does feature the memorandum macros and you want to learn, consult your documentation or read the online-manual pages for **mm**. You can display them by typing the following:

```
$ man mm
```

There's also a common set of macros for creating UNIX-style manual pages. These manual macros (**man**) speed the process of creating online manual pages like you see for the standard UNIX commands. We don't find the online-manual pages very informative for a new user, but they can be lifesavers for experienced users.

In addition to the macro packages, a number of other programs have grown up around **nroff** and **troff**. **Eqn** is used to typeset equations through its own set of dot commands. You normally pass a file through **eqn** first, then pipe the output of **eqn** to **troff**:

```
$ eqn testfile.tr | troff | lp
```

Another common utility, called **tbl**, typesets tables. Again, **tbl** acts as a filter that operates on its own dot commands and passes the rest of the commands on to **troff**:

```
$ eqn testfile.tr | tbl | troff | lp
```

Commercial Packages

Professionals—editors, technical writers, documentation specialists—may not want to rely on the admittedly crude troff-based tools. Commercial text-processing software that we can recommend includes:

▼ Wordperfect for UNIX, which has been upgraded to support a WYSIWYG interface via support for the X Window System and Motif.

▼ FrameMaker, the most popular electronic-publishing and documentation package on the market.

▼ Island Write, part of an X Window-based suite of graphical applications.

Summary

You can select from many brands of commercial word processors that provide WYSIWYG (what-you-see-is-what-you-get) computing, even though this chapter concentrates on a set of typesetting tools that definitely *doesn't* provide any form of WYSIWYG.

You start with original text files created with any text editor, such as **vi** or **emacs**. You then feed these files to **troff**, or the related **nroff** or **ditroff**. **Troff** translates dot commands in text files and outputs formatted text.

Some of these dot commands include **.ad** to run off text justification, and **.ce**, which centers lines of text. To speed your work with **troff**, you can use a set of prebuilt macros, such as the memorandum macros, or **mm**. These macro packages include a number of shorthand macros for the longer **troff** commands.

Shell Programming Basics

This chapter covers:

- ▼ Shell scripts
- ▼ Changing shells
- ▼ Using **vi** and shell scripts
- ▼ Making the script file executable with **chmod**
- ▼ Executing scripts
- ▼ Command-line parameters and shell scripts
- ▼ Shell variables
- ▼ Setting up loops
- ▼ Using the **test** statement
- ▼ Using the **case** statement
- ▼ Using standard input and output with shell scripts
- ▼ Troubleshooting shell scripts
- ▼ Tracing the execution of shell scripts

Creating a Script

UNIX commands involve a lot of typing. If you're not a typist and don't want to remember the strange UNIX syntax for commands, you may want to bundle a number of commands together into what is called a *shell script.*

Shell scripts contain a series of commands for a UNIX shell, like the Bourne shell, **sh**, or C shell, **csh**. These scripts are stored in files and act much like DOS batch files. As you execute a shell script, each command in the text file is passed to the shell to execute, one at a time. When all of the commands in the file are executed, or if an error occurs, the script ends.

These shell scripts can execute UNIX commands and can also use built-in functions provided by the shell. Like most UNIX commands, these built-in functions tend to the cryptic side. We don't expect you to be a programmer, but as you use UNIX, you'll soon find the need to write small shell scripts to make up for the places where the traditional UNIX commands don't do what you want. Shell scripts can be a powerful tool, or a cryptic mess. In this chapter we guide you through that mess and provide a gentle introduction to shell scripting.

Most users run **sh, csh,** or the Korn shell, **ksh,** as their command-line interpreter. (**Ksh** is an enhanced Bourne shell, at least in most respects. See Chapter 4 for more on this.) You can program the shell that you're running right now, but we'll start with the Bourne shell, **sh,** first. While few users actually use the Bourne shell for their shell, virtually all shell scripts are written for the Bourne shell. In addition, the Bourne shell is the most widely available shell.

C Shell Users: Changing Shells

You must be in the Bourne shell to use Bourne scripts, of course. What happens if you're not? If you, for example, run the C shell, **csh**, you can switch to the Bourne shell for the rest of this chapter by simply executing the command **sh**:

```
% sh
$
```

Note how the command prompt changes from the **csh %** to the **sh $**. This shows we're in the Bourne shell. You can later exit the Bourne shell by typing **exit** or **Ctrl-D**; both should exit **sh** and return you back to your **csh** prompt.

NOTE We're running a new shell, **sh**, as a subprocess of the first shell, **csh**. This tends to get complex, but just remember that in UNIX the shell is just another program. Because you can run programs from a shell, there's nothing to stop you from running shells within a shell.

Now that we're all running the Bourne shell, we'll start by creating some simple shell scripts. A shell script is nothing more than a text file that contains a series of commands, just as you'd type in at the prompt. Each line in the text file is interpreted as another UNIX command. That's it. (Well, not really. There's some extra niceties called *syntax* built into the shells to aid writing shell scripts, which is what we cover in this chapter.)

Shell scripts are stored in UNIX text files, so use your favorite text editor (such as **vi** or **emacs,** described in Chapter 11) to create a new file **example1:**

```
$ vi example1
```

In the file **example1**, enter the following text:

```
echo This is my first shell script.
ls
```

Save this simple two-line file under the name **example1.**

There are two lines in our first shell script. The first command, **echo**, prints out the rest of the line to the screen. Since shell scripts are really shell commands stored in a text file, to see what any command does, you can simply type it in at the prompt:

```
$ echo This is my first shell script.
```

And you'll see echoed back:

```
This is my first shell script.
```

Easy, huh?

The second command is the **ls** command we introduced in Chapter 2. It will print out a list of the files in your current directory. As you can tell, we're not breaking any new computational ground here with this first shell script.

Now that we know what the shell script should do, it's time to actually run it.

Running Shell Scripts

There are two main ways to run a shell script. The first is to pass the script as a parameter to the shell program, **sh,** on the command line. The second method involves marking the script executable, which we cover as follows.

To ask a shell to run a script, put the name of the script file, in our case **example1**, on the command line:

```
$ sh example1
```

When you execute this command, you'll see the following output:

```
This is my first shell script.
1995          example3     example6      example9
myls2         example1     example4      example7
mybackup      report.1995
example2      example5     example8      myls
```

Note that you'll see the files in your current directory, not ours.

Making the Script File Executable with Chmod

To actually use our shell script as a UNIX command, we need to mark the file as being executable. We can do this with the **chmod** (*ch*ange *mod*e) command. First, we'll list the file **example1** to see what the file permissions are:

```
$ ls -l example1
-rw-rw-r--   1 erc  bigfun   39 Dec  8 15:42 example1
```

Then, we'll mark the file as executable with **chmod:**

```
$ chmod u+x example1
```

The *u* stands for user and the *+x* for adding the execute permission. All UNIX commands need to have the execute permission set in order to run. We can verify that **chmod** did its work by using **ls** again:

```
$ ls -l example1
-rwxrw-r--   1 erc  bigfun   39 Dec  8 15:42 example1
```

NOTE

If you're using the C shell, **csh**, you'll need to enter the **rehash** command:

```
% rehash
```

This rebuilds the **csh**'s internal table of all available commands. You'll need to run **rehash** each time you add a new command to your system. Remember that each shell script is indeed a command.

Executing Scripts

Now that the file **example1** is marked as executable, we can actually execute the shell script and see what it does. We covered the basics of the **example1** script above. Here's its full output.

```
$ example1
This is my first shell script.
1995           example3    example6    example9
myls2          example1    example4    example7
mybackup       report.1995
example2       example5    example8    myls
```

Commenting in Shell Scripts

The **#** at the start of the line indicates a comment that goes to the end of the line. Comments are used to tell whoever reads your shell scripts what the heck is going on. This might seem obvious now, but if you try to reread a complex shell script a year from now, you may have trouble. That's why most comments are really aimed at telling yourself what you did. (Comments also help to tell others the same thing, if you provide your shell scripts to other users.) We'll use comments in the rest of the examples in this chapter to help you get the hang of things.

Getting the Right Shell to Run your Script

At the start of this chapter, we suggested you run the Bourne shell, **sh**, for shell programming. The problem is that each shell uses a different syntax (we know that this is stupid, but that's the way things are). What works in one shell, like **sh**, may error out in another shell, like **csh.** But, how can you be sure that the shell script you labored over for so long will actually get executed in the proper shell?

Since your system may support many shells, including **sh, csh, ksh, bash,** and many more, there's a special magic syntax to tell your shell which of the many shell programs should execute the script. This magic line is placed at the very top of the file, in the first line, and technically, it's a comment. To use the Bourne shell, **sh,** insert the following line at the start of your shell scripts:

```
#! /bin/sh
```

The # is used as a comment character. See "Commenting in Shell Scripts," below.

N O T E

To use the C shell, insert the following line:

```
#! /bin/csh
```

Not all shells will read these magic comments. Still, include them anyway, since most shells read the comments. Since the magic comments use a comment character, **#**, the comment will be ignored if your shell does not support the **#! /bin/sh** syntax.

More on Echo

You can also place the arguments to **echo** in quotation marks, like this **echo** command:

```
echo "You can also use quotation marks with echo."
```

This command will print out:

```
You can also use quotation marks with echo.
```

We strongly advise you to place the text you want to **echo** in quotation marks, especially since common punctuation characters like ? and ! mean nonintuitive things in shell commands (? matches any single character in file names, while the C shell uses ! for its command history).

If you pass the -*n* command-line parameter to **echo,** then **echo** won't end its output with a newline. The following two commands will print out one line of output, when used in a shell script:

```
echo -n "first message"
echo " second message"
```

The output will look like:

```
first message second message.
```

If you don't place these commands in a shell script, **sh** intervenes with its command prompt between the commands:

```
$ echo -n "first message"
first message$ echo " second message"
 second message
```

Sounds easy, right? The **echo** command is one of the simplest commands, but it can be useful in shell scripts.

Echoing Command Output

You can also use the output of UNIX commands with **echo,** to print out the results. For example, we can use the **pwd** command (which was initially covered in Chapter 2) with **echo.** The **pwd** command prints the working, or current, directory. Thus, if you're in a directory named **/u/erc/teachux,** you should see the following output for the **pwd** command:

```
$ pwd
/u/erc/teachux
```

We can put two commands together, as in the following example:

```
echo "The current directory is `pwd`."
```

The accent marks surrounding the **pwd** command mean that the shell should execute the command between the accent marks and then substitute that command's output in the string passed to the **echo** command. When we execute that command, we'll see output like the following example:

```
$ echo "The current directory is `pwd`."
The current directory is /u/erc/teachux.
```

You can print out the date and time with the **date** command:

```
$ date
Thu Dec  8 15:53:46 CST 1994
```

Note that **date** uses a military 24-hour clock. That means that hours after noon will appear as numbers above 12. To convert to the wall-clock time, subtract 12 from the hour. For example, 10 a.m. will still appear as 10:00, but 3:53 p.m. (the time shown above) will instead appear as 15:53.

We now have a text file with **sh** commands, but we don't yet have a working shell script.

Shell Variables

You can introduce variables in your shell scripts, using the following syntax, as we first described in Chapter 4:

variable=value

Don't put any spaces on either side of the equal sign (=). Variable names must begin with a letter or an underscore character (_). You can use letters, underscores, or numbers for the rest of the variable name.

To later retrieve the value of a variable, place a dollar sign ($) in front of the variable name:

```
variable1="Yow, are we having fun yet?"
echo "The variable is $variable1."
```

When you execute these commands, you'll see the following results:

```
The variable is Yow, are we having fun yet?.
```

You can place the output of a command into a variable, using the accent marks we discussed above:

```
datetoday=`date`
echo "The date is $datetoday."
```

And print out the results:

```
The date is Thu Dec  8 15:57:59 CST 1994.
```

We can then put this all together and create the following shell script, which we call **example2:**

```
#! /bin/sh
#
# Example 2 from Chapter 13 of Teach Yourself UNIX.
#
# More on echo.
#
echo "You can also use quotation marks with echo."

# Note the space after the quotation
# mark and before second.

echo -n "first message"
echo " second message"

# Use a command with echo.
echo "The current directory is `pwd`."

# Use a variable.
variable1="Yow, are we having fun yet?"
echo "The variable is $variable1."

# Set a variable to a command output
datetoday=`date`
echo "The date is $datetoday."
```

To run this shell script, mark it as executable, or just run with the **sh** program:

```
$ sh example2
```

You can read input from the user into variables with the **read** command.

Shell Input with the Read Command

The **read** command reads in user input and places whatever the user types into a shell variable:

```
$ read variablename
```

When used with **echo,** you can prompt the user to enter data, as in the following example:

```
#! /bin/sh
#
# Example 3 from Chapter 13 of Teach Yourself UNIX.
#
# Using read.
#
echo -n "Enter your first name: "
read firstname

echo -n "Enter you last name: "
read lastname
echo "Your name is $firstname $lastname."
```

Enter the previous commands into a file named **example3** and then mark **example3** as executable. When you run this script, you'll be prompted to enter in your name:

```
$ example3
Enter your first name: Eric
Enter your last name: Johnson
Your name is Eric Johnson.
```

Command-Line Parameters to Shell Scripts

Most UNIX commands support a plethora of command-line parameters, all sorts of options for changing what the command does. You can use command-line parameters for your shell scripts, too.

Shell scripts can read up to nine command-line parameters, or arguments into special variables. Anything more than nine is silently ignored. (You can get around this with **$***, as we show below.) Even so, nine command-line parameters is a lot. Inside shell scripts these command-line parameters appear as specially named shell-script variables. The command-line parameters are named *$1, $2, $3,* and so on to *$9.* There's no *$10.*

A special variable holds the name of the executable script, as invoked by the user. This variable is *$0.* In the above file, **example1,** the value of *$0* would be **example1**. But, if we executed the file **example1** with the following command:

```
$ /u/erc/teachux/example1
```

then *$0* would hold **/u/erc/teachux/example1.** Here's a sample shell script to print out up to nine command-line parameters to a shell script:

```
#! /bin/sh
#
# Example 4 from Chapter 13 of Teach Yourself UNIX.
#
# Command-line parameters.
#
echo "The first parameter was $1."

echo -n "The full parameters were (up to 9) "
echo $1 $2 $3 $4 $5 $6 $7 $8 $9
echo "The shell script is $0."
```

Enter the above commands into a file named example4, and then mark example4 as an executable file:

```
$ chmod u+x example4
```

We can now run **example4:**

```
$ example4 1 2 3 4 5 6 7 8 9

The first parameter was 1.
The full parameters were (up to 9) 1 2 3 4 5 6 7 8 9
The shell script is example4.
```

Note the trick of placing a blank space after the data inside the quotation marks earlier. This old programmer trick makes for better-looking output. We can also try the following:

```
$ ./example4 1 2 3 4


The first parameter was 1.
The full parameters were (up to 9) 1 2 3 4
The shell script is ./example4.
```

Or,

```
$ /u/erc/teachux/example4 1 2 3 4
```

```
The first parameter was 1.
The full parameters were (up to 9) 1 2 3 4
The shell script is /u/erc/teachux/example4.
```

If we pass more than nine command-line parameters, the extra parameters will be ignored:

```
$ example4 1 2 3 4 5 6 7 8 9 10 11 12 13
The first parameter was: 1
The parameters were: 1 2 3 4 5 6 7 8 9
The shell script command was: example4
```

If we pass fewer than nine command-line parameters, the extra variables have a null value:

```
$ example4 1 2 3 4
The first parameter was: 1
The parameters were: 1 2 3 4
The shell script command was: example4
```

How can you tell the number of command-line parameters? The special variable $# contains this value. Put the following command in a file named **example5:**

```
#! /bin/sh
#
# Example 5 from Chapter 13 of Teach Yourself UNIX.
#
# Number of command-line parameters.
#
echo The number of parameters was: $#
```

Again, mark this file executable with **chmod** and then run the following command:

```
$ example5 1 2 3 4
The number of parameters was: 4
```

NOTE The C shell doesn't like the *$#* variable for the number of command-line parameters, which we used in **example5.** Use *$#argv* instead.

There's also a special variable, *$**, which contains *all* the command-line parameters. The variable *$** can hold more than nine parameters. Create a file named **example6** and insert the following command:

```
#! /bin/sh
#
# Example 6 from Chapter 13 of Teach Yourself UNIX.
#
# All command-line parameters.
#
echo "All the parameters were $*"
```

Again, mark this file executable with **chmod** and then run the following command:

```
$ example6 1 2 3 4 5 six 7 8 9 10 oh boy
All the parameters were: 1 2 3 4 5 six 7 8 9 10 oh boy
```

We've summarized the shell variables in Table 13.1.

Table 13.1 *Sh Command-Line Parameters*

Variable	Meaning
$0	The name of the script, as passed on the command line.
$1	The first command-line parameter.
$2	The second command-line parameter.
$3..$9	The third through ninth command-line parameters.
$#	The number of command-line parameters.
$*	All command-line parameters (can have more than nine).

Loop-the-Loops

You can place commands in a loop to be executed again and again until some condition is met, using a **for** loop. A **for** loop loops *for* a given number of times and the syntax is:

```
for variable
        in list_of_values
do
        command1
        command1
        command2
...

        lastcommand
done
```

For example (pardon the pun), to list all of the files that start with *example* and followed by a single letter, we could use the following commands:

```
#! /bin/sh
#
# Example 7 from Chapter 13 of Teach Yourself UNIX.
#
# For loops
#
for filename
    in example?
do
    echo "Example file is $filename."
done
```

You can store these commands in a file named **example7** and mark the file as executable—as you've done with every example so far. When you run this example, you'll see the following:

```
$ example7
Example file is example1.
Example file is example2.
Example file is example3.
Example file is example4.
Example file is example5.
Example file is example6.
Example file is example7.
Example file is example8.
Example file is example9.
```

For this simple example we could have used the **ls** command:

```
$ ls example?
```

In real shell scripts you'll do much more than **ls** can, though.

In our previous example , we used the **in** statement to list the set of values to iterate over. If you omit the **in** statement, **sh** will loop over all of the parameters passed to the command line for the script. In other words, if you omit the **in** statement, the results are the same as if you used *$**, for example:

```
for filename
    in $*
do
    echo $filename
done
```

The above script forms a *very* primitive **ls** command.

The If Statement

In addition to the **for** loop, **sh** provides for tests to check if something is true. The **if** statement uses the following syntax:

if (*command*) then
    command1
    command2
    ...
    lastcommand
else
    command1
    command2
    ...
    lastcommand
fi

The **if** statement ends with a **fi** command. (*Fi* is *if* backwards, get it?) **Sh** executes the code between the **then** and **else** if the first command is true. **Sh** also executes the code between the **else** and the **fi** if the first command results on a nontrue, or false, value. The **else** part is optional, so you could have an **if** statement more like the following:

```
if (command) then
        command1
        command2
        ...
        lastcommand
fi
```

Most commands are considered to result in a true value, unless an error occurs in the command. For example, if we make up a nonexistent command, **frazzle,** then the following shell script will result in a not-true value for the **if** statement:

```
if (frazzle) then
    echo "frazzle is true."
else
    echo "frazzle is not true."
fi
```

If you run this as a script, you'll see the following output:

```
frazzle: not found
frazzle is not true.
```

First we get an error for the nonexistent command, **frazzle**, then we note that the result of **if (*frazzle*)** is not true.

The Test Command

To gain more flexibility with if statements, you can use the Bourne shell **test** command. This command returns true or false depending on the command-line parameters used with **test,** as we cover in Table 13.2.

Table 13.2 *The test Command with Files*

Command	Returns
test -r *filename*	True if you have permission to read *filename*.
test -s *filename*	True if *filename* has at least one character.
test -w *filename*	True if you have permission to write to *filename*.
test -x *filename*	True if you have permission to execute *filename*.

All of the above examples of **test** return false if the named file does not exist. There's also an *eq* command-line parameter to test for equality, as explained in Table 13.3.

Table 13.3 *Using test to Check for Equality*

Command	Returns
test *variable1* -eq *variable2*	Returns true if the variables are equal.
test *variable1* -ne *variable2*	Returns true if the variables are not equal.

We can combine loops, the **if** statement, and the **test** command to create our own version of the UNIX **ls** command. In the following file, named **myls**, we read in each filename passed as a command-line parameter and then use the **if** statement to test if the file is readable, writable, or executable. The results are printed out with the filename.

Enter the following commands into a file and name the file **myls**:

```
#! /bin/sh
#
# myls from Chapter 13 of Teach Yourself UNIX.
#
# Using test.
# This script acts something like ls.
for filename
do
    if (test -r $filename) then
        r="read"
    else
        r=""
    fi
    if (test -w $filename) then
        w="write"
    else
        w=""
    fi
    if (test -x $filename) then
        x="execute"
    else
        x=""
```

```
        fi
        echo "$filename has $r $w $x permissions."
    done
```

The magic here is that you have to call **myls** with the names of the files that you want it to test. The *for filename do* line just places each command-line parameter passed to **myls** in the variable **filename,** one at a time, as if we wrote *for filename in $* do.* This isn't very intuitive, but it forms an easy means to search through a directory.

Here's an example of **myls,** passing the files that begin with example and end with any single letter:

```
$ myls example?
example1          has read write execute permissions.
example2          has read write execute permissions.
example3          has read write execute permissions.
example4          has read write execute permissions.
example5          has read write execute permissions.
example6          has read write execute permissions.
```

Checking the same files with **ls** reveals that the **myls** script is accurate for the user's permissions:

```
$ ls -alx example?
-rwxr--r--    1 erc    users     378 Jul 29 18:38 example1
-rwxr--r--    1 erc    users     268 Jul 29 18:49 example2
-rwxr--r--    1 erc    users      39 Jul 29 19:05 example3
-rwxr--r--    1 erc    users      33 Jul 29 19:11 example4
-rwxr--r--    1 erc    users      76 Jul 29 21:25 example5
-rwxr--r--    1 erc    users     137 Jul 29 21:30 example6
```

A Shorthand for the Test Command

There's also a shorthand alternate form for the **test** command. This form looks kind of odd, but is used in a great many shell scripts, so you need to be aware of it. Basically, **test** is replaced with a bracket, *[.* The final form looks like:

```
if [ -r $filename ]
then
    command
```

```
else
  command
fi
```

Between the brackets, you place the parameters for **test**, in this case, *-r $filename*. The result is the same as the following code:

```
if (test -r $filename) then
  command
else
  command
fi
```

NOTE With the short-hand notation for the **test** command, you must put the **then** statement on the next line.

We can rewrite our original **myls** script using the shorthand method for the **test** command. We call this one **myls2** (an original name):

```
#! /bin/sh
#
# myls2 from Chapter 13 of Teach Yourself UNIX.
#
# Using the alternate form of test, [ ].
# This script acts something like ls.

for filename
do
    if [ -r $filename ]
    then
        r="read"
    else
        r=""
    fi

    if [ -w $filename ]
    then
        w="write"
```

```
    else
         w=""
    fi

    if [ -x $filename ]
    then
         x="execute"
    else
         x=""
    fi

    echo "$filename has $r $w $x permissions."
done
```

Testing for Success

You can test for the return status of a command using the **if** statement. Be careful, for UNIX commands return 0 (false) on success and nonzero (true) on failure.

Thus we can borrow the **cat** command from the above script and test it for successful completion with the following code:

```
if cat $filename >> $backupdir/report.backup
then
# failed....
else
# Success!
fi
```

Don't name this script **test**! That's the name of the **test** command.

NOTE

We put in the **cat** command to check an **if** statement. You also use the more convenient || operator:

```
cat $filename >> $backupdir/report.backup || exit 1
```

The || symbol means to execute the command on the right if the command on the left fails.

Returning an Exit Status

If your script detects an error, the convention is to echo a message to the user explaining the situation and then running **exit,** which stops your shell script. You can pass an error code, a number, with **exit** and here the convention is to return 1 on errors.

The case Statement

If you have really complex conditions, the **if** statement tends to break down. For more complex conditions, you probably want to use the odd-looking **case** statement, which uses the following syntax:

```
case word
in
value1)
    command1
    command2
    ...
    lastcommand
;;
    value2)
    command1
    command2
    ...
    lastcommand
;;
*)
    command1
    command2
    ...
    lastcommand
;;
esac
```

This looks confusing—and it is. The case statement tries to match the word following "case" with one of the values. If a value matches the word, then the commands after the value are executed, up to the double semi-colons (;;). If nothing matches, then the commands after the *) are executed, again, up to the double semi-colons (;;). The whole statement ends with *esac,* which is case backwards.

Here's an example that should clear things up:

```
#! /bin/sh
#
# Example 8 from Chapter 13 of Teach Yourself UNIX.
#
# Using case.
#
echo "Which do you like better, a dog, cat, or platypus?"
read animal

case $animal
in
    dog)
        echo "You like dogs best."
    ;;
    cat)
        echo "Cats ARE the best."
    ;;
    platypus)
        echo "What planet are you on?"
        echo "Why did you pick a platypus?"
    ;;
    *)
        echo "Can't you pick one of a dog, cat, or platypus?"
    ;;
esac
```

After getting grief from the Platypus Society because of our comments regarding platypi in the second edition of this book, we want to be very clear that we in no way advocate any sort of bad feelings, negative attitudes, or low self-esteem at the vertically challenged critters.

The shell script above presents a simple "choose an animal" game. If we name this script **example8,** here's what happens when we try entering different values for the animal:

```
$ example8
Which do you like better, a dog, cat or platypus?
```

```
cat
Cats ARE the best.

$ example8
Which do you like better, a dog, cat or platypus?
dog
You like dogs best.

$ example8
Which do you like better, a dog, cat or platypus?
platypus
What planet are you on?
Why did you pick a platypus?

$ example8
Which do you like better, a dog, cat or platypus?
aardvark
Can't you pick one of a dog, cat or platypus?
```

You can see that the *) choice at the end is very useful for providing the user of your shell script hints about bad input.

Input and Output

You can use the shell redirection and pipe operators, <, >, >>, and | in shell scripts as well as with commands you type in at the command line. For example, to copy the contents of all report files into a target backup directory, you could use the following script:

```
#! /bin/sh
#
# Example 9 from Chapter 13 of Teach Yourself UNIX.
#
# Input and output.

#
echo -n "Enter name of backup directory: "
read backupdir
```

```
for filename
    in report*
do
    cat $filename >> $backupdir/report.backup
done
```

When we run this, we must enter in the name of a subdirectory, such as 1995, to back up the data to.

```
$ example9
Enter name of backup directory: 1995
```

Then we check in the backup directory and find:

```
$ ls 1995
report.backup
```

The above script copies the contents of all files that start with *report* into a backup directory that you name. All the report files are concatenated together and appended to a file named **report.backup** in the backup directory.

Putting It Together

We can put all this together with the following example shell script. The purpose of the **mybackup** script is to back up all files with a similar extension, such as *.1995*, into a backup directory for the year in question, in this case also 1995. The script takes care of creating the directory and finding all of the files that match the criteria in the current directory. You can use this script as an example to help you create your own scripts. (Note also the heavy use of comments.)

```
#! /bin/sh
#
# mybackup from Chapter 13 of Teach Yourself UNIX.
#
# Backs up reports to directories.
#
# This script assumes that files are named with .year,
# as in .1994 or .1995. It will copy all such files
```

```
# to a backup directory, named for the year.
#
# Usage is:
#     mybackup year
#
# For example:
#     mybackup 1994
#        -- Copies all files ending in .1994 to 1994/
# Or,
#     mybackup 1995
#        -- Copies all files ending in .1995 to 1995/
# Check that we have the right number of arguments.
if [ $# -ne 1 ]
then
    echo "ERROR: Usage is:"
    echo "    mybackup year"
    echo "Where year is a year number, like 1995."
# Exit the script on errors.
    exit 1
fi
# Use variables for years, so you can update it easier.
year=$1
# Note how we combine a $year with "*." below:
for filename
    in *.$year
do
    echo "Copying $filename to $year."
    cp $filename $year
done
echo "Done copying files."
```

Once you get your scripts to run, the next step is to get them to run correctly.

Troubleshooting Shell Scripts

There's a lot that can go wrong with a shell script, but most problems are merely typos. The first step is always to examine the file with a text editor like **vi.** Correct any errors (always easier said than done.)

You may have a problem with individual commands in the shell script. In UNIX, each command should return a number to test for success. Commands return zero (0) for success and nonzero for failure. The shell variable *$?* holds the return value of the last command. You can check this variable to see if all went well. Here's a simple example, which you can place in a file named **example10:**

```
#!/bin/sh
make
echo "The result of the command was $?"
```

We call the command **make,** which is used in building, or making, programs. Since we haven't properly configured **make,** the command should fail. (See the next chapter for an introduction to **make** and explanation for configuring the necessary **Makefile.**)

If you run the **make** command in a subdirectory without a **Makefile,** this should generate an error:

```
$ example10
Make: No arguments or description file.  Stop.
The result of the command was 1
```

Note that **make** printed out its error message and that our shell script also detected the error from the *$?* variable, which held a nonzero value (1). You can use *$?* in your own shell scripts to make them more robust when errors occur.

Don't name a shell script **ls** if it calls the **ls** command, for example, as this could lead to an infinite loop. If the script is named **ls,** then it may try to re-execute itself, and on and on and on.

It's also a good idea to place shell scripts in a directory, along with any executable programs you develop. A common name for this directory is **bin** (most UNIX commands are in directories named **bin,** short for *binary*) as a subdirectory of your home directory. Keeping commands in such a directory gives you two things: (1) that a given file is a command (if the file is stored in the **bin** directory), and (2) that it's not a good idea to mess with the file (since it is presumably a *working* command). Make sure this **bin** directory is in your path.

Tracing the Execution of Shell Scripts

If you still have problems with your shell scripts, you might want to try tracing the scripts. You can use the tracing facility of **sh** to watch each command in a shell script execute. To do this, we pass the shell script in question as a command-line parameter to **sh**, along with the *-v* or *-x* option. The **sh -v** command prints out the lines in the shell script as they are read and then executes the script. The more useful **sh -x** command prints out each shell script command as it executes. This should help you narrow down any problems and determine which line holds the offending command.

Going back to our first example, you can trace the execution of the shell script file **example1,** using the -x command-line parameter to **sh**:

```
$ sh -x example2
+ echo You can also use quotation marks with echo.
You can also use quotation marks with echo.
+ echo -n first message
first message+ echo  second message
  second message
++ pwd
+ echo The current directory is /home/erc/books/teachux3.
The current directory is /home/erc/books/teachux3.
+ variable1=Yow, are we having fun yet?
+ echo The variable is Yow, are we having fun yet?.
The variable is Yow, are we having fun yet?.
++ date
+ datetoday=Thu Dec  8 23:14:54 CST 1994
+ echo The date is Thu Dec  8 23:14:54 CST 1994.
The date is Thu Dec  8 23:14:54 CST 1994.
```

Summary

In this chapter we've just provided the basics of shell programming. If you want to delve into this more deeply, there are many books available on shell programming. You can also try your UNIX manuals, as well as the **sh** or **csh** online manual pages.

Most shell scripts are written for the Bourne shell, as this is the most widely available shell. Other common shells include the C shell, **csh**, and the Korn shell, **ksh** (an enhanced Bourne shell).

Shell scripts are text files, which you can edit with **vi** or **emacs**. To run a shell script, though, you must mark it as executable with the **chmod** command:

```
$ chmod u+x filename
```

The **echo** command prints text to the screen. The **read** command reads in user input into a variable.

You can set a variable to a value using the following syntax:

variable=value

The **if**, **for**, and **case** statements allow you to control which commands in a shell script get executed. The **test** command enhances the usefulness of the **if** statement.

You can trace the execution of a shell script with the **sh -x** command.

C Programming Tools

This chapter covers:

- ▼ Basic programming with the C language
- ▼ File names and types
- ▼ Compiling with the **cc** command
- ▼ Building an executable program
- ▼ Troubleshooting **cc** errors
- ▼ Using **make** to build programs
- ▼ Using **imake** to build programs
- ▼ Debugging your applications
- ▼ Other C-based tools
- ▼ Checking for performance bottlenecks

277

Speaking the Language

Computer programmers write programs in special languages, languages oriented to the needs of computers and somewhat to the needs of programmers. UNIX supports more computer languages that you'd ever think possible, including Ada, APL, BASIC, COBOL, C, Modula-2, Eiffel, Objective-C, Fortran, Pascal, Perl, Tcl, and C++.

The most common programming languages used on UNIX, though, is the C programming language. C and UNIX share the same team of inventors at Bell Labs, and the evolution of both C and UNIX are tightly intermixed. One of the reasons UNIX is so popular, in fact, is that UNIX runs on most available computers. The reason for this is that most of UNIX is written in C and it's very easy to get the C language up and running on new computer platforms. (At the time, most operating systems were written in a language particular to a machine or architecture, such as assembly language for a particular processor. Because of this, the task of getting an operating system to work on different computer hardware proved extremely tough. Compared to this, UNIX, written mostly in the C language, was relatively easy to *port* to other platforms.) Once you get C up and running, it's a lot easier to get UNIX ported.

Because of the tight connection between C and UNIX, you'll find a plethora of C programming tools on most UNIX platforms. (We say *most* because the latest trend in UNIX is to strip out all nonessentials to make the smallest version of UNIX possible. Many new systems charge extra for software development tools, like the C compiler, so your system may not have a C compiler.)

This chapter covers the basics of UNIX tools for C programming.

C Programming

C programs—and in fact, most programs in general—usually start in plain old text files. (UNIX makes extensive use of simple text files, as you've seen throughout this book.) These text files are created with text editors like **vi** or **emacs.** Once created, C programs must be *compiled* with, naturally enough, a C compiler, which is a UNIX command. This C compiler converts the text file, which the programmer wrote, into object, or machine, code for your programming platform. Then, object modules (files of object code) are *linked* together to make an executable program, a brand new UNIX command. Once the process is successfully completed, you can execute this program like any other command you type at the command line. Being able to create your own commands is neat. However, by writing shell scripts, as we described in the last chapter, you can do essentially the same thing. In fact, to solve your particular task, there may already be a UNIX command ready and waiting. So, from the plethora of UNIX tools, you need to choose what is the appropriate tool for any given task.

Even if you never write C programs, though, it is important to know about the process of compiling and linking C programs because the vast majority of UNIX freeware comes in source-code format, which you must compile to be useful.

Free UNIX Programs

UNIX preceded the generous freeware traditions of DOS and Macintosh systems. There are thousands of free UNIX programs (some more useful than others). Unlike DOS and Macintosh systems, though, there are a wide variety of UNIX systems, so that you usually won't find an executable program for your system. Instead, you'll usually get C program source code, which you must somehow figure out how to compile and link into a program. (Some freeware packages make this easier than others. You can look in Appendix A for books that cover UNIX freeware in depth.)

To keep track of all these C text files, object modules, and executable programs, most C programmers use a few conventions for naming files. These conventions are especially useful when you're examining an unknown freeware program.

File Names and Types

Most C programming files use special suffix to tell what type of file they are. A few of the most common are listed in Table 14.1.

Table 14.1 C program file types.

File Suffix	DOS Equivalent	Meaning
.c	.c	C program.
.h	.h	C include file.
.o	obj	Object module (compiled from a .c file)
s	.asm	Assembly code.
.a	.lib	Library.
a.out	.exe	Executable (no one uses the **a.out** name).
.C	.cpp	C++ file (note uppercase *C)*.

.cc	**.cpp**	C++ file.
.cpp	**.cpp**	C++ or C preprocessor file.
.cxx	**.cpp**	C++ file.
.c++	**.cpp**	C++ file.
.f	**.for**	Fortran program.
.for	**.for**	Fortran program.

Most C programs are stored in one or more files that end with *.c*, like **inventory.c** and **checkin.c**, for example. When you compile a C file, the C compiler, **cc**, creates an object file, usually ending with *.o*. The linker (called *linkage editor* in UNIX parlance), **ld,** then links the .o files together to make an executable program. The default name for this program is **a.out**, although no one really uses **a.out** for their program names. Instead, programs end up with names like **ls, cp,** or **mv**. All of this is controlled by the **cc** command.

The Cc Command

The **cc** command executes the C compiler, which can compile and link C programs into executable commands. The myriad of options to **cc** controls exactly what the compiler does. We won't cover all of the many **cc** options; instead, we'll introduce the most important ones and let you read the online manual for **cc** for the rest. Use the following command to read the manual pages for **cc**:

```
$ man cc
```

We must warn you that you'll see a *lot* of output.

Getting a C Compiler

Many modern UNIX systems don't come with the tools you need to write your own programs. In that case, you're out of luck unless you can somehow acquire one. For many of us stuck in these circumstances (C compilers typically cost thousands on dollars on UNIX systems), there's a nice alternative. The Free Software Foundation, creators of **emacs** (see Chapter 12), also have created a neat-o *free* C compiler. (It also compiles C++ and Objective C, if you're interested.) This compiler, called **gcc** (for GNU C Compiler), is available over the Internet from **prep.ai.mit.edu** and a host of other sites (see Chapter 10 for more on the Internet). The GNU C compiler is available in source-code form, which leaves you with a chicken-and-egg problem: You need a C compiler, the **cc** program, to compile the source to this C compiler. So, you'll need to get both the binary version for your hardware platform as well as the source code.

Writing a Small C Program

To test your C compiler (and ensure that you have one), you can enter the following program:

```
#include  <stdio.h>
main()
{
    /* main */
    /* This is a comment */
    printf("This is the famous hello world program.");
    printf("It prints out a message:");
    printf("Hello world!");
    /* main */
}
```

Figure 14.1 *A small C program*

The program is short, and you can probably type it in using **vi** or **emacs** or another text editor, in under one minute. Type in each line one at a time, exactly as presented above. If you name the file **hello.c**, then you can use the following **vi** command to start editing the file:

```
$ vi hello.c
```

Then, in **vi** (or **emacs**), enter in the program listed previously.

Always name C program files with a **.c** extension. This isn't required, but following conventions like this makes UNIX easier to use.)

N O T E

Save the file and quit **vi** (or **emacs**). Next, we'll compile the program.

After you type in this short program, you can follow through the following simple steps to create a working executable program from this C file.

The program you typed in was simply a text file. There's nothing in it to make it an executable command. C programs aren't like shell scripts (covered in the last chapter), so we can't simply mark the text file with the execute permission to make it a working program (would that it were this easy). Instead, we need to compile and link the program. Both steps are accomplished by the following **cc** command:

```
$ cc -o hello hello.c
```

The above command runs the C compiler, **cc**. The *-o* option tells **cc** to build a program named *hello*. The **hello.c** part of the command tells **cc** to compile the file named **hello.c**. The **cc** command both compiled and linked the program.

Now, you should have an executable program named **hello**. You can execute this program by typing **hello** at the command line. When you do, you'll see the following output:

```
$ hello

This is the famous hello world program.
It prints out a message:
Hello world!
```

Now you're a bona-fide C programmer and ready for a new lucrative career.

Compiling the Long Way

The **cc** command first compiled the program into an object module, then linked the object module to create an executable program, the file named **hello.** This is very important if you have more than one file to compile together into your program. Most C programs require a number of *.c* files, all of which must be compiled and then linked together to form one program. One of the main reasons for separating C programs into multiple files is simply sanity: reading a one-megabyte program in one file is ludicrous. And yes, C programs get to this size and even much bigger than one megabyte.

To use the long method of compiling and linking, we split the tasks into two steps. First, you compile all of the *.c* files you require. Then, you link the resulting *.o* files (we'll get into this below) into your executable program. Since we have a very small C program typed in already (you did type it in, didn't you?), we'll start with that.

To compile **hello.c** into an object module, a *.o* file, use the following command:

```
cc -c hello.c
```

If successful, you should see a file named **hello.o** in your directory. The *.o* file is called the object file (or object module). Using the **ls -l** command, you should see this file:

```
$ ls -l hello*
-rw-r-r—   1 erc   users   235 Jul 28 21:11 hello.c
-rw-r-r—   1 erc   users   646 Jul 28 21:11 hello.o
```

The next step is to link the object files (usually there's more than one) into an executable file. To do this, we again use the *-o* option to **cc,** but this time we pass a *.o* file at the end of the command line, rather than the *.c* file we used above:

```
cc -o hello hello.o
```

This command links together the file **hello.o** into the executable program **hello.** You can place more than one object file name on the command line, as in the following example:

```
cc -o hello hello1.o hello2.o hello3.o
```

We're not trying to torture you. You need to know how **cc** operates to compile a large amount of the UNIX freeware you'll find.

Working with Cc

In normal operation, the **cc** command executes a number of other commands under the hood. One such command is **cpp.** The **cpp** command is the C preprocessor. This reads a C program file, a *.c* file, and expands any *#* directives. In the short program listed previously, the *#include* directive means to include the file **stdio.h.** That is, **cpp** reads in **stdio.h** and inserts the contents right at the *#include* directive. Most C programs use one or more include files.

These include files are normally stored in **/usr/include**. If you use the angle brackets, (<) and (>), around an include file name, like **<stdio.h>,** this means that **cpp** looks for a file named **stdio.h** in the standard places, of which **/usr/include** is the default (the *-I* command-line parameter can add more directories to the include file search path, as you'll see later in this chapter). You can also use quotation marks (") around the file name.

All C programs are built around the section labeled *main()*. The *main()* section (called a *function* in C parlance) is executed when the program starts. Our *main()* function has three C program statements, all of which call the *printf()* function, which prints out the text between the quotation marks to your screen. As you can tell, this is not a sophisticated program.

Each \n character passed to *printf()* in our example source code means that a *newline* character is printed. This starts a new line. If you're used to a DOS machine, you'll note that UNIX uses a newline character where DOS uses a carriage return and then a newline. The backslash, \, is used as a special character in C programs. Usually, a backslash is combined with another character to make a nonprintable character, such as \n for a newline or \a for a bell.

Does this sound familiar? It should, as we pointed it out when you first learned about the C shell, which is closely patterned after the C programming language.

N O T E

Troubleshooting Cc Errors

If you entered the example program exactly as we wrote it, you should get no error messages from **cc**. If you made a typo perhaps and the **cc** command found any errors, though, then you'll see some cryptic error messages. Many of the error messages won't make sense. However, the best part of these error messages is that each message tells you the line number in which **cc** detected an error. (Note that this line number isn't always accurate—the error may be a number of lines above, but **cc** does give you a starting place from which to look for problems.)

For example, if we add the word "blech" into our sample program, this will generate an error. Just type in *blech* on a line of its own and run **cc** again:

```
$ cc -c hello.c
```

You'll see something like the following output:

```
"hello.c", line 10: blech undefined
"hello.c", line 10: syntax error
"hello.c", line 10: illegal character: 134 (octal)
"hello.c", line 10: cannot recover from earlier errors:
goodbye!
```

If you get errors like this, go back into **vi** or **emacs** and correct the problem. Make sure your program looks like the example program. You have a more serious problem, though, if you get an error message like the one below:

```
cc: Command not found.
```

What this means is that your system cannot find the C compiler. All is not lost, though. You may have a system that provides a different name for the **cc** command. For example, a commercial compiler vendor like LPI may name their C compiler **lpicc**. If you use the free C compiler from the GNU project, then the **cc** command may be named **gcc** instead.

The worst problem is if your system does not come with a C compiler at all. In days past, *every* UNIX system came with a C compiler. But in recent years many vendors omit the C compiler to cut costs and to create a version of UNIX that doesn't use up all your hard disk space. If you don't have a C compiler, you won't be able to complete the examples, but you can still follow through the text.

Using The Cc Command and Command-Line Parameters

The **cc** command uses a number of command-line parameters to tell it what to do and to allow you to fine-tune the process of building executable programs from C language text files. Table 14.2 lists commonly used **cc** command-line parameters.

Table 14.2 Cc command-line parameters

Parameter	Meaning
-I*directory*	Search the given *directory* for include files, as well as **/usr/include**
-c *filename.c*	Compile the file *filename.c* and build the object module *filename.o*. Do not create an executable command.
-o *progname*	Name the executable program *progname*. The default name is **a.out**.
-g	Compile with debugging information.
-O	Optimize the program for best performance.

Note that you usually cannot mix the *-g* (include debugging information) with -O (optimize) options. (The GNU C compiler allows this, but most other C compilers don't.)

Using Make

Any large programming project, which includes just about any commercial software package, involves a large number of C program files with complex rules for putting the whole thing together into executable programs. Because C programmers tend not to be skilled typists, you'd expect there to be some shorthand for controlling this build process for larger software projects. One of the basic UNIX tools for this is called **make**.

Make is a command that helps build or "make" UNIX programs from the C language text files. **Make** proves itself especially useful when you make small, incremental changes to just a few of the various files that make up your program.

Make uses a set of rules, written by you, to try to do the minimal amount of work necessary to rebuild the program, based on what you changed. These rules are most effective for large programs made up of many files.

The rules used by **make** are stored in a special file named **Makefile**. You keep a **Makefile** in each directory where you develop C programs. This **Makefile** requires a rigid syntax, and **make** complains about the slightest variances. In fact, according to UNIX legend, the creator of **make** never knew his tool would catch on so fast, or he would have invented a looser, easier syntax.

The basic **make** syntax is deceptively simple. (There's a lot of newer enhanced versions of **make** floating around. We'll just cover the basics in this chapter.)

You start out with a so-called *target*. The target is something that you want to build, such as our program **hello** from the previous example.

To create a target in the **Makefile**, begin with a new line, you name the target—what you want to build—then place a colon (:), a tab, and then a list of the files that the target depends on. Starting on the next line, begin with a tab, then place the UNIX command used to build the target. You can have multiple commands, each of which should go on its own line, and every command line must start with a tab.

In the abstract, the **Makefile** rules look like the following:

what_to_build: what_it_depends_on
    command1_to_build_it
    command2_to_build_it
    command3_to_build_it
    ...
    lastcommand_to_build_it

In the abstract, this looks confusing. Here's a more concrete example, using the **hello** program we provided above.

The target we want to build is the **hello** program.

The **hello** program, the target, depends on the object module **hello.o**. Once we have the object module **hello.o,** then the command to create the **hello** program is **cc -o hello hello.o:**

```
hello:    hello.o
    cc -o hello hello.o
```

The above **make** rule states that if **hello.o** has a more recent date, then execute the **cc** command to build the **hello** program from the object module **hello.o.**

This is just part of the task, as we still have to compile **hello.c** to create the object module **hello.o.** That is, the file **hello.o** is said to depend on the file **hello.c.** You build **hello.o** from **hello.c.** To do this, we use another **make** rule.

This time, the object module **hello.o** depends on the text file **hello.c.** The command to build the object module is **cc -c hello.c:**

```
hello.o:  hello.c
    cc -c hello.c
```

Thus, with this **make** rule, if you edit **hello.c,** you'll give the file **hello.c** a more recent date/time than the object module **hello.o.** This causes **make** to trigger the **cc** command to compile **hello.c** into **hello.o.**

You've discovered the secret to **make**'s rules. Everything depends on the date/time of the files, a very simple—but clever—idea. The idea is that if the text of the program *.c* file is modified, then you better rebuild the program with **cc.** Because most users are impatient, if the **.c** file hasn't been changed, there's simply no reason (at least in our example) to rebuild the program with **cc.**

A Make Example

To try out **make**, enter in the following text into a file named **Makefile:**

```
#
# Test Makefile
#
# The program hello depends on hello.o.
hello:    hello.o
```

```
    cc -o hello hello.o

# The object module hello.o depends on hello.c.
hello.o:  hello.c
    cc -c hello.c
```

The above **Makefile** should be in the same directory as your sample C program file, **hello.c.** To use **make,** we need to tell it what to make, that is, what target we want to build. In our case we want **make** to build the program **hello**. The following command will build this program:

```
$ make hello
        cc -c hello.c
        cc -o hello hello.o
```

We should now have the **hello** program ready to run. If we try **make** again, it—being very lazy—tells us that there's no new work to do:

```
$ make hello
`hello' is up to date.
```

Why? Because the **hello** program was built and nothing has changed. Now, edit the **hello.c** file again, or use the **touch** command to bump up the date/time associated with the file:

```
    $ touch hello.c
```

When you call **make** again, it knows it now needs to rebuild the **hello** program, because presumably the **hello.c** file has changed since the last time **hello.c** was compiled with cc. But, since **touch** only updates the date/time associated with the file and doesn't change the internals of the file in any way, we've just fooled **make**. **Make** doesn't bother checking if a file is different—it merely checks the time the file was last written to, blindly assuming that no one would ever write to a file without modifying its contents. Normally, though, you don't want to fool **make,** but use its simple rules to make your life easier.

Make supports a number of useful command-line parameters, as listed in Table 14.3.

Table 14.3 *Make command-line parameters*

Parameter	Meaning
-f filename	Uses the named *filename* instead of **Makefile** for the rules.
-n	No execute mode—only prints out the commands, but doesn't execute them.
-s	Silent mode—doesn't print out any command that **make** executes.

Imake

In addition to **make**, there's a relatively new program called **imake**, which is used to generate **Makefiles** on a variety of systems. **Imake** uses an **Imakefile** for its rules. These rules then help generate a **Makefile.** This **Makefile** is then used by **make** to build the program. Sound like circular reasoning? You bet it does. The main reason **imake** exists is because of radically different system configurations, especially where the X Window System is concerned.

You'll find **imake** especially popular with programs for the X Window System (see Chapter 7 on the X Window System). The problem with X is that there are so many options, as every UNIX platform is configured slightly differently. There's simply no way you could write a portable **Makefile** that could work on all such platforms. Thus, **imake** uses an **Imakefile**, along with configuration files that are local to your system. Together, the **Imakefile** and the local configuration files generate a **Makefile** that should work just dandy on your system.

If you need to compile programs for the X Window System and you see an **Imakefile**, here's what you should do. First, run the **xmkmf** shell script. This script is merely a simple front-end to **imake:**

```
$ xmkmf
mv Makefile Makefile.bak
imake -DUseInstalled -I/usr/lib/X11/config
```

The above commands should make a backup of any **Makefile** you have (to **Makefile.bak**) and then create a new **Makefile** based on the commands in an **Imakefile.**

Imake isn't easy to grasp, so if you have problems with **imake,** you should check with your system administrator, or look up **imake** in a book on the X Window System (such as *Using X*, MIS: Press, 1992; see Appendix A for a list of books on using the X Window System).

Debugging

When you write programs with the C language (or with any programming language for that matter), the programs often won't work the first time. Many times this is just a typo in the program's text files. But sometimes you find very subtle problems. To aid in tracking down these problems, you can use a UNIX debugger. The debugger is supposed to help you remove the problems—bugs—from your programs.

To work with a debugger, you must first compile your programs with the *-g* command-line parameter to **cc.** This *-g* option places special debugging information into your program, and the debugger, naturally enough, uses this information.

The most common debugger programs include **sdb, adb, dbx, xdb,** and **gdb.** Each of these debuggers uses its own cryptic syntax, so be sure to check with your system's documentation and the online manual pages.

You may also have some graphical programs that act as front-ends to these debuggers, such as **xdbx, dbxtool,** the SunPro debugger (on Sun workstations), or **edge** (on Silicon Graphics workstations). Hewlett-Packard's Softbench environment also comes with a graphical debugger.

In addition to debuggers, UNIX comes with other tools for aiding the process of developing C programs.

Other C Tools

The program called **lint** flags any so-called "lint" it discovers in your programs. **Lint** complains about places in your C programs where you bend and warp the rules. Even if your code is legal C, you may still have problems, and **lint** tries to warn about potential problems.

SCCS (Source Code Control System) and RCS (Revision Control System) aim at keeping older versions of your C program text files. As you can tell, it's easy to make a mistake in a text editor like **vi** or **emacs**, or accidentally call **rm** to remove too many files. What happens if you make such a blunder and you destroy a file that's key to your company's business? You lose. As we mentioned in Chapter 2, there's not a lot you can do if you accidentally delete a file in UNIX.

To help avoid this problem, many companies use one of these two file controls systems (SCCS or RCS). Both work much the same. What you do is check in a key file. If you want to edit the file, you must check it out, and only one person at a time can check a file out. When you're done making changes, you check the file back in. If you made a mistake, you can check out an older version of the file. Both SCCS and RCS keep records of *every* version of the file that you've checked in. To save on disk space, both packages use what are called *delta* files. That is, for any version of a file, SCCS and RCS only have to keep the changes or differences from the last version. (SCCS and RCS act slightly differently in this regard, but to users, the result is the same.)

Checking for Performance Bottlenecks

UNIX comes with a number of tools to check your programs for performance bottlenecks. Two of the most common of these tools are **prof** (short for profiling) and **gprof. Gprof** is an extended form of **prof** that includes more detailed output.

These profiling tools help you find out what parts of your programs take the most time to execute. To use these tools, you must compile with **cc** using the *-p* option **(prof)** or *-pg* option **(grof)**. Note that many systems have only one (or none) of these tools.

Once you've compiled with *-p* or *-pg*, then you run your program like normal. You'll notice the program runs slower than you're used to because of the way **prof** and **grof** monitor the time it takes your program to perform tasks also takes time.

When you're done running your program, use **prof** or **gprof** to compile the data from the run of the program. The end result is a chart showing every function that the program executed, along with the average time each call to a given function took to complete, the total cumulative time spent in that function, and the total number of times the function was called. **Gprof** shows more information.

Summary

In this chapter we covered the basics of compiling C source code files into working executable programs. Whether you intend to write your own C programs or simply use the thousands of free UNIX programs, you'll need to know the basics of how to compile and link C programs with the C compiler, **cc**.

Not all systems come with a C compiler, but if you have one, you can compile and link a program, named **hello.c** for example, with the following command:

```
$ cc -o hello hello.c
```

The C source code files are simply text files created with a text editor like **vi** or **emacs**, which you then turn into executable programs through the magic of **cc.**

The program **make** exists to make your life easier and to build programs using only the minimum number of necessary steps. **Make** gets its knowledge from a set of rules written by you and stored in a file name **Makefile**.

If you work with X Window programs, you'll also need to worry about a cryptic beast called **imake**. **Imake** uses the rules in an **Imakefile** to generate a **Makefile** configured properly for your system. **Imake** then runs **make** to build the program using the newly created **Makefile.**

System Administration 101

This chapter covers:

- ▼ System administration
- ▼ Setting up a new system
- ▼ Logging in as the root user
- ▼ Setting the system name
- ▼ System states
- ▼ Backing up your data
- ▼ Using the **tar** command
- ▼ Shutting down a UNIX system

Heeding Your Own Advice

This book has been geared toward the true beginning UNIX user. As such, we've avoided any advanced topics; when in doubt, we have always advised you to seek the advice of your system administrator.

Not everyone is going to have a system administrator available 24 hours a day. In some situations system administration happens between other tasks. If you're a workstation user, you're both the end user and the system administrator in many cases—at least the system administrator assigned to your personal workstation. Quite honestly, there are some simple acts that don't necessarily require the intervention of a system administrator. If you're a new UNIX user with a new UNIX system, you certainly won't have a system administrator handy; your wits and your documentation are your only guides. And while we can't speak to the condition of your wits, we can speak to the condition of UNIX documentation—it makes books like these necessary.

In this chapter we cover some simple, basic system administration to be performed with a new UNIX machine. If you've not read the preceding chapters and are not at ease performing the basic tasks we have enumerated, we advise you to go back and start reading this book from scratch; you should know the basics of shell commands, text editor, and command lines before embarking with this chapter. The commands we cover here are available only to system administrators, not to every user. And they may not even be available to you as a system administrator. One of the great strengths of the UNIX operating system is that it's not controlled by one large corporation; customization among vendors is rampant. And many UNIX vendors have been known to greatly customize systems, especially with such simple tasks as basic, new-user installation. While the procedures described here should be available on your system, we can't guarantee their availability.

What we describe here are not heavily involved tasks, requiring a ton of time on your part. But they will help you to run your UNIX system more smoothly from Day One. And they'll give you a taste of power, should you want to continue down the path to UNIX gurudom by becoming a full-fledged system administrator.

Setting Up Your New System

In this book we've assumed that you began computing on an existing UNIX system. However, there are cases when you'll need to set up your system from scratch. For instance, you may have the pleasure of setting up a standalone UNIX workstation for your own use. Or you may have a PC plunked on your desk, with some version of UNIX waiting for your personal configuration.

Unfortunately, there's no one way to install UNIX software—either the actual operating system or any applications. The best-case scenario is the purchase of a system with UNIX preinstalled. But in the case of a new installation, all we can really tell you is to follow the directions and keep a phone line open for support.

After you've installed your particular brand of UNIX, it's time to perform some simple housekeeping details—and these form the reason for this chapter's existence. Generally, after installation you must shut your computer off and then start it again, allowing the operating system to load. When UNIX loads itself into your computer, it runs through a series of processes and system checks that may or may not mean anything to you as you see the verification messages roll by. Unless something went horrendously wrong with your installation, you'll eventually see a login prompt something like this:

```
Login: root
Password:
#
```

During the course of your system installation, you probably will have been asked to supply a password to the root user account. You'll begin your first UNIX session by entering *root* as the login name and then hitting the **Enter** key after the password. This logs you on as the root user. (Again, this may be different depending on your particular system configuration.)

Why log in as *root*, and not with the login names and passwords we covered in Chapter 1? Here, we are working under the assumption that your new system doesn't have any login names installed yet. So the login name will be utterly meaningless to the new system.

The *root user*, or *superuser*, has access to all parts of the UNIX operating system. There are no files that cannot be read by the superuser, there are no portions of the file system inaccessible to the superuser, and there are no UNIX commands unavailable to the superuser. The superuser controls all aspects of UNIX system usage and configuration—which is why you're logging in as the root user.

As superuser, you're entitled to your own, special prompt: #.

Because you have no restrictions, as the root user you can seriously damage your UNIX system. A simple accident can cause you a lot of grief. So be very careful when you are logged in as the root user.

WARNING

Setting the Settings

Your UNIX machine at this point is like a tabula rosa: It's up to you to educate it, by telling it who it is, what time it is, and what day it is.

First off, you must name your system in two ways: with a *system name* and a *communications node name*. Generally the system name is set to whatever version of UNIX you happen to be running, while the communications node name is a unique name used to identify your system if you communicate with other computer systems. You can set both at the same time using the same command, **setuname**, with two options signifying the system name (*-s*) and node name (*-n*):

```
# setuname -n attila -s SVR4
```

Then you must set the time and date. This is done by using the **date** command, which we covered earlier. You must be exact with this command. The syntax looks like the following:

```
# date mmddttttyy
```

where *mm* refers to month, *dd* refers to date, *tttt* refers to time (using 24-hour military notation, of course), and *yy* refers to year. To set a system with a date of August 12, 1992, at 7:26 P.M., use the following:

```
# date 0812192692
Wed Aug 12 19:26:00 CDT 1992
```

Some PC Unices automatically set the clock from the PC configuration information.

The State I'm In

Most UNIX systems are designed to boot into multiuser state, where other users can login the system and the entire file system is accessible. (The term for making the file system accessible in UNIXdom is *mounting* the file system.) However, this is not always true (Apple's AU/X, for instance, boots in the administrative state, belying its orientation as a single-user system). We've listed the basic system states in Table 15.1. Most of the time you'll want to work in the multiuser state. (There are additional, advanced system states also available; we've listed the ones you're most likely to use.)

WARNING

Not all versions of UNIX support states.

Table 15.1 *System states*

State	Meaning
0	*Shutdown.* The machine is off.
1	*Administrative.* The full file system is available to the superuser, but other users cannot login. Background tasks can run.
2	*Multiuser.* Other users can login the system and access the file system.
3	*RFS.* If you're mounting file systems from other machines, this state connects your machine to the RFS network and makes it accessible to all users. This state is also multiuser.
S	*Single-user.* The file system is unavailable, other users cannot login, and only the root file system is available.

Depending on your needs, you may want to use the system in a different state. As we said earlier, it's most desirable to work in the multiuser state. At some point in the login sequence, you'll be told what state you're in. If you're in the administrative state, you'll see something like:

```
# init 1
```

Before you change to a single-user state, you probably want to warn any other users logged in to the system. In fact, it's a good idea to give users a chance to log off before you unceremoniously cut them off from their work.

To change to multiuser state, type the following:

```
# init 2
```

Backing Up Your System

We advise that you back up your work often—as often as possible. There isn't a computer user anywhere who hasn't accidentally erased an important file at one time or another. In many ways, the regular and systematic backup of files is the most important task a system administrator fulfills—a task that you should perform regularly if you lack a system administrator.

What kind of files should you back up regularly? Essentially, your system contains three types of files: system files, configured system files, and data files. System files rarely change and can be reinstalled from the original floppies or tape (though, admittedly, not without a little bit of sweat), so you don't need to back up these files often. System files that you've configured and data files, on the other hand, are key to the success of your enterprise. Data files form the core of your daily computer work. If you lose 20 files that took all day to create, you have essentially wasted the labor of a full day. And who wants to do that?

Luckily, UNIX—the newer versions, at least—features a powerful, yet easy-to-use command for archiving and storage: **tar**.

Tar stands for *ta*pe *ar*chiver, and it started life as a tool for backing up files to a tape drive—still the predominant back-up storage device on UNIX systems. Today **tar** can be used to back up to any storage device—tape drive, floppy drive—supported on your UNIX system. Specifics may differ from system to system; our examples will cover backups to both tape drives and floppy disks. (We strongly advise you to check your system documentation or **tar**'s online-manual page before embarking on a backup.)

A glimpse of **tar** in action: Let's say you wanted to back up all the files in an important directory—**/usr/erc/data/reports**—to make sure that you don't lose any of your work to date. Before using **tar**, make sure that your current directory is **/usr/erc/data/reports**:

```
# cd /usr/erc/data/reports
```

Then back up the files in the directory, using the following:

```
# tar -cvf archive.fil .
```

In this command we have run **tar** with the following:

▼   *c*, which *creates* the archive;

▼   *v*, which tells tar to be *verbose*—that is, report to us periodically about its progress;

▼   *f*, which specifies the *file* name of the archive;

▼   ., which designates that all of the contents of the current directory should be copied.

If, for example, we wanted to back up only those files ending with *c*, we could invoke a wildcard:

```
# tar -cvf archive.fil *c
```

The above command stores all of the files ending with *c* into the **tar** archive file named **archive.fil**. In this case **archive.fil** is just a standard UNIX file. Since UNIX treats hardware devices as files (remember that abstraction), we can back up our files to a tape, by replacing the file name **archive.fil** with the name for the tape device, usually **/dev/tape**. (Refer to your system administrator or your system documentation for the device name of your tape drive—assuming of course, you have a tape drive.) The following command line backs up all of the files ending with *.txt* to the device **/dev/tape**, which is normally configured as a tape drive:

```
# tar -cvf /dev/tape *.txt
```

Note that you should insert a blank tape into the tape drive *before* issuing the previous **tar** command. (Some tape drives spin the tape heads for a short while after you insert a new tape. Make sure this process is also complete before executing the **tar** command.) In addition to tapes, there are other backup devices. On Sun SPARCstations, for example, the internal floppy drive is mounted under the directory **/pcfs**, for PC file system. You can use **tar** if you'd like, or simply use **cp** to copy files to the **/pcfs** directory.

To restore files from the archive, use **tar** as in the following:

```
# tar -xvf archive.fil
```

The previous command extracts (the *-x* option) the files stored in a **tar** archive file and places these extracted files into your current directory. The *-f* option is followed by the name of the **tar** archive file, in this case **archive.fil**. And, the *-v* option again sets **tar** into verbose mode, providing important status information. To restore from the tape drive named **/dev/tape**, use the following command:

```
# tar -xvf /dev/tape
```

The more important options associated with the **tar** command are listed in Table 15.2.

Table 15.2 *Tar options*

Command	Result
c	Creates an new archive.
o	Overwrites file permissions associated with the files in the archive.
t	Provides a listing of the contents of archive.
u	Updates files in the archive. If the files do not need updating, no action is taken.
w	Asks for confirmation before backing up an individual file.
x	Extracts files from the backup device.

Tar is not the only backup tool available in UNIX, though we find it the most widely used. Another backup tool is **cpio**, which has been called the most difficult-to-use UNIX command by many astute observers and users. If you're interested in **cpio**, check your system documentation or the **cpio** online-manual page.

Shutting Down Your System

Because it takes so long to boot a UNIX machine, most are left on 24 hours a day, seven days a week, with only the monitors or terminals turned off.

However, there are times when you want to turn off your system. You may need to move it; if you're moving it across the office or across the country, you should turn it off or be prepared to use a *very* long extension cord. You may need to attach a new peripheral or remove an existing one. Your office may be getting too hot for computer use; generally, it's good to shut off computer systems when the temperature in a room rises over 85 degrees. Or you may be leaving for vacation and don't want to waste electricity running your UNIX workstation when no one will be using it.

Earlier we mentioned the shutdown state of 0. A better way of shutting down your system is through the command **shutdown**. If used correctly, **shutdown** will shutdown the system and alert other users that the system is shutting down:

```
# shutdown
```

If for some reason you get an error message when you run these commands, you may want to try specifying the full pathname of the commands. On older (pre-SVR4) systems, the command line is:

```
# /etc/shutdown
```

On SVR4 systems the command line is:

```
# /usr/etc/shutdown
```

After using the **shutdown** command, the system will ask you if you want to send a message before shutting down, and how long to wait before shutting down. It will also confirm that you really want to shut the system down. If you're working by yourself on a UNIX workstation, you don't need to send a message, and you can shutdown immediately. If you're working on a multiuser system and want to give the users some warning, you can send a message to them, and you can give them 60 seconds before shutting down (60 seconds is the default; any other period would be specified by you).

The **shutdown** command does differ somewhat from system to system. If your system doesn't work in this exact fashion, check your online-manual pages or documentation.

With System V UNIX, you can speed up the **shutdown** command using the following command-line parameters:

```
# shutdown -g0 -y
```

The *-g* option specifies the grace period before shutting down, in seconds. The zero (0) means that we don't want to wait at all. The *-y* answers yes to the question do we really want to shut down. Thus you won't be prompted to confirm the shutdown operation.

After **shutdown** runs, it displays something like the following:

```
Safe to Power Off
     -or-
Press Any Key to Reboot
```

or

```
Reboot the computer now.
```

Your system may contain a shell program, **sysadmsh**, that combines many of the operations described here. (SCO UNIX, for example, allows system administration via **sysadmsh**.) This menu-based program is designed to make the process of system administration less cryptic and easier. If you feel more comfortably with pull-down menus and an organized hierarchy, check if your system features **sysadmsh** or something similar. Another common name for **sysadmsh** is simply **sysadm**.

Many newer UNIX systems, that is, System V Release 4.2, that feature a graphical interface will also feature a Shutdown procedure attached to an icon. In these cases shutting down the system is a matter of closing all of your open files and then double-clicking on the shutdown icon, which is shown in Figure 15.1.

Figure 15.1 *The Shutdown icon from UnixWare.*

You'll be asked if you want to save the current configuration of the system (that is, if you want any windows that are open to be open when you login again) and whether you really, truly want to shut down the system.

Summary

Most system administration tasks are performed as the root user, also called the superuser. Superusers have the privilege to do anything on the system: read any file, write to any directory, and delete anything. This last part means it's easy to shoot yourself in the foot as the root user. Common superuser commands include:

- ▼ **date**, which sets the system date and time
- ▼ **init**, which changes the system's run state, for example, to single-user state
- ▼ **tar**, which acts as a tape archiver
- ▼ **shutdown**, which, naturally enough, shuts down the system

All users can run **date** and **tar**, but only the superuser can use **date** to change the system's time. The **init** and **shutdown** commands are restricted to the root user.

The root user is also responsible for adding new users to the system and installing the UNIX operating system in the first place. Unfortunately, the bane of many system administrators is that every brand of UNIX uses different methods for installation and adding new users, among other differences.

This chapter provides only the barest basics of system administration. But, after becoming more familiar with UNIX, your system's manuals should describe this area as seen by your UNIX vendor.

Additional and Advanced UNIX Tools

In this chapter we cover:

Moving Up to Advanced Levels

As we've repeated throughout this book, perhaps the greatest strength of the UNIX operating system is that it's a collection of small, useful tools that can be combined to form even more powerful tools. The majority of our discussion, therefore, has centered around tools that are applicable to your needs and skill level as a beginning UNIX user.

You won't be a beginner forever, however. In this chapter we'll describe what we feel are advanced tools. While we don't expect you to rush out and start programming with **awk** tomorrow, there's a pretty good chance you may want to look at it in the future. This chapter deviates from the rest of the book in that it's not strictly based on tutorials (though we will be using some of the commands and tools in tutorial form) and will instead merely describe the advanced tools, alerting you to their existence. When you're ready to tackle the use of these tools, we suggest checking out some of the more advanced books described in Appendix A.

Awk

Developed by three Bell Labs researchers (Alfred *A*ho, Peter *W*einberger, and Brian *K*ernighan—hence the acronym *awk*), **awk** is technically a programming language (with some strong similarities to the C programming language, discussed in Chapter 13), but used much in the same manner as other UNIX tools. Hence its inclusion in this chapter.

Awk's primary value is in the manipulation of structured text files, where information is stored in columnar form and information is separated by consistent characters (such as tabs, spaces, or other characters). **Awk** takes these structured files and manipulates them through editing, sorting, and searching.

Let's think back to Chapter 3, when we discussed UNIX tools that allowed you to edit and manipulate similarly structured files. We used a data file named **workers**; we'll use it again here:

```
Eric      286    555-6674    erc       8
Geisha    280    555-4221    geisha    10
Kevin     279    555-1112    kevin     2
Tom       284    555-2121    spike     12
```

Let's sink into the trap of abstraction for a minute and compare our example file output to a two-dimensional graph. Each row across is called a *record*, which in turn is made up of vertical *fields* or *columns*, almost like a database. **Awk** allows us to manipulate the data in the file by either row or column, which makes it more powerful and useful than the tools described in Chapter 3.

Using the **awk** command is not a complicated process. The structure of the **awk** command looks like this:

```
$ awk [option] 'pattern action'
```

(The only options available with **awk** are *-F*, which allows you to specify a field separator other than the default of white space, and *-f*, which allows you to specify a filename full of **awk** commands instead of placing a complex pattern and action on the UNIX command line.) Here we should define our terms. A *pattern* can be an ASCII string, a numeral, a combination of numerals, or a wildcard, while *action* refers to an instruction we provide. So, essentially, **awk** works by having us tell it to search for a particular pattern; when it has found that pattern, then **awk** is to do something with it, such as printing the pattern to another file.

The simplest **awk** program merely prints out all lines in the file:

```
$ awk ' print ' workers
Eric     286     555-6674      erc      8
Geisha   280     555-4221      geisha   10
Kevin    279     555-1112      kevin    2
Tom      284     555-2121      spike    12
```

Continuing our previous example, let's say we wanted to pull all records that began with the string *Geisha*. We'd use the following:

```
$ awk '$1 ~ /Geisha/ print $0' workers
```

Here's what the command means, part by part:

- ▼ *$1*: Tells **awk** to use the first column for the basis of further action. **Awk** will perform some action on a file based on either records or fields; a number beginning with a $ tells **awk** to work on a specific field. In this case *$1* refers to the first field.

- ▼ ~: Tells **awk** to match the following string.

- ▼ */Geisha/*: The string to search for.

▼   *print $0.* Tells **awk** to print out the entire record containing the matched string. A special use of the *$* sign is with the character *0*, which tells **awk** to use all of the fields possible.

▼   *workers:* The file to use.

In our case, **awk** would print the following to the screen:

```
Geisha    280    555-4221    geisha    10
```

Not every action needs to be the result of matching a specific pattern, of course. In **awk**, the tilde (~) acts as a relational operator, which sets forth a condition for **awk** to use. There are a number of other relational operators available to **awk** users that allow **awk** to compare two patterns. (The relational operators are based on algebraic notation.) **Awk** supports the same relational operators as found in the C programming language; they are listed in Table 16.1.

Table 16.1 *Awk relational operators.*

Operator	Meaning	Usage
<	Less than	*$1 < "Eric"* returns every pattern with an ASCII value less than *"Eric"*.
<=	Less than or equal to	*$1 <= "Eric"* .
==	Equals	*$1 == "Eric"* returns every instance of *"Eric"*.
!=	Does not equal	*$1 != "Eric"* returns every field not containing the string *"Eric"*.
>=	Greater than or equal to	*$1 >= "Eric"* returns every field equal to or greater than *"Eric"*.
>	Greater than	*$1 > "Eric"* returns every field greater than *"Eric"*.

We could increase the sophistication of **awk** searches in a number of ways. Firstly we could incorporate the use of compound searches, which uses three logical operators:

▼   *&&,* which works the same as the logical AND

▼   *| |,* which works the same as the logical OR

▼   *!,* which returns anything NOT equaling the original

For example, let's say we wanted to know how many workers had a value in the fifth field that is greater than or equal to 10:

```
$ awk '$5 >= 10   print $0  ' workers
Geisha  280     555-4221      geisha  10
Tom     284     555-2121      spike   12
```

We can also combine tests, to print out, for example, all workers who have the fifth field less than 10 and the second field greater than 280:

```
$ awk '$5 < 10 && $2 > 280   print $0  ' workers
Eric    286     555-6674        erc     8
```

While these examples are obviously contrived, you can use **awk** to help pull out all entries that share certain postal (ZIP) codes, or all employees who have a salary in a certain range. We're just scratching the surface with **awk**.

Awk can also be used to return entire sections of data, as long as you can specify patterns that begin and end the section. To return the records of Eric and Kevin and all between, use the following:

```
$ awk '$1 ~ /Eric/,/Kevin/ print $0' workers
Eric    286   555-6674   erc      8
Geisha  280   555-4221   geisha  10
Kevin   279   555-1112   kevin    2
```

If we don't want to print the whole record, we can print just a few of the fields, as in the example below, which prints out fields 2 and 1:

```
$ awk '$1 ~ /Eric/,/Kevin/ print $2, $1' workers
286 Eric
280 Geisha
279 Kevin
```

As with other UNIX commands, **awk** can be used in pipes, and its output can be directed to other files or directly to the printer. For example, if we were looking through a large file and expecting many matches to a particular string (such as salary ranges or employment starting dates), we might want to direct that output to a file or to a printer.

For example, to use **awk** with the UNIX **sort** utility, we can sort the output of the last example:

```
$ awk '$1 ~ /Eric/,/Kevin/ print $2, $1' workers | sort
279 Kevin
280 Geisha
286 Eric
```

(Note that this is sorting on the leading number.)

Awk also provides some summary abilities as well. The **NR** symbol in an **awk** command returns the number of records, for example.

We can combine this with **awk**'s ability to total fields in an **awk** program.

Awk Programs

You're not limited to what fits on the command line with **awk**. You can also store a series of **awk** commands in a file and then use **awk** to execute the file.

For example, we can store our simplest **awk** command, {**print**}, in a separate file and use the following **awk** command:

```
$ awk -f awk.1 workers
Eric      286     555-6674      erc      8
Geisha    280     555-4221      geisha   10
Kevin     279     555-1112      kevin    2
Tom       284     555-2121      spike    12
```

In this case we're assuming the file **awk.1** contains our very simple **awk** "program":

```
{ print }
```

You can combine this with the **awk BEGIN**, **END**, and **NR** commands to make a more complex **awk** program. When working with this, it's good to remember that **awk** applies each **awk** command to every record; that is, every line of text, in the input file. A program like {**print**} says that for each line in the input file, print it.

The **awk BEGIN** command lists what to do before reading the first line of text. For example:

```
BEGIN  { print "Workers for Spacely's Sprockets"; print "" }
{ print }
```

The above **awk** program will print out the text "Workers for Spacely's Sprockets" before printing each line in the **workers** file. On the command line, this will look like the following (if we stored the above **awk** program in a file named **awk.2**):

```
$ awk -f awk.2 workers
Workers for Spacely's Sprockets

Eric     286      555-6674      erc      8
Geisha   280      555-4221      geisha   10
Kevin    279      555-1112      kevin    2
Tom      284      555-2121      spike    12
```

The **print** "" prints a blank line.

The **END** statement similarly lists commands to execute after data is all read. Here's where the **NR** command, number of records (or lines), comes in handy, as in the following example:

```
BEGIN  { print "Workers for Spacely's Sprockets"; print "" }

{ print }

END  { print "There are ",
       NR,
       " employees left after the latest wave of layoffs." }
```

The previous example uses cleaner formatting for the **END** statements. It makes no difference in the output if we had instead placed the entire **END** command on one line. We can name this file **awk.3** and then execute the following command:

```
$ awk -f awk.3 workers
Workers for Spacely's Sprockets

Eric     286      555-6674      erc      8
Geisha   280      555-4221      geisha   10
Kevin    279      555-1112      kevin    2
Tom      284      555-2121      spike    12
There are  4  employees left after the latest wave of
layoffs.
```

This brief explanation covers **awk** in the simplest terms. For example, **awk** includes most of the trappings of a full programming language, including loops, variables, string operations, numeric operations, and the creation and manipulation of arrays. If you're interested in a useful programming language that can be mastered relatively quickly, we would recommend further reading on **awk**; our recommendations can be found in Appendix A.

Perl

Perl is a freeware scripting language developed to handle a number of system administration tasks. **Perl** stands for Practical Extraction and Report Language. The whole point of the language is to make it easier for you to extract data from UNIX and output reports on things such as Usenet news (see Chapter 10), disk usage, and a list of all users on your systems, sorted in order of largest disk usage.

Perl is also one of the few computer languages in which people try to write poetry. While this may sound about as silly as translating the Bible into the Klingon language of Star Trek fame (know any Klingons to convert to Christianity?), at least the aspiring **perl** poets are keeping off the streets when they write their sonnets in perlese.

As a scripting language, **perl** has a lot in common with the C and Korn shell languages discussed in Chapter 12.

When approaching **perl**, the first question to ask is: Do you have **perl** on your system? Many UNIX systems, such as Linux, come with **perl** built in. To check this out, simply type in:

```
$ perl -v
```

If you have **perl** on your system, you should see the version number for **perl**. If not, you'll get an error like the following:

```
$ perl -v
perl: Command not found.
```

See the section on acquiring **perl**, below, for more on getting **perl** if you don't already have it.

Once you make sure you have **perl**, you can try a few **perl** scripts to get a flavor of the language. As with so many parts of UNIX, there are usually a number of ways to get things accomplished. For many of the tasks **perl** is suited for, you could also write a Bourne or C shell script, write an **awk** command, create a program in C, or use a number of other UNIX scripting languages. UNIX gives you a lot of choice but little guidance.

Our best recommendation is to look around at the choices and see which one you think best fits your task. Your background and ability also impacts this decision. For example, if you write C programs for a living and don't bother with shell scripts, then C is probably the way to go. While you may want to stick to what works for you, you may also want to look around and see what's available in the wide world of UNIX.

Perl tends to be good at tasks that revolve around reporting system information.

A First Perl Script

Perl, like most UNIX scripting languages, uses the # as a comment marker. Any line with # is ignored from the # onward. (See Chapter 12 on shell scripting for more on comments and their usefulness.)

Like the **echo** command in shell scripts, **perl** offers the more versatile **print** statement, as we show in the following example:

```
#! /usr/bin/perl
# My first perl script.
print "This is my first perl script.\n";
print "Oh, joy!\n";
```

When you run this script, you'll see the following output, as you'd expect:

```
This is my first perl script.
Oh, joy!
```

The \n stands for a newline, or linefeed character, and is typical UNIX parlance.

You can also prompt for data in **perl**, using the following odd syntax:

```
#! /usr/bin/perl
# Prompting for input in perl.

print "What is your first name: ";

# <STDIN> stands for standard input: the keyboard.
$first_name = <STDIN>;

# Remove trailing linefeed.
chop($first_name);

printf "What is your last name: ";
$last_name = <STDIN>;

chop($last_name);

print "Your name is $first_name $last_name.\n";
```

When you run this script, you'll see the following prompts:

```
What is your first name: Eric
What is your last name: Johnson
Your name is Eric Johnson.
```

From the above example, you'll note that **perl** seems more difficult than the Bourne shell for getting input from users.

Where **perl** excels, though, is in arrays, UNIX process control, and string handling. **Perl** offers a string set of array operations, which allow you to have a set of data treated as one unit, for example:

```
(1,2,3,4,5,6)
```

The above array has the values 1 through 6. You can also intermix text and numeric values, as shown below:

```
(1,2, 3, "Text")
```

You can assign this array to a variable and then access any element in the array. A great strength of **perl** is its associative arrays, where you can use a key value for an array index and associate this with a data value. For example, you can have a **perl** array for a first name, last name, and street address. You could then access the street address as shown below:

```
#! /usr/bin/perl
# Associative arrays in perl.

# bill is an associative array.

$bill"firstname" = "Bill";
$bill"address" = "1600 Pennsylvania Ave.";

# Print the data.
print $bill"firstname";
print "'s address is ";
print $bill"address";

# End with a carriage return.
print "\n";
```

The previous example stores a first name and an address in the associative array named **bill**. Associative arrays form a very powerful feature and can be used effectively in a lot of system administration tasks.

The output of the above script looks something like the following:

```
Bill's address is 1600 Pennsylvania Ave.
```

In addition to associative arrays, **perl** has a lot of commands to format text to allow you to create reports (the original reason for **perl**'s existence). **Perl** is intimately tied in with UNIX and provides a number of shortcuts for common UNIX activities, like accessing the password file (described in Chapter 1):

```
#! /usr/bin/perl
# Accessing the password file.

# Get Eric's password entry and print it.

@erc_entry = getpwnam("erc");

($username, $realname, $homedir) = @erc_entry[0,6,7];

print "User $realname has";
print " a home directory of $homedir";
print " and a username of $username.\n";
```

When you run this script, you'll see output like the following:

```
User Eric F. Johnson has a home directory of /home/erc and a
username of erc.
```

Naturally, you'll want to use a username that is available on your system.

There's a lot more to **perl**, which fills more than one book on the subject. If you're interested in learning more about **perl**, see Appendix A.

Acquiring Perl

The source code for **perl** is free. You then need a C compiler to compile and link the **perl** sources to create the **perl** command.

You can acquire the **perl** source code from a number of UNIX Internet FTP sites that contain free UNIX software or from a number of CD-ROM collections of

UNIX freeware, such as the UNIX Freeware and Shareware, also published by MIS: Press. See Appendix A for more information.

Sed

The **sed** (*streams editor*) command can be likened to the text editors we covered in Chapter 11—**vi**, **emacs**, and **ed**. However, the Chapter 11 editors are *interactive*, which means that you supply filenames, operations, and text on the fly; not so with **sed**.

Sed can be thought of as a filtering text editor; procedurally, you use the **sed** command with the following steps:

▼   Read in text from file

▼   Make changes in the text

▼   Display new text on screen or save to file

These procedures are specified all in one command line. (Since every installation of UNIX should include access to **sed**, you can follow along at your own keyboard and type the command lines as they appear later in this chapter.) A typical **sed** command line should look something like this:

```
$ sed -n -e operation -f scriptfilename filename
```

where *-n* refers to a specific line or lines, *operation* refers to one of the many available **sed** operations, *scriptfilename* refers to a file that contains a longer list of **sed** operations, and *filename* refers to the file that **sed** works on.

The various command-line options are explained in greater detail in Table 16.2.

***Table 16.2** Sed command-line options.*

Command	Result
-e	Explicitly tells **sed** that what follows is an operation. If you only use one operation, then you can omit the **-e**.
-f	Specifies a script file. If you plan on using many operations regularly, then it's best to save them in a script file for future use.
-n	Specifies a specific line number or a range of line numbers to use.

Keeping with our habit of recycling previous works of art when applicable, let's flash back to Chapter 11, when we discussed text editing. We used a file that we called (imaginatively enough) **test**. To jog your memory, here's what that file ended up looking like when we were through with it:

```
This is a test of the Emergency UNIX system. This is a test.
If this were an actual document, we probably would take it
more seriously than we do this flippant, unorganized memo.
We are typing this test in order to test the capabilities of
the vi editor. Really. This concludes our test of the
Emergency UNIX System.
```

Let's begin by using **sed** to display only a portion of the file test, like the second and third lines. Do so with:

```
$ sed -n '2,3p' test
```

On your display, you'd see the following:

```
If this were an actual document, we probably would take it
more seriously than we do this flippant, unorganized memo.
```

If we wanted to write the results of our command to a file, we could do so as follows:

```
$ sed -n '2,3p' w filename test
```

where *filename* is the name of a file.

Some things to note in our little examples:

- ▼ Because we used only one operation, we omitted the *-e* option.
- ▼ We listed the command within single quotes, which tells **sed** that everything contained in the quotes is part of the same operation.
- ▼ We specified certain lines for **sed** to work on. If no lines are specified, **sed** assumes that it is to work on the entire file.

Printing, of course, is not the only operation available to **sed** users. We list the major operations in Table 16.3.

Table 16.3. *Sed operations.*

Operation	Result
a\string	Adds the *string*.
c\string	Changes specified lines to the specified string.
d	Deletes specified lines or strings.
i	Inserts specified string before specified lines.
l	Lists the file or specified portions thereof. Useful because it displays characters normally used for formatting; for example, tabs are printed with the > character.
p	Prints to standard output—unless specified otherwise, your screen.
r *filename*	Inserts an entire file after a specific line.
s/string1/string2/	Substitutes *string1* for *string2*.
w *filename*	Writes specified lines to *filename*.

Like most UNIX commands, **sed** can be used with pipes and other commands. As with **awk**, we're not going to spend too much time with **sed**. If you want more information about **sed**, we suggest that you consult the other references cited in Appendix A.

The Nice Command

Sometimes you'll run a command and not care too much when it's completed, such as when you issue a command right before you leave for lunch. When time is not of the essence—especially on large, multiuser systems that may not contain quite enough hardware firepower to support so many users—you may want to use the **nice** command in conjunction with other commands, so named because you're being *nice* to the system. Use it at the beginning of the command line:

```
$ nice command filename
```

For example, if you're performing an extremely complicated sort with many files, you may want to launch the sort using **nice** before that typical two-hour lunch.

The At Command

Of course, some lunches can expand to three or even four hours, depending on the libations involved. If you're not sure you'll be back to the office in time to run an important command, you can use the **at** command.

Seriously, you're more likely to use the **at** command to relieve pressure on the system by running system-intensive commands in the middle of the night, to send mail messages involving long-distance charges when rates are lowest, or to backup a large hard disk at some regular interval.

 Not every user can use **at**, as system administrators have the power to deny users—usually beginners—access to **at**. If you try to use **at** and are denied permission, check with your system administrator.

Using **at** is simple, as you first specify a time for execution, followed by the command line. To set up a specific command, type the following:

```
$ at 11am
```

At is very flexible about defining the time when the command is to be run; you can use a time as in our example, or you can use a more precise number based on military time.

After you hit the **Enter** (or **Return**) key, you'll be placed on the following line, without a prompt. As you recall, this is the UNIX method of asking you for additional input. (Usually, anyway; there are exceptions.) This is where you provide the command that **at** is to execute; end each command by hitting the **Enter** (or **Return**) key. When you're through, type **Ctrl-D**.

The system's response is a single line of information that confirms when the command (designated by the system with a job-ID of many digits) will be run. This job-ID is very valuable information. Should you need to see a list of pending job-IDs, use **at** with the *-l* (ell) option:

```
$ at -l
```

If you want to cancel a pending command scheduled with **at**, use **at** with the *-r* (remove) option:

```
$ at -r job-ID
```

WARNING If you plan on using **at** regularly, make sure your system's date and time are set correctly, using the procedures outlined in Chapter 15. Furthermore, for procedures you need to perform again and again, **cron**, covered later in this chapter, is likely to be a better tool than **at**.

The Batch Command

We've already discussed the early days of UNIX usage, when instantaneous inter-action between users and the UNIX system wasn't always possible. Out of this need arose the **batch** command, which allows you to combine many commands into one command line, which is then run in the background without any prompt-ing on your part. Use **batch** as follows:

```
$ batch
```

End the command by hitting the **Enter** (or **Return**) key. As with **at**, you'll be placed on a new line, as **batch** waits for additional input. Go ahead and type in the commands, ending each by hitting the **Enter** (or **Return**) key. When you're finishing entering commands, type **Ctrl-D**.

You'll then be presented with a command prompt, so go ahead with your other work as your **batch** commands are quietly executed by the system. If your commands require some sort of confirmation message or output delivered to you, the message will be conveyed as a mail message; you won't find messages pop-ping up on your screen while you're in the middle of some other action.

Elsewhere in this book, we have discussed running programs in the back-ground using the ampersand. There are some fundamental differences between background tasks and **batch**:

▼   Commands issued to **batch** are accorded even less priority than com-mands run in the background.

▼   With **batch**, commands will continue to execute even if you log off the system (shades of **nohup**!). Background tasks are killed if you log off the system.

▼   Background will interrupt you should your background command specify some kind of output or confirmation. **Batch** does not; as we noted, con-firmation or output is sent as a mail message.

The Cron Command

System administrators have all the fun—or used to, anyway, as evidenced by the **cron** command. **Cron** started life as a tool for system administration, allowing the system administrator to schedule regular tasks unattended. These tasks were stored in a file called **crontab**, usually found in the **/usr/lib** directory. Some versions of UNIX, either pre–System V or Berkeley, still allow **cron** privileges only to the system administrator. However, if you're using a newer version of UNIX, you'll have access to **cron**.

If you're not using System V UNIX, you won't have access to the **cron** command unless you're a system administrator with superuser capabilities. Also, system administrators have the power to deny users access to **cron**. If you're using a newer version of UNIX and still are denied access to **cron**, consult your system administrator.

Why use **cron**? As we said above, it allows you to schedule regular tasks unattended. You may want to back up your data to tape drive weekly or even daily. You may want to send yourself a mail message to remind you of important non-computer chores. Or you may want to send electronic mail to other UNIX systems late at night when the long-distance rates are lower.

In some ways the **at** command accomplishes the same as the **cron** command. So why use **cron**? Because you can set it up to perform regular tasks. With **at**, you can only set up a single task to be performed at one specific time. Because **at** is much easier to use, we recommend using it in one-time situations, and **cron** in repetitive situations.

There are two parts to **cron**: The **crontab** file and the actual **cron** command. We'll cover each.

Creating a Crontab File

As we said earlier, the **crontab** file contains the tasks that are to be performed regularly. You have your own personal **crontab** file, stored in the **/usr/lib/crontab** directory.

NOTE Some systems don't use a **/usr/lib/crontab** directory. Instead, you'll often find the **cron** files stored in the **/usr/spool/cron/crontab** directory, and permission files, which specify who can and who can't use **cron**, in **/usr/lib/cron**. If in doubt, check the online-manual pages for **cron**. In any case **cron** stores its jobs in a **crontab** file.

Such a file is not created automatically when your account is created; instead, it's up to you to create the file—though not directly. The **crontab** file installation, as well as the structure of the actual file, can be a tad confusing.

You can use **vi** or **emacs** to create a **crontab** file. However, you can't save the file directly in the **/usr/lib/crontab** directory; instead, you must save it under a different name and use the **cron** command to install it. We'll guide you through a typical file creation and installation.

There are six fields to a **crontab** file, each separated by a space. The first five fields specify exactly when the command is to be run; the sixth field is the command itself.

Let's say that we wanted to run a command every morning at 8:30 a.m. The structure of the **crontab** line looks something like this:

```
30 8 * * * command
```

The exact values associated with the five fields are listed in Table 16.4.

Table 16.4 *Fields in a crontab line.*

Field	Meaning
1	Minutes after the hour.
2	Hour, in 24-hour format.
3	Day of the month.
4	Month.
5	Day of the week.

Some things to note when creating a **crontab** file:

▼ Asterisks (*) are used to specify when commands are to be run in every instance of the value of the field. An asterisk in the third field means to run the command every day of every month, an asterisk in the fourth field means to run the command every month, an asterisk in the fifth field means to run the command every day of every week.

▼ Days of the week are notated somewhat strangely. The week begins with a 0 for Sunday and ends with a 6 for Saturday. (Computer people, especially on UNIX, are famous for starting to count with 0 rather than the more common 1 used by real people.)

▼ Times are specified in military (24-hour) time. Thus 10 p.m. is specified as 22.

▼ Ranges can be specified, instead of specific days and times. For instance, you can perform the command only on the 15th and 30th days of the month by using 15,30 in the third field. (Just make sure you adjust it in February.) Or you can specify that a command be run only the fall months by using 10-12 in the fourth field. These two methods can be combined: Running a command in spring and summer means using 4-6,10-12 in the fourth field.

After creating our **crontab** file (which must be saved under a filename of anything but **crontab**; we'll call it **ourfile**), we can then install it, using the **crontab** command:

```
$ crontab ourfile
```

Crontab then takes **ourfile**, copies it, and saves the copy under our username in the **/usr/lib/crontab** directory, with a filename of **/usr/lib/crontab/ourname**. If we want to make changes to our **cron** configuration, we must edit our original file (which still exists—remember, **cron** only makes a copy) and then reinstall it using **crontab**. If we want to totally remove the file, we must use the **crontab** command with the *-r* option:

```
$ crontab -r
```

To prevent mischief or some unintended damage, we are allowed access to only our own **crontab** file.

Some Crontab Examples

The **crontab -l** command lists out the **crontab** entry for your username. For example:

```
$ crontab -l

15 3 * * * sh /u/erc/my_backup
```

In this example, every night at 3:15 a.m., **cron** will invoke the Bourne shell, **sh**, and will execute a shell script called **my_backup** that is stored in the **/u/erc** directory. Presumably, this script will back up certain directories to tape. The reason it's performed at 3:15 a.m. is because at this time the machine is mostly idle.

If you only wanted to back up on Mondays, you'd use the following **crontab** entry:

```
15 3 * * 1 sh /u/erc/my_backup
```

Again, we've left the time to execute the script at the arbitrary time of 3:15 a.m.

If you wanted to only perform backups on the first and 15th of each month, you could use the following **crontab** entry:

```
15 3 1,15 * * sh /u/erc/my_backup
```

The Bc Command

Even though the proliferation of ubiquitous and inexpensive calculators have made this command somewhat obsolete, the **bc** command can still be used as a calculator. Use it as follows:

```
$ bc
1+1
2
quit
```

This simple equation shows how to use **bc**: Type it as a command line, hit **Enter** (or **Return**), enter your equation, hit **Enter** (or **Return**), read the calculation, and type quit when you're through. Obviously, other more advanced features are available, such as square roots, converting numbers from one base to another, determining prime factors, control statements for writing programs, and more. Consult your system documentation or the online **man** page for further information.

Summary

The **awk** language helps process UNIX text files, especially formatted or structured text files, such as a list of employees. You can write **awk** programs or just issue **awk** commands at the command-line prompt.

The streams editor, **sed**, acts as a batch text editor. **Sed** becomes really useful when you want to automate changes to text files.

The **at**, **batch**, and **cron** commands all allow you to run commands in the background. **At** runs a command at a specified time. **Cron** allows you to set up commands to run at certain times of the day or days of the week. For example, you might want to run a daily production report at the end of the business day. You might also want to configure your system via **cron** to dial out to other computer systems in the wee hours of the morning, when long-distance telephone rates are their lowest. To configure **cron**, you create a **crontab** file and then issue the **crontab** command.

When you issue the **nice** command, you're being nice to the other users of the system by running your programs at a very low priority.

Finally, the **bc** command provides an interactive calculator, so you can balance your checkbook and solve complex equations.

Learning More About UNIX

Obviously this book serves as a brief introduction to a very complex operating system. To learn more about the UNIX operating system, we'd highly recommend the following as part of your core reading list.

▼ *Life with UNIX: A Guide for Everyone.* Don Libes and Sandy Ressler. Prentice Hall, 1989. This book is a hoot. Though you'll find little in this book to make your day-to-day computing tasks simpler, the history of UNIX as outlined in this book is tremendously entertaining and provides valuable insights as to why UNIX ended up the way it did.

▼ *UNIX System V Release 4: An Introduction for New and Experienced Users.* Kenneth Rosen, Richard Rosinski, and James Farber. Osborne McGraw-Hill, 1990. Weighing in at close to 1,200 pages and a little over 4 pounds, UNIX System V Release 4 is the most thorough documentation of SVR4 in one volume. It should be—the three authors all work for AT&T and have been working with UNIX for years.

325

▼ *UNIX in Plain English.* Kevin Reichard and Eric F. Johnson. MIS:Press. 1994. This book is a quick reference for the UNIX command set. Each major command is covered in its own page, and entries are cross-referenced by type and with DOS commands.

MIS:Press has embarked on a series of books focusing on UNIX fundamentals. These books are in some ways more introductory than this one, but the later books in the series focus on specific topics:

▼ *UNIX Fundamentals: The Basics.* Kevin Reichard. MIS:Press, 1994. This covers the basics of UNIX on a far more introductory level than the book you're holding. If you're still confused about some aspects of UNIX, you may want to take a step back and read this book.

▼ *UNIX Fundamentals: UNIX For DOS and Windows Users.* Kevin Reichard. MIS:Press, 1994. This covers UNIX from the point of view of the DOS and/or Windows user, translating common DOS/Windows actions into their UNIX counterparts.

▼ *UNIX Fundamentals: UNIX Communications and Networking.* Kevin Reichard and David Burnette. MIS:Press, 1994. UNIX was built from the ground up to include networking, which is directly responsible for the Internet. This book covers the basics of UNIX networking and moves on to glamorous topics like the Internet, the Usenet, and the World Wide Web.

▼ *UNIX Fundamentals: UNIX Shareware and Freeware.* Kevin Reichard. MIS:Press, 1994. Freeware and shareware is a proud tradition in the UNIX world, and this book contains the best of UNIX freeware in source-code form on a CD-ROM.

Over the last few years a number of specialized UNIX books cropped up. For the **vi** text editor, you could try:

▼ *The Ultimate Guide to the vi and ex Text Editors.* Hewlett-Packard Company, Benjamin Cummings, 1990.

And for more than you ever wanted to learn about **nroff**, **troff**, and an entire family of related programs, there's:

▼ *Text Processing and Typesetting with UNIX.* David Barron and Mike Rees. Addison-Wesley, 1987.

For more on the Internet, read:

▼   *The Whole Internet User's Guide and Catalog*, second edition. Ed Krol. O'Reilly & Associates, 1994.

If you need to know more about the X Window System, check out:

▼   *Using X.* Eric F. Johnson and Kevin Reichard. MIS: Press, 1992.

▼   *The UNIX System Administrator's Guide to X.* Eric F. Johnson and Kevin Reichard. M&T Books, 1994.

You can find out more about the **perl** scripting language discussed in Chapter 16 by looking up the following books:

▼   *Programming Perl.* Larry Wall and Randall Schwartz. O'Reilly and Assoc.

▼   *Learning Perl.* Randall Schwartz. O'Reilly and Assoc.

If you're not only learning UNIX as a user but also find yourself a reluctant system administrator, we recommend:

▼   *UNIX System V Release 4 Administration*, second edition. David Fielder, Bruce Hunter, and Ben Smith. Hayden Books, 1991.

▼   *UNIX Administration Guide for System V.* Rebecca Thomas and Rik Farrow. Prentice Hall, 1989.

Other texts we find useful include:

▼   *!%@:: A Dictionary of Electronic Mail Addressing and Networks.* Donnalyn Frey and Rick Adams. O'Reilly and Assoc., 1989.

▼   *Inside SCO UNIX.* Steve Glines, Peter Spicer, Benjamin Hunsberger, and Karen Lynn White. New Riders Press, 1992.

Usenet Newsgroups

In Chapter 10 we covered the Internet and the Usenet quite extensively. The Usenet, specifically, features many newsgroups geared for UNIX users of all sorts. We present an introductory list in Table A.1.

Table A.1   *Usenet newsgroups covering UNIX*

Newsgroup	Purpose
comp.unix.admin	Administering a UNIX-based system.
comp.unix.advocacy	Arguments for and against UNIX.
comp.unix.aix	A discussion of IBM's AIX.
comp.unix.aux	A discussion of Apple's A/UX.
comp.unix.bsd	A discussion of the Berkeley Software Distribution UNIX.
comp.unix.dos-under-unix	Running MS-DOS under UNIX.
comp.unix.misc	Miscellaneous UNIX topics.
comp.unix.programmer	Q&A for people programming in UNIX.
comp.unix.questions	Discussion of UNIX geared for beginners.
comp.unix.shell	Programming UNIX shells.
comp.unix.sys5.r4	Discussion of System V Release 4.

User Groups

We've learned a lot by attending our local meetings of UNIX Users of Minnesota. And you certainly could learn a lot by attending a meeting of your local UNIX user group. Most groups follow the same format: Meetings for beginners, followed by general meetings with guest speakers and Q&A sessions.

Unfortunately, there's no centralized list of UNIX user groups. We'd recommend checking out a local computer publication for a listing of local user groups. If you live in Minneapolis/St. Paul, Seattle, Philadelphia, Kansas City, Phoenix, New Orleans, Indianapolis, Denver, or Detroit, look for your local edition of Computer User. If you live in San Francisco, check out Microtimes. If you live in Los Angeles, San Jose, San Francisco, Boston, or Atlanta, look for your local edition of Computer Currents.

Organizations

There are two professional organizations devoted to the UNIX operating system:

UniForum
2901 Tasman Dr., Suite 201
Santa Clara, CA 95054
800/255-5620

USENIX
2560 9th St., Suite 215
Berkeley, CA 94710
415/528-8649

Finally....

We've mentioned the Free Software Foundation several times throughout this book. Here's the address should you want further information:

Free Software Foundation
675 Massachusetts Ave.
Cambridge, MA 02139
617/876-3296

APPENDIX

B

Some Basic UNIX Commands

UNIX is made up of literally thousands of commands and variations. In the course of the summary, we did not have the chance to cover every command and variation. Here we have the chance to cover the major commands in some detail. As always, this doesn't cover every possible command. We do differentiate between the various shells: The default is the Bourne shell, while **csh** refers to the C shell, and **ksh** refers to the Korn shell. Unless noted otherwise, a command should work with every shell. Should you require additional information about these commands (or those we fail to list), refer to the online-manual pages or your system's documentation.

This is a truncated listing; a full listing of UNIX commands and their many options fill entire books. If you're looking for a complete reference to the UNIX command set, check out UNIX in Plain English (see Appendix A for details).

alias

Description

Displays and sets command aliases. **Alias** by itself will give a summary of current aliases.

Syntax

```
alias name=cmd (csh and ksh)
alias name=cmd (ksh)
```

at

Description

Performs specified commands at given times, as long as the commands require no additional input from you. For instance, you may want to print a series of long documents at midnight, so you don't need to tie up the laser printer for hours when other people may need it. You don't need to interact with the laser printer at midnight (although you should make sure its paper tray is filled before leaving work!), so you can use the **at** command to print at midnight.

Syntax

```
at time
at [options] job-ids
```

The system assigns job IDs when you use the **at** command.

Options

-l	Lists current job.
-r	Removes specified job.
time	Obviously, the time when the commands should run. Unless you specifyotherwise (with **a.m.** or **p.m.** as a suffix), the system assumes military time.

banner

Description

Displays up to ten characters in large letters using asterisks (*) or number signs (#), depending on your system. For instance, the command **banner kevin** would display the following on your screen:

Syntax

```
banner text
```

bg

Description

Resumes a suspended job.

Syntax

```
bg PID
```

cal

Description

Displays the current month in calendar form.

Syntax

```
cal
cal month year
cal year
```

cancel

Description

Cancels pending printer jobs. You can either specify the job ID or by printer to be canceled.

Syntax

```
Cancel
Cancel ID
Cancel printer
```

cat

Description

Combines or displays files.

Syntax

```
cat [options] filename
```

Options

-u	Output is unbuffered.
-v	Prints nonprinting characters.

cc

Description

Compiles C language programs.

Syntax

```
cc options filename linkoptions
```

Options

-c filename	Specify the name of the file to compile, to generate a *.o* file.
-g	Generate debugging information.
-o filename	Specify the name of the executable file to generate.
-O	Optimize while compiling.
-llibrary	Links in the given library, e.g., -lX11.

cd

Description

Change current directory to a new directory.

Syntax

```
cd directory
```

chgrp

Description

Changes a file's group ID, which is used for the group access permissions.

Syntax

```
chgrp groupname filename
```

chmod

Description

Changes the access permissions on a given file. The *mode* is an octal number in the following format:

Number	Meaning
400	owner has read permission.
200	owner has write permission.
100	owner has execute permission.
040	group has read permission.
020	group has write permission.
010	group has execute permission.
004	world has read permission.
002	world has write permission.
001	world has execute permission.

Add together the numbers for the permissions you want. For example, 423 means that you, the user, can read the file, users in your group can write the file, and the rest of the world can write and execute the file.

Syntax

```
chmod mode filename
```

chown

Description

Changes the ownership of a given file.

Syntax

```
chown owner filename
```

Options

-h   Changes the ownership of a symbolic link.

compress

Description

Compresses a file (or files), creating *filename.Z.*

Syntax

```
compress filename
```

cp

Description

Copies the contents of one file into another file.

Syntax

```
cp [options] filename newfilename
```

Options

-i	Makes sure you don't overwrite existing file.
-p	Retains existing permissions.
-r	Copies entire directory.

crontab

Description

Tells **cron** to run a set of commands at specified times.

Syntax

crontab *filename*   Where *filename* is the name of a *crontab* file.

csh

Description

Starts the C shell.

Syntax

```
csh
```

date

Description

Displays current date. Or, if you have superuser status, can be used to set the system date and time.

Syntax

```
date [options]
```

Options

mmddHHMMMMYY   Sets month (**mm**), date (**dd**), hour (**hh**), minute (**MM**), and year (**YY**).

diff

Description

Compares two files.

Syntax

```
diff options filename1 filename2
```

Options

-b   Ignores blanks at the end of line.

-c   Generates a context **diff**.

-e   Creates a script for the **ed** editor to make *filename1* the same as *filename2*.

du

Description

Displays how much disk space is used by a directory (and all its subdirectories), in blocks (usually 512 or 1,024 bytes each).

Syntax

```
du options directories
du options filenames
```

Options

-a   Displays all information.

-r   Reports on files and directories du cannot open.

-s   Silent mode. Displays only totals.

echo

Description

Echoes text to standard output.

Syntax

```
echo text
```

env

Description

Displays the current user environment variables with their values.

Syntax

```
env [options]
```

Options

    ENV=VALUE   Sets environment variable (ENV) to VALUE.

exit

Description

Quits the current session.

file

Description

Describes file type of given file.

Syntax

```
file filename
```

find

Description

Finds a file.

Syntax

```
find / -name filename -print
```

Options

    -print   Prints the results of the search.

grep

Description

Searches files for a pattern.

Syntax

```
grep options pattern filenames
```

Options

-c	Only displays the number of lines that match.
-i	Ignores case.
-l	Lists only filenames that have matching lines.
-n	Lists each matching line with its line number.
-v	Lists lines that *don't* match.

head

Description

Displays the beginning of a file. The default is ten lines.

Syntax

```
head filename
```

Options

    -n   Specify the number of lines to display.

history

Description

Display previous command lines. Used with the C and Korn shells.

Syntax

```
history
```

jobs

Description

Display all current jobs.

Syntax

```
jobs
```

kill

Description

Kills a current process by ID number.

Syntax

```
kill process.id
```

ln

Description

Links two or more files.

Syntax

```
ln filename1 filename2
```

Options

-s   Creates a symbolic link.

lp

Description

Sends a print request to a printer. Can be used to print multiple files with one request. On some systems, you may need to use the **lpr** command instead.

Syntax

```
lp filename
```

Options

-c	Copies the file before sending the request.
-d	Specifies a printer other than the default printer.
-m	Sends a message to the user when the file is printed.

lpstat

Description

Returns the status of print requests.

Syntax

```
lpstat options
```

Options

-d	Copies the file before sending the request.

ls

Description

Lists the contents of the specified directory. If no directory is specified, the contents of the current directory are listed.

Syntax

```
ls names
```

where *names* refers to filenames or pathnames.

Options

-a	Lists all contents, including hidden files.
-d	Lists only the name of the directory, not the contents.
-l	Lists the contents of a directory in long form.
-m	Lists the contents across the screen, separated by commas.
-q	Lists contents with nonprinting characters represented by a question mark (?).
-r	Lists the contents in reverse order.

-t	Lists the contents in order of time saved, beginning with the most recent.
-1	Lists contents one entry to a line.

make

Description
Builds programs from a set of rules stored in a makefile.

Syntax
```
make options targets
```

Options
-f *makefile*	Use *makefile* instead of file named **Makefile** for make's rules.
-n	No execute mode. Only print out commands, don't execute them.
-s	Silent mode. Don't print out any commands **make** executes.

man

Description
Displays the online-manual page for a command.

Syntax
```
man command
```

mkdir

Description
Create a new directory.

Syntax
```
mkdir dirname
```
where *dirname* refers to the name of the new directory.

Options

-m *mode*   Specifies the *mode* of the new directory.

more

Description

Displays all or parts of a file. Type *q* to quit, Spacebar to continue.

Syntax

```
more filename
```

Options

-c   Clears the screen before displaying the file.

mv

Description

Moves a file or multiple files into another directory or to a new name in the current directory.

Syntax

```
mv filename directory
```

or

```
mv filename newfilename
```

Options

-f   Moves file without checking for confirmation in case of an overwrite.

-i   Prompts users if action would overwrite an existing file.

news

Description

Displays all news items distributed systemwide.

Syntax

```
news
news newsitem
```

Options

-a	Displays all of the news items.
-n	Displays the names of all of the news items.
-s	Displays a count of all of the news items.

nice

Description

Runs a command nicely, by giving it a very low priority.

Syntax

```
nice options command
```

where command refers to the command to execute nicely.

Options

-n	Specifies **n** as the decrement in priority. The default is 10.

nohup

Description

Keeps a command running even if you log off the system.

Syntax

```
nohup command
```

page or pg

Description

Displays a file one page at a time.

Syntax

```
pg filename
```

Options

+n   Starts the display at line number n.

+/string   Searches for the string string.

passwd

Description

Sets the user's password.

Syntax

```
passwd user
```

pr

Description

Prints a file or files to the default printer.

Syntax

```
pr filename | lp
```

Options

-d   Double-spaces the text.

-h text   Prints the header *text* at the beginning of the output.

-l   Sets the page length.

-w   Sets the page width.

ps

Description

Returns the status of all current processes.

Syntax

```
ps
```

Options

-e	Displays expanded information about all current processes.
-f	Displays full information about processes.

pwd

Description

Returns the current working directory.

Syntax

```
pwd
```

rcp

Description

Copies files to and from remote systems.

Syntax

```
rcp host1:filename host2:filename
```

resume

Description

Starts a suspended job.

Syntax

```
resume PID
```

rlogin

Description

Logs in to a remote system.

Syntax

```
rlogin hostname
```

Options

-l **username**   Remotely login under the new *username*.

rm

Description

Removes files.

Syntax

```
rm filename
```

Options

-f   Removes files without verifying action with user.

-i   Removes files after verification from user.

rmdir

Description

Removes a directory.

Syntax

```
rmdir directory
```

set

Description

Returns the values of all current environment variables.

Syntax

```
set
```

setenv

Description

Sets an environment variable. (Used only with C shell.)

Syntax

```
setenv variable newvariable
```

spell

Description

Returns incorrectly spelled words in a file.

Syntax

```
spell filename
```

Options

-b	Checks for spelling based on British usage.
+s *filename*	Creates a sorted file (filename) of correctly spelled words.

stop

Description

Suspends a currently running process.

Syntax

```
stop PID
```

stty

Description

Sets your terminal configuration and options.

Syntax

```
stty
```

Options

    -a   Displays current options.

tabs

Description

Sets the tab settings.

Syntax

```
tabs
```

Options

    -filename   Inserts tab information in the file *filename*.

    -n   Sets tab every *n* characters.

tail

Description

Displays the final ten lines of a file.

Syntax

```
tail filename
```

Options

    -n   Specifies the number of lines from the end of the file to be displayed.

tar

Description

Archives files to `tar` files, often on backup tapes.

Syntax

```
tar options filenames
```

Options

c	Create a new tar archive.
f *filename*	Write archive to *filename,* often /**dev/tape**.
t	Print out a table of contents
v	Verbose mode: print out status information.
x	Extract files from within the **tar** archive.

telnet

Description

Logs in to a remote system.

Syntax

```
telnet hostname
```

uncompress

Description

Uncompresses a file, usually with a name ending in .**Z**.

Syntax

```
uncompress filename
```

unset

Description

Unsets a specified variable.

Syntax

```
unset variablename
```

unsetenv

Description

Unsets an environment variable. (Used only in the C shell.)

Syntax

```
unsetenv variablename
```

wc

Description

Counts the number of words, characters and lines in a text file or files.

Syntax

```
wc options filenames
```

Options

-c	Only print the number of characters.
-l	Only print the number of lines.
-w	Only print the number of words.

who

Description

Displays the names and other information about users on the system

Syntax

```
who
```

Options

am I	Displays your user account information.

write

Description

Sends a text message to another user. Use **Ctrl-D** to exit.

Syntax

```
write username
```

Glossary

absolute pathname The complete name of a file, replete with the total path of directories indicating the file's location on the directory tree. For instance, the absolute pathname of the file *file1* is **/usr/users/kevin/docs/file1**.

address Either the name of a specific machine on a network or the name of the entire UNIX system. Both meanings are used in discussions of electronic mail and communications.

aging Used by the system to determine when passwords or files are old enough to be changed or deleted.

alias A substitute for a command set up by the user, often a short substitute for a longer, often-used command.

anonymous ftp A remote login that requires no password; used for downloading files from a remote machine. See **ftp**.

append To attach text to the end of an existing text file.

application Software that supplies specific functions to end users; for example, Wordperfect is a word-processing application.

argument Used to modify a command on the command line.

ASCII (American Standard Code for Information Interchange) A standard format used to communicate data between different types of computer types. An ASCII file created on a UNIX computer will be readable on other kinds of computers.

at Command that lets you schedule tasks to be run at a future date.

awk A programming language geared toward text manipulation.

BSD (Berkeley Software Distribution) A still-popular version of UNIX originated at the University of California-Berkeley that was noted especially for its advanced networking capabilities.

353

background   When programs are run in this mode, the user can perform other tasks and will be notified when the background program is completed. Background commands are notated with an ampersand (&) at the end of the command line.

backup   An archived copy of user-specified files, kept as an insurance policy should the original files be damaged or corrupted. The UNIX operating system uses the **tar** command to create backups.

bang path   A type of electronic-mail address that relies on an exclamation point (!) to separate parts of the address. Derives its name from the UNIX nickname for the exclamation point, which is bang.

batch   Command that allows you to input many commands to be run unattended in sequence. The command that allows **batch processing**.

batch processing   Where the system is given a series of commands (some of which may depend on the output of other commands) and performs these commands without any interaction with the user. Although a throwback to the olden days of computing, much of what can be done in UNIX can be done with batch processing.

bc   Command that turns a $10,000 workstation into the equivalent of a $20 calculator.

bin   Directory that contains most of the standard UNIX programs and utilities.

binary file   A machine-readable format that usually cannot be read directly by other computers.

bitmap   A method of displaying graphics where the machine maps out every specific point (called pixels) on a display.

boot   Starting the computer and loading the operating system into memory.

Bourne shell   A commonly used shell (**sh**) created by Steven Bourne of Bell Labs. The original shell.

buffer   A section of random-access memory (RAM) used to temporarily store data for future use.

bug   Errors in software. Sometimes called *unanticipated features.*

C   A programming language created by Dennis Ritchie (Bell Labs) in the 1960s. Most UNIX programming utilizes the C programming language (as well as the C++ language), since most of UNIX is written in C.

C++   An enhanced version of C written by Bjarne Stroustrup (Bell Labs) that is gaining in popularity in both the general computing world and among UNIX programmers.

C shell   A commonly used shell created by Bill Joy and others at University of California–Berkeley.

CPU (Central Processing Unit) The brains of the computer; usually a processor that performs much of the actual work of the computer, including processing data and carrying out instructions.

cal   Command that displays a one-month calendar.

cat   Command used to concatenate files, though the most common usage may be the simple viewing of files.

cd   Command that changes your current directory.

child process   A process started by a parent process through a fork. Every UNIX process is a child of another process, except for **init**.

chmod   Command used to change file permissions.

client   In a distributed file system, a computer that accesses the files and services on a server. In the X Window System, an application that runs on the local machine (as opposed to the server).

command   An instruction sent to the shell, which interprets the command and acts upon it.

command history   See **history**.

command line   One or more commands, arguments, and options strung together to create a command.

command mode   In a text editor, the mode where the user supplies commands for saving and editing files.

command substitution   Using the output of one command as input for a new command.

comments   Text included in script or programming files that is not meant to be acted upon by the computer, but rather used to illuminate commands for someone reading the file.

communications node name   Unique name given to a UNIX system for networking and communications purposes.

compiler   A program that turns source code into programs that can be executed by the computer. For example, C source-code files must be run through a compiler before being run by the computer as a full program.

compressed file   File that has been shrunk by compression software.

conditional execution   A construction where one action won't be taken unless another action is performed satisfactorily (if this, then that).

console   Two meanings: A terminal that is the mother of all terminals, displaying all the system error messages; or, more generally, the terminal used by the system administrator.

core dump   A very bad thing. If an error occurs that a program can't deal with, the program will display all of the content of the memory before shutting down; this is the core dump.

cp   Command used to copy a file from one directory to another.

cpio   Command used to backup files.

cron   Command used to schedule routine and regular tasks, such as backing up files.

crontab   The file that contains settings for the **cron** command.

csh   Command that launches the C shell.

current directory   Your current location on the file system. The **cd** command is used to change current directories.

cursor

A symbol used to display the current position on a screen. Older terminals use blinking squares; X Window System users can use just about anything, including (our favorite) a Gumby character.

DOS (Disk Operating System)

An operating system designed for personal computers by Microsoft and sold under the MS-DOS and PC-DOS names.

daemon

Despite the title, a good thing. A daemon (pronounced *demon*) is set up to perform a regular, mundane task without any user initialization or supervision. See **cron** for an example of a daemon.

database management

A structured way of storing information so it can be easily sorted and otherwise managed by the computer.

date

Command used to print out or change the current date and time.

debugger

A program that provides information about bugs in software.

default

A value or state assumed when no other is supplied.

delimiter

A marker used to distinguish between sections of a command or a database. With UNIX, spaces are used as delimiters between portions of a command line.

destination

As you might expect, the target for a directed command.

dev

Directory containing device files.

device

A physical device attached to the computer system, such as a printer or a modem. UNIX's device drivers allow the system to talk to these devices.

device file

A file that contains a description of the device so the operating system can properly send data to and from the device.

device independent

Having the ability to perform a task without regard for a specific computer or peripheral. The text processor **ditroff** is device independent because it will work with many different printers.

directory

A grouping of files and other directories; analogous to a folder residing in a file cabinet.

display

The physical part of the computer system used to communicate back and forth with the user.

distributed file system

A group of two or more physical computers containing files and programs that appears as one contiguous system to the end user. Also refers to the software introduced in System V Release 4 that accomplishes this goal.

distributed processing

A theory of computing that allows resources to be allocated efficiently on a network; for instance, a PC user could use a more powerful workstation on the network for computational-heavy processing.

ditroff

A device-independent version of the text processor **troff**.

Documenter's Workbench

A group of UNIX programs (**troff**, etc.) used for various forms of text processing. Some AT&T licensees treat **troff** et. al. as a separate package; others do not.

domain

Best envisioned as a pyramid, a domain is a group that has control over all groups—other domains or no—beneath it.

domain addressing

Electronic-mail addressing scheme that specifies a specific address within a larger domain; if the address name is *reichard@mr.net*, the domain would be *mr.net*.

dot command

Just what the name implies: A command preceded by a dot. Used to tell the shell to execute the commands in a file; also used by **troff** and other text-processing tools to indicate formatting commands.

echo

A UNIX command used to print standard input to standard output.

ed

Retro text editor that edits an ASCII file one line at a time.

edit buffer

A section of RAM used to contain a file while you edit the file with a text editor.

editor

A program used to edit ASCII files, such as **ed**, **vi**, and **emacs**.

editing mode

In a text editor, the mode where editing changes (like inserting new text, cutting, pasting, etc.) occur. Also known as *command mode*.

electronic mail   The ability to send and receive mail from different computer systems.

emacs   Full-screen text editor. Widely distributed, though not standard on all UNIX implementations.

encryption   A method of encoding a file so that it's not readable by other users, used as a security measure.

end-of-file (EOF) character   The character, surprisingly enough, that indicates the end of a file. The combination **Ctrl-D** is the EOF character in UNIX.

environment   The sum of all of your shell variables, which are set individually by you and either stored in your .profile file or set manually by the user as need be.

environment file   Specific to the Korn shell, this file also contains environment settings.

environment variable   An individual shell setting that makes up part of your environment. For instance, you can designate a directory as your **HOME** directory as an environment variable.

eqn   Dot commands used to typeset equations in conjunction with **troff**.

error message   In a nutshell, a message that tells you something is awry.

escape key   Character labeled **Esc** on a keyboard and used for a variety of functions.

etc   Directory containing everything but device files and program files.

executable file   A program file that runs simply by typing its name on the command line.

execute permission   A setting for an executable file that denotes who can run the program.

exit   Quitting a running program; in UNIX, technically you are terminating a process.

export   To make environment variables available to other users.

extension   A suffix to a filename that helps identify the data contained in the file. A C source-code file usually ends with a *.c* suffix.

field
A vertical column of data in a structured data file, with all the entries of the same type. If we were to create a file containing the names, phone numbers, and salary of every employee, with each employee's phone number contained in the second column, we would call that column a field.

file
A defined set of characters (called bytes) referenced by its filename.

file sharing
The mechanisms (RFS and NFS) used to make files on one system available to users on another system.

file system
The pyramid-like method used in UNIX to organize files and directories: A root directory (analogous to the top of the pyramid) contains several subdirectories, and these subdirectories in turn may contain further subdirectories. Any directory can hold files.

filename
The obvious: the name given to a file. Files in the same directory cannot have the same filename, but files in different directories may have the same name.

filling
An action in a text processor where as much text as possible is crammed onto a line.

filter
A type of UNIX program that takes input from one file and provides output to the display or another file based on parameters set up by the user.

find
Command used to find a file.

finger
Command that provides information about another user.

foreground
Commands that have the full attention of the system and do not return control to the user until the command is completed. In UNIX, the default is to run commands in the foreground.

fork
When a program starts another program, called a child process.

ftp
Command used to connect to any other computer on your network running **ftp**; when connected, **ftp** can then be used to transfer files to your computer. Can also be used to access files anywhere on the Internet provided you have access to the Internet.

full pathname The full description of the location of a file on the directory tree, from the root directory down.

function key A key (usually marked as **F1**, **F2**, etc.) that can be defined by the operating system and/or applications to perform any number of functions. The actions attached to the key usually differ from program to program and operating system to operating system.

gateways Computers that forward mail, news, or other stuff to other connected machines.

global To make changes to all occurrences of a given object; to change every instance of *Word* to *word* in a file with **emacs** would be an example of a global search and replace.

graphical user interface A metaphoric display of a computer system, with icons, windows, and scrollbars. Motif, Open Look, the Macintosh, and Windows are all examples of graphical user interfaces.

graphical windowing system See **graphical user interface**.

grep A UNIX command that searches for user-specified strings in a file or files.

group A defined set of users.

head Command used to display the beginning of a file.

header The beginning area of a file that contains vital statistics about the file. A mail file contains a header that specifies, among other things, the sender of the message and the route it takes.

header file A C-language file used to include system-specific information. Sometimes called include files, as they are specified in a source-code file with the include command.

hidden file A file beginning with a dot (**.profile**, for example) that is not returned by the **ls** command unless ls is told to return the names of all files in a directory, including hidden files.

hierarchical file system See **file system**.

history

A record of previous commands maintained in your computer's memory. Available only in the C and Korn shells.

history substitution

Plucking a command line from a history list and using it again by typing the number assigned to the command. Available only in the C and Korn shells.

home directory

The directory the user is placed in after logging in. This directory is set in the **.profile** file with the **HOME=** command.

hostname

The name of your UNIX system.

icon

A graphical representation of a program or file.

inbox

The storage area for electronic mail that has not been read.

init

The initial process, which launches when you boot a computer running the UNIX operating system. All processes are children of the init process.

inode

The location of information about files in the file system.

input mode

The mode where a text editor will accept input and includes it in the edited file. The opposite of editing mode.

interactive

Involves a dialogue of sorts between user and computer; the computer does not perform future tasks until given approval by the user. Most UNIX work can be done with the opposite of interactive computing, batch processing.

Internet

The umbrella name for a group of computer networks that distributes newsgroups and electronic mail around the world. Computers with access to the Internet are said to be **internetworked**.

Internet address

The name given to a computer system that allows it to receive Internet news and mail.

job

Another name for process or program running.

job control

Changing the status of a job, such as killing it or resuming a suspended job.

job shell	A superset of the Bourne shell (sh) devoted to job control.
kernel	The core of the UNIX operating system that interacts directly with the computer.
keyboard	That big thing with keys used to provide input. If you really looked up the definition of *keyboard* in a UNIX tutorial, we strongly advise you to take a remedial "Introduction to Computers" class before proceeding with any UNIX usage.
kill	Command that stops a running process.
kill buffer	A section of RAM devoted to storage of deleted text, which can then be called back into the text editor for further editing.
Korn shell	The shell (**ksh**) created by David Korn that improved on the older, popular Bourne shell.
language	Instructions that are translated into commands a computer can understand. Popular languages include C, BASIC, PASCAL, and FORTRAN.
library	A set of commonly used C-language functions.
line editor	A text editor that processes one line at a time, like **ed**.
link	Instead of wasting disk space on multiple copies of a commonly used file, one copy of the file is maintained and other filenames are linked to the original file.
ln	Command used to link files.
local-area network	In the PC world, a group of personal computers connected via cable to a central computer (the server) that distributes applications and files. Novell NetWare is an example of a local-area network software package.
login	Establish a session on the main UNIX system after providing a login name and a password.
login name	The truncated, unique name given to all users on a UNIX system.
login shell	A shell launched before the C shell, which allows the user to login and set environment variables.

logname	See **login name**.
logoff	Quit a UNIX session, typically by typing EXIT, logout, or **Ctrl-D**.
look and feel	The specific arrangement of elements on a screen (scrollbars, title bars, etc.)
loop	A state where commands are to be executed again and again until some condition is met.
lp	Command used to print a file.
lpstat	Command used to view the current status of print requests.
ls	Command that lists the files in a directory.
macros	Short instructions that are expanded by the shell to mean longer, more explicit commands.
mail	Command used to send and receive mail from other users.
mailbox	The file area used to store electronic-mail messages.
make	A UNIX program used to create applications based on system-specific information.
man	Command that displays online-manual pages.
man pages	See **online-manual pages**.
manual macros	Macros used to create formatted online-manual pages.
memorandum macros (mm)	Macros used in conjunction with **troff** to create stylized business letters, resumés, and reports.
mesg	Command that lets you block messages from other users created with **talk** or **write**.
Meta key	A specified key used in conjunction with other keys to create additional key combinations. On a PC keyboard, the **Alt** key is the **Meta** key; on a Sun keyboard, the **Alt** key is *not* the **Meta** key.
more	Command used to display a file one page at a time.
Motif	Created by the Open Software Foundation, Motif is a style guide that defines a particular look and feel for programs. Based on the X Window System.

mount	Make a file system available to users, either locally or remotely.
multiprocessing	Run more than one task or process at a time; one of the great strengths of the UNIX operating system.
multitasking	Run more than one task or process at a time; one of the great strengths of the UNIX operating system.
multiuser	Allow more than one user to be active on the system at once; one of the great strengths of the UNIX operating system.
mv	Command that moves a file from one directory to another.
NFS (Network File System)	Software developed to create a distributed file system for use with both UNIX and non-UNIX computers.
networking	Connecting computers via phone line or direct link so that they can share data.
newline	Character placed at the end of every line in a text file, usually created by pressing the **Return** (or **Enter**) key.
news	Command that displays text files containing news items.
news feed	On the Usenet, all the incoming message files from the worldwide newsgroups.
news readers	Software dedicated to reading Usenet newsgroups.
newsgroup	On the Usenet, public discussions of various topics.
nice	Command that allows you to assign a lower priority to a process, thus relieving the stress somewhat on an overstressed UNIX system.
noclobber	Condition set where a new file cannot overwrite an existing file with the same line unless the action is approved by the user.
nroff	Text-processing software, used to output formatting documents on a line printer.
online-manual page	Technically detailed information about a command, accessed by the **man** command.

Open Look Created by Sun Microsystems and AT&T, Open Look is a style guide that defines a particular look and feel for programs.

operating system Software that controls a computer, acts as an interface for a user, and runs applications. UNIX is an operating system.

options Characters that modify the default behavior of a command.

ordinary file A text or data file with no special characteristics; the most common file type in the UNIX operating system.

orphan A process that runs even though its parent process has been killed.

owner The user with the ability to set permissions for a file.

paging A memory-management scheme that divides RAM into 4K segments for more efficient shuffling of data to and from RAM and a hard disk.

parent process A process that generates another process.

parsing Logically dividing a command so that we can divine its meaning.

partition A section of a hard disk treated as a separate area by the operating system.

passwd Command that allows you to change your password.

password A unique set of characters designed to confirm your status as a legitimate user of a system.

path A list of directories the system uses to search for executables.

pathnames A description of where a file resides in the file system. All pathnames flow from the root directory.

permissions A security tool that determines who can access a file.

pipes A device that allows standard output from one command to be used as standard input for another command.

pg Command used to view a file one page at a time.

PostScript	A system-independent page-description language developed by Adobe Systems.
process	Essentially, a program running on the computer.
process identification number (PID)	A unique number assigned to a program so that it can be tracked and managed by the operating system and user.
profile	A description of a user's environment variables, stored in the **.profile** file.
program	A set of instructions for the computer to carry out.
prompt	A character used by the shell to indicate that it is waiting for input. In addition, some programs (like **ftp**) supply their own unique prompt.
ps	Command that shows what processes are running on your system.
pwd	Command that prints the working, or current, directory.
RAM (Random-Access Memory)	A physical area of the computer used for short-term storage of data and programs. When a computer is turned off, the data in RAM disappears.
RFS (Remote File System)	Software developed to create a distributed file system for use only with the UNIX operating system.
read	Command reads in user input and places whatever the user types into a shell variable.
record	A row in a structured data file. If we were to create a file containing the names, phone numbers, and salary of every employee, with each employee's information contained in a single row, we could call that row a record.
recurse	See **recurse**.
redirection	See **standard input and output**.
relational operator	A symbol that sets forth a condition in a programming language, such as **C** or **awk**. These conditions are based on algebraic notation.
relative pathname	The location of a file in relation to another location in the file system.

rlogin   Command that allows you to remotely login another computer on your network.

rm   Command that deletes a record of the file from the file system.

root directory   The topmost directory in a file system that contains all other directories and subdirectories. Indicated in all pathnames as a slash (/).

root user   See **superuser**.

screen editor   A text editor that allows the user to view a document one screen at a time and to edit anywhere on that screen through movement via cursors or mouse.

secondary prompt   A character used by the shell to indicate that additional input is needed before a program can run.

sed   Filtering text editor that requires you supply filenames, operations, and text before running it.

server   In a distributed file system, a computer that supplies files and services to other computers.

sh   Command used to switch shells.

shell   A program that interprets commands from the user into instructions the computer can understand. Popular shells include the Bourne, Korn, and C shells.

shell script   A file containing a series of commands for a UNIX shell.

shutdown   Command used to shutdown a UNIX system before powering down.

signal   An instruction sent by the operating system to a program, telling it to shutdown or otherwise modify its behavior.

sort   Command used to sort files.

SPARCstation   Popular UNIX workstation sold by Sun Microsystems.

spell   Command that generates a list of words not contained in a dictionary file.

standard error   The default location for error messages, usually your screen.

standard input and output	The path that the data takes: Input usually comes from your keyboard or another program, while output is usually sent to your screen, to a file, or to a printer. When you specify output to anything but the defaults, you are redirecting the input and output.
state	See **system state**.
status line	A portion of the screen used to provide feedback to the user. Not supported by all UNIX programs.
stty	Command that allows you to assign different meanings to a key.
superuser	The user who can do just about everything possible within the UNIX operating system.
swapping	Using the hard disk as a slower form of RAM when there's no RAM available to run programs or to store data.
symbolic links	An advanced form of a linked file that allows links between files located on remote file systems.
system administrator	A worker officially assigned to oversee housekeeping details on a UNIX system, including adding new users and scheduling system backups.
system call	Actions available to programs only after communicating with the kernel, such as printing files or saving data to disk.
system name	Name used to identify a UNIX system, usually the version of UNIX used.
system state	The state of the operating system: single user, multi-user, administrative, and more.
TCP/IP (Transmission Control Protocol/ Internet Protocol)	Protocols used to link UNIX and non-UNIX computers worldwide via phone lines.
tail	Command used to display the final ten lines of a file.
talk	Command that lets you send instant messages to other users logged on the system.
tar	Command that archives files and data to a backup device, such as a tape drive or floppy disks.

tbl
Dot commands used to create tables in conjunction with **troff**.

telnet
Command that allows you to remotely login another computer on your network.

terminal
Originally used to describe a dumb machine consisting of little more than a keyboard and a screen that relies on the larger system for its computing power; now used to describe any computer used to communicate with a UNIX system.

test
Command used to check variables under the Bourne shell.

text editor
A UNIX program, like **vi** or **emacs**, used to create ASCII text files.

text-formatting program
A program, like **troff**, that takes a text file created elsewhere and prepares it with formatting command for output to a printer.

thrashing
A condition where the computer is slowed down because the system is writing extensively to and from hard disk when all the RAM is in use.

tmp
Directory used by the system for temporary storage of working files.

toggle
Turning features on or off in the C and Korn shells.

troff
Text-processing program that processes text files for output on a typesetting machine. The original **troff** was upgraded to support all output devices (typesetting machines, laser printers, etc.) and renamed **ditroff**, though most users still refer to **ditroff** generically as **troff**.

UUCP (UNIX-to-UNIX System Copy)
Program that copies files from one system to another via communication on ordinary telephone lines.

UUCP Network
A series of UNIX computers that pass along electronic mail and files all around the world.

UNIX
The greatest operating system in the whole wide world. You should be commended for your astute and informed selection of such a great operating system.

Usenet   A loose confederation of computer systems (both UNIX and non-UNIX) that transmits electronic mail and newsgroups.

userid   See **login name**.

utility   A very specialized program that performs only a few actions.

vi   A text editor that ships with virtually every UNIX system.

virtual memory See **paging**.

wc   Command that returns the number of words in a given file.

who   Command that displays other users logged on the system.

wildcards   Special characters within a filename that tells the shell to search for all files with similar filenames: ***r**, for example, would tell the shell to return all files ending with the character *r*.

window manager X Window program that defines how other programs actually appear and act on the display.

word processor Software that combines the powers of text editors and text processors into single packages.

workstation   Usually a powerful, networked, single-user computer running the UNIX operating system.

write   Command that lets you send instant messages to other users logged on the system.

WYSIWYG (what-you-see-is-what-you-get) A term describing word processors and electronic-publishing packages that display exactly how a document will look before it is printed.

X terminal   Computer that runs a local X server, but relies on a machine elsewhere on the network for most of its computing power.

X Window System Graphical windowing system created by MIT that can be described as building blocks for fuller user interfaces, like Motif or Open Look. It is not tied to any particular operating system, but it has been popularized with the UNIX operating system.

XENIX   Older version of UNIX developed by Microsoft for microcomputers.

xterm   Popular X Window program that provides a command-line interface to the UNIX operating system.

zombie   Process that is not active, but not yet killed by the parent process.

Index

V